A SHORT HISTORY OF
SOUTH-EAST
ASIA

5TH EDITION

A SHORT HISTORY OF
SOUTH-EAST
ASIA

5TH EDITION

EDITED BY PETER CHURCH

WILEY
John Wiley & Sons (Asia) Pte Ltd

This publication is designed to provide accurate and authoritative information with regard to the subject matter covered. It is sold with the understanding that the Publisher is not engaged in rendering professional services. If professional advice or other expert assistance is required, the services of a competent professional person should be sought.

Other Wiley Editorial Offices
John Wiley & Sons, Inc., 111 River Street, Hoboken, NJ 07030, USA
John Wiley & Sons Ltd, The Atrium, Southern Gate, Chichester PO19 BSQ, England
John Wiley & Sons (Canada) Ltd, 5353 Dundas Street West, Suite 400, Toronto, Ontario M9B 6H8, Canada
John Wiley & Sons Australia Ltd, 42 McDougall Street, Milton, Queensland 4064, Australia
Wiley-VCH, Boschstrasse 12, D-69469 Weinheim, Germany

Library of Congress Cataloging-in-Publication Data:

ISBN-13   978-0-470-82481-8

Typeset in 11/15, Galliard by Thomson Digital
Printed in Singapore by International Press Softcom Limited
10 9 8 7 6 5

CONTENTS

"... to understand the present
and anticipate the future,
one must know enough of the past,
enough to have a sense
of the history of a people."

Lee Kuan Yew,
then Prime Minister of Singapore,
in January 1980 on the occasion of the 25th anniversary
of the founding of the People's Action Party

PREFACE

I had already been involved with South-East Asia for many years when I read former prime minister of Singapore Lee Kuan Yew's thought-provoking words set out on the facing page. Although I was an indifferent student of history at school in Australia, the words hit me like a sledge hammer. Whilst I was well aware of the importance to business of understanding the different cultures of South-East Asia, I had not given a lot of thought to the relevance of history to the future in general, or to business in particular.

Since that time I have read a lot of history on the region and what I have learnt has reinforced over and over again Lee Kuan Yew's message. Unfortunately, I have found much of the history of the region has either been written by scholars absorbed by their topics and at a much greater depth than is required to get that broad under-standing of history of the people or has been written in an abbreviated form for tourists or others needing only an outline of the past.

This book is our fifth edition of *A Short History of South-East Asia* and we continue to attempt to find a middle path which will give business and other readers enough detail to have a sense of the history of the different countries and their people. The first edition of this book was published in 1995 under the title "Focus in Southeast Asia". The original book was written substantially by two leading Australian historians who specialise in the ASEAN region, Professor (now Deputy Vice Chancellor at the University of Western Sydney) John Ingleson and Dr Ian Black of the University of New South Wales. They immediately understood what it was that we were trying to achieve and, through their skill, sensitivity and experience, the original book was published.

There have been significant historical developments in much of South-East Asia since 1995 and this led us to bring the material up to date in 1999, 2003, and 2006 for subsequent editions and again now in 2009 for the fifth edition. For this edition we turned once more to Daniel Rantzen and are extremely thankful to him for his profession-alism and expertise. I must also thank my long time assistant, Daphne

Lim, for her painstaking work in reviewing and proofing the text. Any mistakes which remain are mine.

The original project proved to be a far more difficult exercise than at first envisaged. Not only is it difficult to condense thousands of years of history to a few pages but, at all times, we wanted to test the material against the objective that by the end of each chapter a reader should have a feel for the history of the particular people.

As this edition goes to press the whole world is being battered by the Global Financial Crisis (GFC). While South-East Asia came out of the Asian Economic Crisis relatively quickly, I fear the current crisis is likely to have a much deeper impact on the political and economic environments in most, if not all, of the countries covered. Only time will tell.

Above all, we hope you come away from reading our book with a deeper understanding of the history of South-East Asia which might, in a small way, better enable you to understand the present and interpret the future with respect to your South-East Asia business and other interests.

Peter Church OAM,
Chairman, Asean Focus Group
Sydney, 1 June, 2009

INTRODUCTION

INTRODUCTION TO THE 2009 FIFTH EDITION

The first sentence of my introduction to the fourth edition has been reinforced by the market since then. More than 150,000 copies of "this little book" have now been sold and here we are with a fifth edition. That it fills a need is more than ever obvious. Busy people who need a basic history of one or more of the countries of South-East Asia have been well-served by it.

The region, like the rest of the world in January 2009, faces formidable difficulties. Demand for exports is drying up, as is foreign investment. Economies that have a major exposure to earnings sent home by workers who have jobs in other countries are likely to be adversely affected. For example, some eight million Filipinos work overseas and their repatriated earnings are a significant part of the country's national income. The competence of governments everywhere will be tested. Some will manage better than others, but all will come under strain. A major question is whether regional cooperation will be more effective than in 1987–88. Their histories do not enable us to predict with certainty how South-East Asian that Asian countries will be affected. But some knowledge of history certainly helps.

2009

Rawdon Dalrymple AO
Chairman, Advisory Board of Asean Focus Group

INTRODUCTION TO THE 2006 FOURTH EDITION

The continuing and increasing demand for this little book reflects not only the quality of its contents and the relevance of its format but also the prominence of South-East Asia in events which have engaged worldwide attention. Thus Islam in South-East Asia has been much discussed and many outside the region have become aware that there are more adherents of that religion in Indonesia than in any other country in the world. Political changes and developments in Indonesia, with a new and very different president, have appeared to hold out new promise, as has the change of leadership in Malaysia. Security incidents and concern about threatening networks have prompted unprecedented cooperation between the countries of the region including Australia. Most recently the natural disaster of the tsunami wave originating off Sumatra has focused world attention on the region and brought a huge supportive international response.

The East Asian solidarity movement, based on ASEAN, Japan, China and Korea, is still in an early stage, with difficulties between Japan and China, and reservations in ASEAN about both the giant northern neighbours, seeming likely to complicate prospects. But South-East Asia continues to seek to shape this regional cooperation by, for example, insisting that candidates sign on to its Treaty of Amity and Cooperation. Both Japan and the Republic of Korea found ways of doing so without prejudice to their alliance arrangements with the United States, and the government of Australia appears to be considering doing so. Economically, South-East Asia is far from demonstrating the dynamism of China and indeed China's growth increasingly raises questions of the effects on the region. The flood of China's low-priced products is damaging South-East Asian exports to major existing markets, especially since the textiles regime changed. But some Chinese industries are investing in production facilities in South-East Asia and Chinese demand for raw materials and energy resources is benefiting some parts of the region. In any case, the rise of China seems certain to be a major influence on the region in the years ahead. The countries of the region, and especially perhaps Indonesia and the Philippines, will need to address present constraints on their economic performance in order to hold their own.

2006

Rawdon Dalrymple AO
Chairman, Advisory Board of Asean Focus Group

INTRODUCTION TO THE 2003 THIRD EDITION

The success of this book shows that it fills a need, both in Australia and beyond, and that there is continuing interest in learning about the countries of South-East Asia. That is encouraging because there have been major changes in the region since the book was first produced. Those changes probably require qualification of the optimistic last paragraph of the introduction I wrote three years ago. I will try to say briefly why that is so.

In the first place the global climate is more uncertain and even threatening. It is a commonplace that the early post-Cold War euphoria has dissipated. The Western alliance system is divided and possibly even endangered; the enthusiasm for international economic liberalisation has diminished; fear of terrorism has had a major effect, especially on the only superpower; and there is an historically high level of resentment and friction in the global system.

Secondly, South-East Asia has experienced some of the effects of the heightened intensity of Islamic anger spilling out of the Israel/Palestine issue, the slow economic development of the Arab world, and various perceived grievances, especially against the United States. Some countries in the region have taken firm action to prevent violent expressions of that anger, including in the form of international terrorism. Others have been less effective. Domestic religious violence, in some places on a large scale, has also been costly.

Thirdly, recovery from the financial crisis has been patchy and slower than expected. Necessary action on failed banking and financial institutions in Indonesia, for example, is still awaited. Reform and improvement of governance and legal institutions have not been much in evidence.

Fourthly, the dynamism of the Chinese economy and particularly the growth of its exports have overshadowed South-East Asia. Foreign investment has flowed strongly to China while appearing more wary of some of the old favourites in South-East Asia.

Indeed all the last three factors have no doubt played a role in the reduction in FDI into the region in recent years.

South-East Asia has also experienced a diminution of the growth of regional solidarity. This is hard to quantify, but the authority and standing of ASEAN and of its associated FTA seem to have slipped.

If confronted by an external challenge ASEAN would no doubt show renewed solidarity and resilience. But there has been a loss of momentum. This may be partly because the region seems to be waiting to see what comes out of China. Will China emerge in the next ten or 15 years as a new superpower, and if so will it inevitably expand its zone of influence? Will it then become the dominant power in an ASEAN plus Three configuration, a realisation of Dr Mahathir's EAEC concept but with China, and not ASEAN or Japan, as the main driver?

Finally, without wishing to sound a parochial note, something needs to be said briefly about the position of Australia. The Australian perspective has become more reserved, at least at the government level, and the strenuous enforcement of "border protection" measures, as well as confusion about an Australian "deputy sheriff" role and preparedness to undertake "pre-emptive" action to stop emerging threats, have been among the factors seen in the region as evidence of a shift in Australian attitudes away from the "engagement" policy of the previous years. To some extent that perception overlooks the fact that the Australian engagement policy suffered a series of rebuffs by the region which would have made it difficult for any government to maintain. It also needs to be taken into account that Australian public opinion (to which government is highly responsive) was inevitably affected by the extensive and graphic media coverage of events in East Timor. That coverage was far more intensive in Australia, largely because of proximity, than anywhere else in the region.

The biggest challenge for Australia is to combine realistic expectations with a determination to make every reasonable effort to understand and cooperate with the countries of the region. That includes, for example, declining to enter into argument with those like Dr Mahathir who often vilify Australia for domestic purposes or as a proxy for an attack on the United States. It means, more importantly, returning to the policy of previous governments going back 40 years. For decades Australian governments encouraged and promoted the study of South-East Asian languages and the history, politics, economies and societies of the countries of the region. That, unfortunately, has gone backwards in recent years.

Australia in the medium to longer term cannot afford to give up on the national project of building the relationship with its region. That is partly because the region will return to stronger economic growth and will be a growing market for what Australia produces. But beyond that, it would be very uncomfortable for Australia in the longer term to be faced by an indifferent or disapproving South-East Asia. And, as many in the region understand, Australia can make a significant contribution. The role of business in that regard needs to be complemented and supported by addressing the historic task of building up knowledge and linkages across the board.

I see this small book as a contribution to that and hope that it will continue to be widely read by business and other visitors to the region from around the world.

Sydney, 12 June, 2003

Rawdon Dalrymple AO
Chairman, Advisory Board of Asean Focus Group
Former Australian Ambassador to Indonesia,
Japan and the United States

INTRODUCTION TO THE 1999 SECOND EDITION

South-East Asia has for many centuries been a part of the world whose fortunes were largely determined by centres of power elsewhere. It was a theatre for the intersection of Indian and Chinese influence— religious, commercial, cultural and political. Later, it was the eastern-most extension of the spread of Islam. It saw rivalry and conflict for commercial and political control between the rival European colonial powers and then a long period of subservience to those powers until the brief ascendancy of Japanese imperial power in the 1940s.

In the 1980s and up until 1997, South-East Asia experienced economic growth on a scale and at a rate which was unprecedented in world history. The region saw the beginning of a sense of shared purpose, and a confidence that the South-East Asian nations would become prosperous and influential in the world. In the words of the American pioneer of developmental state theory, Professor Chalmers Johnson, they looked forward to achieving not only enrichment but also empowerment. There was a vigorous debate in the international financial institutions and in academic circles about the factors which had made it possible to achieve such spectacular economic progress. One dimension of that debate concerned the influence of the "Japanese model". The "flying geese" theory had it that as Japan moved out of labour-intensive industry it invested in South-East Asia and other emerging economies which were able to take off into export-driven economic growth with a high degree of state direction. Opposed to that was the theory that the South-East Asians had achieved record-breaking economic growth by opening their econo-mies increasingly to the world market which forced them to become highly competitive and made them attractive investment opportuni-ties. On that theory, deregulation and openness were the keys to continuing success.

The crisis which started with the collapse of the Thai baht in June 1997 was widely seen in the West as discrediting the Japanese model and Japanese leadership in the region. The International Monetary Fund's rescue operations in the region were driven by a belief that the crisis economies needed strict control of public expenditure, transparency in regulation of the banking and finance sector, and liberalisation of financial flows in particular and their economies generally. Debate continues about the wisdom of the Fund's policies which were modified after an initial period, especially in Indonesia. It is probably fair to say that no one would now believe that South-East Asia can return to strong growth in the long term without substantial reforms of governance. But there remains in the region a strong belief that these countries cannot afford to place themselves totally at the mercy of international financial markets and that some measures of control are necessary.

It will be some time before these policies and other problems are resolved but, in the meantime, the sense of achievement seen as based on national and more broadly Asian cultural traditions and values, and not simply derived from the West, has been diminished. The sense of regional solidarity based on the shared economic success and on the growing international status of the Association of South-East Asian Nations (ASEAN) has also been affected. ASEAN as a body was shown to be largely irrelevant when the financial crisis struck. Again in September 1999 when East Timor, after voting massively for independence from Indonesia, was plunged into a frenzy of killing and destruction, ASEAN, possibly due to its long-standing policy of not commenting on or being seen to be interfering in the domestic affairs of its members, seemed unwilling or unable to play any substantial role in international efforts to re-establish order. There have been a number of other events over recent years which demonstrate the interdependence of ASEAN's members and how events in one country have the potential to severely affect another. These range from occurrences of ethnic and religious conflict to unchecked forest fires in Indonesia causing havoc in other ASEAN countries such as Singapore, Brunei and Malaysia. Events such as these have led a number of members to express the view that ASEAN needs to review its raison d'etre and one suspects this will have to lead to substantial changes in policies if the grouping is to continue to have relevance.

But in the longer term the present situation is likely to be seen as an interlude, although in some cases—and especially in Indonesia—it might last some years. It should not be seen simply as an interruption of the remarkable economic successes of the last 20 years. High levels of economic growth will not return without substantial reforms and policies to equip these countries for success in a rapidly changing world economy. Moreover, there is substantial political change afoot in South-East Asia. That is perhaps most evident in Thailand, where democracy seems now firmly implanted and working well. There is a sense in Malaysia that change there cannot now be too far off. In Indonesia, the troubled giant of the region, there are elements of major change together with retention of elements from the Suharto New Order era. Of the two great political forces in the country, the Islamic seems to have gained ascendancy over the secular nationalist. But it is a moderate and tolerant Islamic leadership apparently committed to equal rights for all. In that country, much economic and social ground has been lost and it will be a hard task to establish a new political order and the basis for a new era of economic growth and increasing welfare for the population of more than 210 million.

It would, in my view, not take long if stability and economic recovery prevail for the sense of optimism and confidence to return to South-East Asia, and this time it could be enhanced by a much wider public acceptance and sense of participation. In Indonesia, where the outlook is still uncertain, there is already an enormous change in the atmosphere with a novel and unaccustomed frankness and exchange of opinions in the media and a sense of relevance and indeed of power in the elected parliament. If economic recovery takes hold across the region we are likely to see a move to try to enhance the role and relevance of ASEAN. The proposal to establish an East Asian Monetary Fund has support in South-East Asia and the initiatives which flow from the Miyazawa Fund could lead to an invigorated cooperative arrangement supported by Japan. Global currents caused havoc in the region in 1997 and 1998 and that has led some to think in terms of building defences and walls. Globalisation will, however, affect South-East Asia in positive ways—socially, politically and economically. Indeed they cannot afford not to respond to it, and one of the questions which faces them is whether or how they can best support each other in that enterprise.

Sydney, 1 January, 2000

Rawdon Dalrymple AO
Chairman, Asean Focus Group

1 BRUNEI

6th–9th centuries

14th century

1521

16th–17th centuries

18th century

1839

1888

Britain declares
Brunei a
protectorate

Independence
granted. James
Brooke arrives and
becomes the Governor
and "White Rajah" of
Sarawak (then part of
Brunei)

Magellan visits a
flourishing trading
community linked to
South-East Asia
and China

Brunei's area of
economic and
political influence
gradually declines

Brunei claimed as
part of the
Majapahit Empire

Kingdom of Puni, on
the north-west coast
of Kalimantan,
paying tribute to
China

Nationalist Brunei
becomes a major
regional kingdom
extending to
southern
Philippines; Sabah
and Sarawak
movement born

Gold Domed Mosque

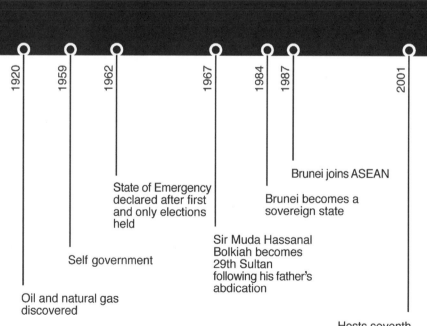

1920

1959

1962

1967

1984

1987

2001

State of Emergency
declared after first
and only elections
held

Brunei joins ASEAN

Brunei becomes a
sovereign state

Sir Muda Hassanal
Bolkiah becomes
29th Sultan
following his father's
abdication

Self government

Oil and natural gas
discovered

Hosts seventh
ASEAN summit
meeting

1 BRUNEI

Brunei is a small state of just 2,226 square miles located on the north-west coast of the island of Kalimantan, or "Borneo" (a Western term derived from "Brunei"). It is an Islamic State where the sultan, Sir Hassanal Bolkiah, the 29th Sultan in the dynasty, rules by decree. Its population is about 400,000, of whom nearly 60 per cent live in urban areas. Malays comprise about 64 per cent of the population, Chinese about 20 per cent and indigenous tribes about 8 per cent. It would be an unremarkable territory were it not that underneath its soil and under its territorial waters lie huge oil and gas reserves which have enabled the country to boast the highest per-capita income in South-East Asia at around US$27,000. This underground wealth has also enabled one of the world's few remaining absolute monarchies to survive into the 21st century. The sultanate has considerable financial reserves invested overseas.

EARLY HISTORY

Little is known of the early history of Brunei. There appears to have been trade between the north-west coast of Kalimantan and China as early as the sixth century and Brunei was influenced by the spread of Hinduism/Buddhism from India in the first millennium. Chinese records make mention of a kingdom of Puni, located on the north-west coast of Kalimantan, which paid tribute to Chinese emperors between the sixth and the ninth centuries. Brunei was claimed by the great Javanese empire of Majapahit in the 14th century, though it was most likely little more than a trading/tributary relationship. Brunei became a more significant state in the 15th century with a greater degree of independence from its larger neighbours. When the Chinese Admiral Cheng Ho visited Brunei in the early 15th century, as part of his exploration of South-East Asia, he discovered a significant trading port with resident Chinese traders engaged in profitable trade with the homeland.

Brunei was a small cog in the early South-East Asia trading networks but well known enough to figure in the records of the major states. The Brunei ruler seems to have converted to Islam in the middle of the 15th century when he married a daughter of the ruler of Melaka. The Portuguese conquest of Melaka in 1511 closed Melaka to Muslim traders, forcing them to look elsewhere in the archipelago. There was an outflow of wealthy Islamic traders who settled in other parts of the Indonesian archipelago taking with them not only their business acumen but also their religious beliefs. The Islamisation of the archipelago was given a great impetus. Brunei prospered from the Portuguese conquest of Melaka as Islamic traders were now attracted to its port in greater numbers. When Magellan's expedition visited Brunei in 1521 it found a prosperous town with a flourishing trading community linked into the South-East Asia—China trading network. Throughout the 16th century it engaged in political and commercial relations with other states in the Malay world, comprising the Indonesian archipelago, the Malay peninsula and southern Philippines.

Brunei became a major regional kingdom in the 16th and 17th centuries, with its influence stretching into the southern Philippines and its territorial claims extending over most of the north coast of Kalimantan, including what are now the Malaysian states of Sarawak and Sabah. As the first Islamic kingdom in the area, Brunei was the base for the Islamisation of the southern Philippines and surrounding areas, frequently coming into conflict with Catholic Spain after the Spanish conquest of Luzon, the central island of the Philippines. In 1578 Spain attacked Brunei and briefly captured the capital. It was unable to hold the town, in large part because its forces were decimated by sickness. Spain continued to try to conquer the Islamic Sultanate of Sulu in the southern Philippine islands, only finally succeeding in the last quarter of the 19th century.

Brunei did well out of the Portuguese conquest of Melaka. Not only did it become an important port for Muslim traders but it was able to negotiate a deal with the Portuguese for cooperation in the

South-East Asian trade with China. Brunei was no threat to Portugal, having no territorial claims outside Kalimantan. It also shared a commercial interest in promoting the China trade. In 1526 the Portuguese established a trading post at Brunei to collect the valued products of Kalimantan and surrounding islands. Brunei became an integral port of call on the Melaka to Macau route.

Brunei's commercial and political power was at its peak in the middle of the 17th century. It had managed to stave off Spain and had reached a mutually beneficial accord with Portugal. From the middle of the 17th century it was increasingly challenged by the Sultanate of Sulu in the islands north-east of Kalimantan. Ostensibly under Brunei suzerainty, the Sultanate of Sulu gradually established total independence, going so far as to acquire from Brunei sovereignty over most of the area which today constitutes the Malaysian state of Sabah.

By the beginning of the 19th century the political and economic power of the Malay rulers in Kalimantan and what is now the southern Philippines was declining sharply. The rule of the once-powerful Sultans of Brunei and Sulu now barely extended outside their capitals. Their decline resulted largely from the development of European entrepots in South-East Asia, which offered local traders a better price for their produce and were free from the taxes of the Malay ports. The development of local trade with European entrepots, especially Singapore, Batavia and Manila, and the decay of the older trading centres of Brunei and Sulu meant a drastic reduction in the Sultanates' revenues, with a consequent decline in political power.

About 40,000 people lived in Brunei town and surrounding areas in the mid 18th century. By the 1830s the population had declined to about 10,000. The northern coast of Kalimantan, except for Brunei town itself, was ruled by local chiefs based at river mouths. The coastal population was predominantly Malay (and Muslim), with a small group of Chinese merchants and pepper growers and a smattering of people of Arab descent. The tribal people who lived in the interior were neither Malay nor Muslim: they were subsistence farmers who traded with the coastal Malays but resisted attempts to bring them under Malay control. To Brunei's south the most significant tribal people were Iban, or Dayak. To the east (in Sabah) the most significant groups were Kadazan-Dusun and Murut.

In addition to its economic decay, the Brunei Sultanate was further weakened by power struggles within the Court. Omar Ali Saifuddin, who succeeded to the throne of the Sultanate in 1828, was a weak ruler. During his reign a bitter power struggle developed between two rival factions led by Brunei Chiefs. The decline in the

Sultan's power was evidenced by the increasing independence of provincial rulers, and by the growth in the power of formerly subservient chiefs. In the late 1830s, Sarawak, the westernmost province claimed by the Sultanate of Brunei, was in open rebellion against the local provincial ruler whose rule had become progressively more oppressive as he became more independent of Brunei. In 1837, the Sultan tried to suppress the rebellion but without success.

THE BRITISH IMPACT
In the first half of the 19th century the interest of the British government and the English East India Company in South-East Asia was limited to the protection of the China trade routes from interference by other European nations and the provision of minimum conditions for the expansion of British trade in the area. The Anglo-Dutch Treaty of 1824, under which Britain acquired Melaka from the Dutch and relinquished Benkulen on the south-west coast of Sumatra and the Dutch withdrew all objections to Britain's occupation of Singapore, contained articles which guaranteed British traders entry to the Dutch-administered ports and laid down maximum rates of import duties. The failure of the Dutch to carry out the commercial clauses of the Treaty led to a growing agitation by merchants in Singapore and Britain that Britain should directly challenge the Netherlands' position in the archipelago by opening an entrepot to the east of Singapore. The unsuccessful settlements in northern Australia—Melville Bay, Raffles Bay and Port Essington—had been made partly with this end in view, but in the late 1830s attention was focused on the north-west coast of Borneo, the only part of the archipelago not recognised as lying within the Dutch sphere of influence.

Into this situation of a decaying Sultanate of Brunei, facing rebellion in Sarawak, and a growing commercial interest in the north-west coast of Kalimantan by the British community in Singapore, arrived in August 1839 a remarkable Englishman named James Brooke. Brooke was in the mould of the early 19th-century Romantics: he admired what he saw as the simple and unsophisticated life of the peoples of the Malay archipelago and wanted to improve it by bringing to them what he saw as the benefits of British civilisation, without destroying the basic simplicity of their lives. He became convinced that he had a divinely appointed mission in the Malay archipelago. With the proceeds of his wealthy father's estate, he bought a boat and journeyed first to Singapore and then to the north-west coast of Kalimantan. His timely arrival at the head of the Sarawak river with an armed yacht in August 1839 brought the rebellion of the local chief to an end. In return he received the Governorship of Sarawak.

Over the next 30 years Brooke established a personal fiefdom in Sarawak, remorselessly extending its borders at the expense of the Sultanate of Brunei. He was adroit at persuading British naval commanders in Hong Kong and Singapore to support him in forcing the Sultan of Brunei to make concession after concession. However, his attempts to persuade the British government to make Sarawak a British protectorate for the moment fell on deaf ears. The "White Rajah" was one of the more colourful oddities in the history of British colonialism.

A weakened Sultan of Brunei made further concessions of territory in 1877. This time it was to a private company, the American Trading Company, owned by an Austrian and an Englishman. The Austrian sold out to the Englishman in 1881. In order to keep the French and the Germans out of a strategically important area, Britain then granted a royal charter for the establishment of the British North Borneo Company. Further Brunei territory was successfully claimed by Sarawak in 1882, reducing the Sultanate to two small areas: the core around Brunei town and a small pocket of land inside Sarawak. In order to protect what was left of the once great Sultanate of Brunei and finally to ensure that rival European powers were kept out, in 1888 Britain declared a protectorate over Sarawak, Brunei and North Borneo. After a series of arrangements between the British North Borneo Company and Sarawak, which saw Sarawak add further territory, in 1906 Britain appointed a Resident to Brunei in order to supervise the state, modernise its administrative structures and ensure its survival against its predatory Sarawak neighbour.

Brunei had been territorially reduced to a shadow of its former self. But oil and gas were discovered beneath its land and under its territorial waters in the 1920s. The history of Brunei from then on has revolved around the enormous wealth created by oil and gas. The Sultan and his family became very rich very quickly. By the 1960s, access to such a strong revenue stream enabled the Sultanate to provide free health, education and social welfare services of a high standard to all its people, and all with very low rates of taxation.

After World War II and the defeat of Japan, Brunei continued to be a British protectorate with the Sultan ruling with advice from a British resident and under the protection of Gurkha troops. As Britain steadily decolonised in Asia and Africa, this arrangement came to be seen in Britain as anachronistic. In 1959 Brunei achieved self-government, at the insistence of Britain. A constitution was drawn up which provided for elections to a legislative council. In 1962 the first elections were held. They were won by the Partai Rakyat Brunei, a party which opposed the monarchical system and demanded full democratic rights. It also advocated that Brunei join the neighbouring states of Sabah and Sarawak in the mooted Federation of Malaysia. The Partai Rakyat Brunei was strongly opposed by the Sultan and the ruling elite. Its demands were rejected. Brunei was to remain a monarchy.

As a consequence, the Partai Rakyat Brunei launched a revolt. This was quickly crushed by the Gurkha troops stationed in Brunei. The Sultan declared a state of emergency, suspended the constitution, declared the recent elections void and banned the Partai Rakyat Brunei.

This was the only election ever held in Brunei. In 1962 and early 1963 the Sultan became involved in discussions about joining the new Federation of Malaysia. But when Malaysia was formed in September 1963 Brunei elected to remain outside. Disagreements over the distribution of oil and gas revenues (Brunei was determined to protect its revenue) and concern about the relative status of the royal family among the other Malaysian Sultans, all of whom were constitutional monarchs with limited powers, finally decided the Sultan to remain a British protectorate.

The protectorate arrangements were changed in 1971, but Britain still retained control of foreign affairs and defence, although all costs were now met by a very wealthy Sultanate. At the insistence of Britain, embarrassed by the continuation of this relic of colonialism, Brunei became a sovereign state on 1 January 1984.

Independence brought with it few perceptible changes for the people of Brunei. Political parties remain banned. State ministries essentially remain in the hands of members of the royal family and trusted members of a tightly knit elite.

Since the 1960s, Brunei has become increasingly involved with its South-East Asian neighbours. Its relations with ASEAN states since the formation of ASEAN in 1967 have been extremely good, although from time to time there has been some debate in sections of Malaysian society about the merits of Brunei's benevolent but authoritarian monarchy, and in 2003 and 2004 the two countries became involved in a dispute over rival claims to oil fields off the coast of Borneo.

In 1987 Brunei joined ASEAN as a full member, thereby formalising the already close relationship, and in November 2001 staged the seventh ASEAN summit meeting, with representatives of

China, Japan and Korea in attendance. In July 2002, the country hosted the ASEAN Regional Forum in which ASEAN's members and the United States signed a pact pledging to "prevent, disrupt and combat" global terrorism. In December the same year, the Sultan met President George W. Bush in Washington and affirmed the two countries' close ties, although Brunei has discreetly sought to distance itself from the US invasion of Iraq.

In 1998 the business empire run by the Sultan's brother, Prince Jefri, collapsed amid allegations of fraud and mismanagement. The failure of his conglomerate is believed to have resulted in debts to the Sultanate of US$15 billion. Prince Jefri had formerly been finance minister between 1986–1997 and was dismissed as head of the Brunei Investment Agency—which manages the country's overseas investments—in 1998.

BRUNEI IN THE NEW MILLENNIUM

Brunei's revenues are almost entirely dependent on royalties from oil and gas. Conscious of the eventual exhaustion of oil and gas (predicted to occur around 2025), since the mid 1980s Brunei's government has placed priority on developing the agricultural sector so that it can cease to be a net importer of food. Efforts have also been made to develop light manufacturing. But realistically, the country's inherent structural and capacity constraints mitigate against the development of a diversified industrial base. These include high labour costs, a shortage of skilled labour, a small domestic market, the lack of an entrepreneurial class and a large (relative to the population) bureaucracy.

In 2003, plans were announced to corporatise the Department of Telecommunications as part of an ongoing programme to corporatise government authorities to encourage them to become more accountable and competitive. Following lengthy delays, this department was finally corporatised in 2006, with its duties shared between a telecommunications carrier set up in 2002 (TelBru) and the Authority for Info-Communications Technology Industry, which took on a regulatory and facilitation function.

Policies aimed at economic diversification and weaning the population off government dependency have been only partially successful and, approximately 70 per cent of the workforce remains on the state payroll. The government has also invested tens of billions of petro-dollars in the West in order that the accrued income will act to cushion the economic—and no doubt, social—effects brought on by declining fossil-fuel revenues. Such diversified long-term investments offshore will also help smooth out unpredictable short-term fluctuations in the global price of oil, which in 2008–9 alone swung between US$147 and US$40 per barrel due to flow-on effects on oil demand caused by the onset of the global credit crisis and the subsequent world economic downtown.

The social composition of Brunei has changed quickly over the past five decades, most noticeable in the growth of an educated middle class. This educated middle class will continue to increase in numbers. Since 1990, in an effort to intertwine a sense of nation-building, culture, a love of the monarchy and an observance of Islam, the Sultan has promoted an ideology encapsulated by the catchphrase *Melayu Islam Beraja,* or "Malay-Muslim-Monarchy".

A small step towards democratisation was undertaken in 2004 when the Sultan announced that a partly-elected parliament of 45 members would convene. However, no timetable has been set for elections.

A question for the future is the extent to which the hitherto quiescent middle class will continue to accept the status quo or whether they will demand greater political involvement and representation commensurate with their own rising educational and financial attainments.

2 CAMBODIA

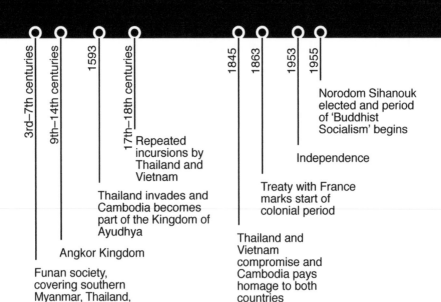

3rd–7th centuries

9th–14th centuries

1593

17th–18th centuries

1845

1863

1953

1955

Norodom Sihanouk elected and period of 'Buddhist Socialism' begins

Independence

Repeated incursions by Thailand and Vietnam

Treaty with France marks start of colonial period

Thailand invades and Cambodia becomes part of the Kingdom of Ayudhya

Thailand and Vietnam compromise and Cambodia pays homage to both countries

Angkor Kingdom

Funan society, covering southern Myanmar, Thailand, Cambodia and southern Vietnam

Angkor Wat

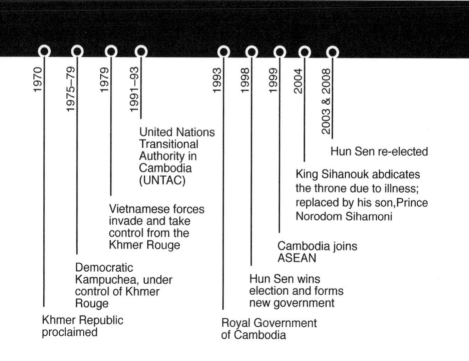

1970 — Khmer Republic proclaimed

1975–79 — Democratic Kampuchea, under control of Khmer Rouge

1979 — Vietnamese forces invade and take control from the Khmer Rouge

1991–93 — United Nations Transitional Authority in Cambodia (UNTAC)

1993 — Royal Government of Cambodia

1998 — Hun Sen wins election and forms new government

1999 — Cambodia joins ASEAN

2004 — King Sihanouk abdicates the throne due to illness; replaced by his son, Prince Norodom Sihamoni

2003 & 2008 — Hun Sen re-elected

2 CAMBODIA

No country in South-East Asia has a more imposing early history than Cambodia. The temples of Angkor, erected between the 9th and 13th centuries, are a testament to the creative energy, wealth and power of Khmer society in that era. But no country in the region has had a more tragic recent history. Ravaged by war and revolution in the 1970s, a decade in which more than one in seven Cambodians died, Cambodia remained a victim of international Cold War rivalries in the 1980s. It is only now, following the turn of the century, that peace and a semblance of economic security is re-emerging in Cambodia.

One striking theme in Cambodia's history is the country's almost-continuous entrapment in the rivalries of outside forces. Until the 19th century, these forces were regional. Since then, Cambodia has been tossed and tormented by world forces, to a degree that sometimes seems inexplicable given Cambodia's small population and poverty. Cambodia's population was assessed at 14.5 million in 2008. Its GDP per capita was US$540.

Another striking historical theme, intertwined with the first, concerns the perennial struggles for power within Cambodia at the expense of the country's general well-being. Traditionally, in a matter of ruling class rivalries, the power struggles have been grotesquely magnified by this century's global ideological collisions.

Cambodia has known peace, sometimes for extended periods, but always under rulers who enforced peace. French colonial rule achieved a kind of peace in Cambodia, as did King Sihanouk in the 1950s and 1960s. Today the Cambodian government works hard to maintain social cohesion while promoting economic growth now that peace seems to have finally come to the country.

EARLY HISTORY AND THE EMPIRE OF ANGKOR

The first glimpses into Cambodian history come from the early centuries of the Christian era. By then Khmers—direct ancestors of Cambodia's modern population—and related Mon peoples occupied a broad band of mainland South-East Asia, stretching across what is today southern Burma, Thailand, Cambodia and southern Vietnam. Early Chinese records mention trade with a society on the lower Mekong which they term "Funan" (perhaps a transcription of the Khmer word *phnom*, meaning "hill"). Funan flourished from the third to seventh centuries, as a port of call on the sea-trading route between India and China. Its Hindu-Buddhist religious life, writing system, irrigation technology for wet rice-growing and other skills were probably developed from Indian sources. Families claiming high Brahman status became a feature of Khmer society, providing priests for Hindu rituals and senior officials for Khmer rulers. Khmer society did not adopt the caste system of Indian Hindu society, but it did become strongly hierarchical in structure.

The Chinese records mention two other early societies in the Khmer area—"water Chenla", in the Mekong delta, and "land Chenla", further up the Mekong, possibly in what is now southern Laos. The records indicate that the latter attacked Funan, bringing about its demise. However, there is insufficient evidence to determine whether the two "Chenlas" and indeed Funan were coherent states, or rather loose collections of farming and trading communities under warlords—albeit warlords aspiring to be seen as divinely ordained warrior kings, identified with Hindu deities such as Siva and Vishnu.

The consolidation of Khmer society is more clear from the ninth century, when the first of the kings to rule over the state now generally known as Angkor, Jayavarman II (reigned c. 802–850), established the state cult of Devaraj, or "god-king". This cult, while incorporating Khmer animist beliefs, centred on the worship of a linga relating the king to Siva and symbolising the king's ability to confer fertility and prosperity on his land and people. A temple built to house the linga represented the mythical Mount Meru, centre of the universe and home of the gods. Thus the king was identified with the divine world, and could lay claim to universal authority. At the king's death his temple could serve as his mausoleum.

Jayavarman II built several such temples at widely spaced sites in what is now Cambodia. For the next four centuries his successors would build their temple-mausoleums, the successive foci of South-East Asia's greatest state until the 13th century. The temples of the Angkor region are still South-East Asia's most imposing historical remains.

From the mid ninth century, Angkor's heartland became the region along the northern end of the Tonle Sap, near the modern city of Siem Reap. The Tonle Sap ("great lake") floods each year, fed by the rushing waters of the Mekong. Angkor's rulers and people gradually built a system of reservoirs and canals to control the inundation and provide year-round water for multiple rice harvests. The system eventually watered an area of about 5.5 million hectares and supported a large population. A "bureaucracy" of regional magnates and officials harnessed the labour and product of this population for the king's projects and their own—temple-building, the lavish decoration and upkeep of temples and palaces, the expansion and maintenance of the irrigation works, trade with merchants sailing up the Mekong/Tonle Sap, and warfare.

The degree of power personally exercised by the "god-kings" remains uncertain, despite the rich information about Angkor provided by temple inscriptions and bas-reliefs. Modern scholars' characterisations of Angkor's rulers vary from Stalinesque tyrants to ceremonial figureheads always in danger from court rivalries and regional challenges. Two men of immensely strong personality stand out from the long line of monarchs—Suryavarman II (reigned 1113–1150) and Jayavarman VII (reigned 1181–c.1219). The former took the empire which Angkor had been developing to its greatest extent. Under him it encompassed much of modern Thailand and Laos, Cambodia and southern Vietnam. For a time he also held the territory of Champa, today's central Vietnam. Appropriately, Suryavarman II initiated the construction of Angkor Wat, sometimes described as the largest religious building in the world, and Angkor's best known monument.

Jayavarman VII, also a triumphant warrior-king, became the most prolific of all Angkor's royal builders. His greatest monument is the massive Angkor Thom and Bayon, but he also established numerous other temples, all in an apparent attempt to promote a form of Mahayana Buddhism. He also initiated a road-building programme and other public works such as hospitals and rest-houses. The mobilisation of labour and resources for warfare and building during the reign of Jayavarman VII must have been enormous. Following his death early in the 13th century no more temples were built and the incising of inscriptions also ceased. Most commentators suggest that his fearsome energies brought social exhaustion. Nevertheless the next major insight into Angkor available to us—the account of a Chinese visitor, Chou Ta-kuan, in 1296—suggests a state still of great power and opulence.

By then, however, the principal religious focus of Khmer society had altered. Varieties of Buddhism had long coexisted with the Hindu Devaraj cults but, during the 13th century, Theravada Buddhism won general allegiance. This form of Buddhism, originally defined in Sri Lanka and possibly Burma, was organised by its *sangha* (order of monks) and clear about what constituted Buddhist orthodoxy, while also being able to subsume Hindu and animist elements. It was rapidly becoming the dominant religion in mainland South-East Asia. The concept of Devaraj, celebrated by Brahmanic officiants, would persist in Khmer society, but a godly king would now demonstrate his virtue primarily through patronage of Theravada Buddhist temples, monasteries and schools. As a consequence, perhaps, interest in the temple-mausoleums of former rulers declined.

In the 1440s, the Khmer ruling class abandoned the Angkor region. Besides the impact of Theravada Buddhism there are other possible reasons for this shift. Court factionalism may have weakened the firm government needed for such an intricately connected "hydraulic society" to work, and hastened ecological deterioration of a region which had been intensively exploited for centuries. The general population of the area may have drifted away as the irrigation system silted up. Malaria has also been suggested as a factor in Angkor's abandonment. The best established factor in the transfer of the kingdom is the rise, from 1351, of the ambitious Thai state of Ayudhya. The Thais insistently attacked Angkor, looting it of wealth and people. A Khmer capital to the south-east (variously in later centuries Phnom Penh, Udong and Lovek) may have seemed more defensible than Angkor. Such cities were also nearer the sea and the booming maritime trade of 15th-century South-East Asia.

THE KINGDOM OF CAMBODIA, 15TH–18TH CENTURIES
Until late in the 16th century the translated Khmer kingdom appears to have been quite strong, an equal of neighbours like Ayudhya, Lan

Xang (Laos) and Vietnam. Intermittent warfare with the Thais continued, but also peaceful trade and cultural exchange. In religion, polity and culture, the Thai and Khmer kingdoms had much in common. In 1593, however, the Thai king Narasuen attacked Cambodia as part of his strategy to reaffirm the power of Ayudhya after a devastating assault on his city by the Burmese. From this time, Cambodia slipped decisively—at least in Thai eyes—to the status of a Thai vassal state.

Shortly after Narasuen's attack, Cambodia demonstrated vividly a feature that would darken its history in the centuries ahead—ruling-class attempts to harness foreign assistance in ruling-class rivalries. In the 1590s, aid was sought from the Spanish, by then ensconced at Manila, against the Thais. Spanish adventurers and missionaries briefly held great influence at the Cambodian court but, in 1599, most were massacred. The king who had favoured them was also assassinated. In 1603, after further upheavals at court, a Cambodian prince aligned with the Thais came to the throne.

Meanwhile, the Vietnamese had long been advancing southwards from their original homeland in the Tonkin delta, overwhelming Champa in the process. In the 1620s, the next Cambodian king turned to the Vietnamese for help against the Thais, permitting the Vietnamese to settle along his kingdom's south-east coast. There the Vietnamese port and stronghold of Saigon would develop. Vietnamese and Chinese adventurers and traders began to dominate other Cambodian ports. European accounts of Cambodia in the late 16th century and first half of the 17th century suggest a cosmopolitan trading life involving Chinese, Japanese, Malay, Arab and other traders, but from the mid-17th century Cambodia became increasingly isolated from the sea, caught in the pincer movement of Thai and Vietnamese expansionism.

The later 17th and 18th centuries saw repeated Thai and Vietnamese incursions, usually connected with rivalries for the throne within the Cambodian ruling class. The 18th century ended with the Thais dominant. From 1771 until the early 19th century the Vietnamese were preoccupied with domestic rebellion and civil war. The Thai general Taksin and the Thai ruler Rama I, the founder of Bangkok, took the opportunity to impose their authority firmly over Cambodia. The north-western provinces of Battambang and Siem Reap were added to Thai territory. The Cambodian kings had their subordinate status made plain by being crowned at Bangkok amidst Thai-dictated ceremonial.

But Thai-Vietnamese rivalry was still to climax. The Cambodian ruler Ang Chan (reigned 1806–35) thought it wise to pay homage not only to the Thais but also to the Vietnamese, by now reunited under a strong new dynasty ruling from the city of Hué. In 1811–12 Thai forces attempted to replace Ang Chan with one of his brothers, but Vietnamese troops repelled the Thais, and Vietnam assumed ascendancy over Cambodia. Ang Chan continued, however, to send tribute to Bangkok as well as to Hué.

In 1833, the Thais staged a major invasion, taking Phnom Penh, but they were again repelled by Vietnamese forces. When Ang Chan died in 1834 the Vietnamese emperor, Minh Mang, decided on a policy of complete absorption of Cambodia within his realm. As a first step, he passed over two male heirs of the late king and appointed their sister, Ang Mei, as a figurehead monarch. Vietnamese officials ran the kingdom, Vietnamese people were encouraged to colonise Cambodia, and Vietnamese language and law, and even Vietnamese costumes and hairstyles, were increasingly insisted upon.

A country-wide rebellion broke out in 1840, and the Thais responded readily to calls for help from Ang Mei's brothers. For five nightmarish years, Thai and Vietnamese forces, and also Cambodian factions, fought an inconclusive war, ravishing the countryside. Finally, in 1845, the Thais and Vietnamese agreed to compromise, placing on the throne Ang Duang, son of Ang Chan, who would pay homage to both Bangkok and Hué. In this uneasy peace, Ang Duang was encouraged by French missions (which had been operating in Cambodia since the previous century) to appeal for French support. In 1853, he sent feelers to the French diplomatic mission in Singapore, but King Mongkut of Thailand made clear his displeasure and the French backed off, for the time being.

THE COLONIAL ERA, 1863–1940

The French began their attack on Vietnam in 1859 and by 1862 had established the colony of Cochin China around Saigon. Cambodia, their new colony's hinterland, naturally interested them. They envisaged the Mekong as a mighty trade route, perhaps even offering access to China. At the same time a new Cambodian king, Norodom (reigned 1860–1904), was seeking allies to support him against the Thais and against domestic rivals for his throne. In August 1863, he signed a treaty of "protection" which established a French Resident at Phnom Penh, gave France control of Cambodia's foreign relations, and opened the country to French commercial interests. King

Mongkut protested but in 1867, reluctantly recognised the French protectorate. The Thais retained Cambodia's north-western provinces, however; these would only be restored to Cambodia in 1907 at the insistence of the French.

For two decades the protectorate meant little change within Cambodia. The French soon realised that the country could offer no rapid economic return, and focussed their development energies on Cochin China. Equally, Norodom proved adept at turning aside French suggestions for administrative or social reform, as he would, throughout his long reign.

In 1884 the French forced Norodom—under threat of being deposed and replaced—to sign an agreement intended to increase the number of French officials in the kingdom, give policy control to the French over all administrative, financial, judicial and commercial matters, initiate a land-titling system, and abolish slavery. The Cambodian ruling class was alarmed at its potential loss of power over taxation, trade, land and labour, and initiated a country-wide revolt. By 1886 the French were willing to acknowledge respect for Cambodian customs and for another two decades change was minimal and cautiously introduced.

At Norodom's death in 1904, however, the French appointed from amongst the possible heirs a king willing to comply with French policies. He was the first of three kings chosen by the French on the basis of their apparent compliancy. The third would be Norodom Sihanouk, who ascended the throne as a shy 19-year-old in 1941. From 1904, therefore, the French were able to establish complete authority over their protectorate. Prior to 1940 they encountered little further opposition. In 1925, the murder of a French official, Felix Bardez, caused a sensation, but only because it seemed an isolated and uncharacteristic challenge to French rule.

Cambodia's economic resources proved to be scanty, even its human resources. In 1921 the population was assessed at about 2.5 million. The main crop was rice, and a Chinese-controlled rice export industry developed, purchasing rice from Khmer farmers, but Cambodian rice was generally considered to be inferior and less efficiently produced than that of Cochin China. Small Chinese timber and pepper industries, and French-financed rubber estates using Vietnamese labour, added to Cambodia's limited exports. Other minor exports included maize, kapok, and dried fish from the Tonle Sap region. The French slowly developed road and rail communications—by 1941 a railway linked Phnom Penh and the Thai border—but the Mekong remained, as it had always been,

Cambodia's main trade route. The port of Saigon dominated this riverine trade.

Around 95 per cent of Khmers remained subsistence farmers. They were characterised by the French—and also by the Chinese, Thais, Vietnamese and often their own elite—as "lazy", "ignorant", "lacking initiative", "fatalistic" and "child-like". Western observers dismissed them as a "decadent race", compared with their ancestors of Angkor. The peasants' options were extremely limited however. French taxation levels were harsh. In addition there is evidence that the peasants' social superiors demand their traditional obligatory dues of product and labour, despite French abolition of formal slavery. In remoter regions, endemic petty violence still made life insecure.

There were further factors deterring any change or development in peasant life. Cambodia was a country where commercial instincts had long been smothered by isolation, war and a ruling class which despised trade, other than as a source of taxation. Under French rule, Chinese and Vietnamese entrepreneurs quickly assumed dominance over trade and money-lending. In colonial Cambodia, no industries of consequence were developed. The country's towns remained small (by the 1930s Phnom Penh's population was about 100,000; Battambang's 20,000) and dominated by aliens—French, Chinese and Vietnamese. Cambodia's elite acquired a French-language education from private tutors or abroad, but for the general population a meagre and essentially traditional education in Buddhist temple schools was all that was available. The first Khmer-language newspaper only appeared in 1938.

Until the 1970s, observers usually saw the lot of Cambodia's peasantry during the colonial era as a relatively happy one. The traumatic events in Cambodia since then have suggested that the countryside harboured much bitter frustration and resentment, waiting to be tapped.

WORLD WAR II, 1940–1945

Such feelings were yet to be coherently expressed, much less given an outlet. In Cambodia politicisation really only began during World War II, and then it was cautious and involved limited numbers. By the 1940s, a tiny Khmer intelligentsia had begun to form, focussed around three institutions—the scholarly Buddhist Institute, Cambodia's sole French-language high school in Phnom Penh, and the Khmer newspaper *Nagara Vatta* (Angkor Wat). Cambodian feelings were outraged in 1940 by the transfer back to Thailand, under

Japanese auspices, of the north-western provinces (these would be returned once more to Cambodia in 1947).

Nationalist stirrings could be tightly controlled by the French, however. The French reached an agreement with the Japanese which allowed them to continue to administer Indochina in exchange for the free movement of Japanese forces. *Nagara Vatta* was strictly censored, and suppressed in mid-1942 following a protest march in Phnom Penh by monks and nationalist-intellectuals over the arrest of a monk implicated in an anti-French plot. A key figure amongst the nationalists, Son Ngoc Thanh, escaped round-up at this point and went to Japan.

The French role in the evolution of Cambodian nationalism was mixed, however. Recognising the need to deflect popular fascination with Japanese power, the French launched a quasi-nationalist movement for young Cambodians, glorifying Cambodia's past and its future "in partnership" with France. They also took steps to raise the status and salaries of Cambodians in government service. Unwittingly, in 1943 they fuelled developing nationalist feelings further by launching a programme to replace Cambodia's Indian-derived form of writing with a roman alphabet. (In Vietnam a comparable reform had been popularly accepted, in the interests of simplicity, efficiency and wider literacy.) The Buddhist *sangha* and the intelligentsia rebelled against what they viewed as an attack on Cambodia's traditional learning and cultural heritage. The Romanisation controversy kept up anti-French feeling until March 1945, when the Japanese seized control of government, interned the French and, amongst other measures, dropped the romanisation programme.

In April 1945 the Japanese, now anxious to harness Cambodian nationalism for themselves, prodded a hesitant Norodom Sihanouk to declare Cambodia "independent'. But when Japan surrendered to the Allies in August 1945, there was no coherent view amongst Cambodia's hereditary or intelligentsia elites about the next step for Cambodia. Cambodia still had no mass anti-colonial movement such as those that emerged in 1945 in Vietnam and Indonesia.

TOWARDS INDEPENDENCE, 1945–1953

After the Japanese surrender, Cambodia drifted. French officials resumed authority and, in October 1945, arrested Son Ngoc Thanh, who had returned to Cambodia in April and had become the main figure trying to organise resistance to the French return. At the same time, the French opened discussions with King Sihanouk about limited Cambodian self-government. Faced with revolution in

Vietnam, they recognised that some gesture towards Cambodia's aroused national feelings would be wise. They also needed the collaboration of Cambodia's elite to restore order in the countryside, where armed bands were flourishing. Some of these armed groups affected a degree of nationalism, calling themselves Khmer Issarak (Free Khmer). Both the strongly anti-French Thai government of the day and the Vietnamese communists were lending them tentative support.

The French, while retaining control of finance, defence, foreign affairs and all key instruments of government, announced elections for a new National Assembly and permitted political parties to form. At the elections, held in September 1946, the winning party proved to be the Democratic Party, which took 50 of the Assembly's 67 seats. The Democrats, though headed by a prince, broadly represented Cambodia's "intelligentsia elite"—schoolteachers, minor government officials, politicised monks and the like—and convincingly demonstrated their ability to organise a strong grassroots vote. Cambodia's traditional royal and aristocratic ruling class, headed by the King, was not amused. Subsequent Democrat attempts to win meaningful powers for the National Assembly and achieve independence would be frustrated not only by the French but also by Sihanouk and those who supported the traditional social order.

By the early 1950s, the lack of political progress was producing acute strains. The National Assembly had become a factionalised talk-shop. A radical fringe of politicised Cambodians were contemplating revolution, some under Son Ngoc Thanh, who established an insurgent movement in the north-west in 1952, and some under the communist, Vietnamese sponsored, KPRP (Khmer People's Revolutionary Party, founded 1951), which was organising guerilla activity in outlying areas. In January 1953, martial law was declared and Sihanouk dissolved the National Assembly.

Sihanouk now executed a dazzling bid for command of his people. Beginning in February 1953 he toured France, the United States and other countries demanding independence. In October 1953, the French—by this time with their backs to the wall in Vietnam—gave in to Sihanouk's campaign. Sihanouk returned to Cambodia a hero.

CAMBODIA UNDER SIHANOUK, 1953–1970

Independence defused most of the insurgency in the countryside. Son Ngoc Thanh dwindled into irrelevance in exile. The leaders of the KPRP retreated to Vietnam, though the party would continue surreptitious recruitment in Cambodia. In 1954, Sihanouk and the conservative elite regarded the Democratic Party as their main challenge, especially as they were obliged to hold national elections in September 1955 under agreements reached at the international Geneva Conference on Indochina in 1954.

Sihanouk responded to this challenge with more strategic brilliance. In March 1955, he abdicated (his father became figurehead king but would die in 1960) and established his own political party, Sangkum Reastr Niyum (People's Socialist Community). His newfound, if vague, commitment to socialism was perhaps designed to distance himself from his conservative background and woo the leftist-inclined intelligentsia. In the same vein, he announced that Cambodia would be unaligned with either the communist or anti-communist world blocs, though he continued to accept the United States' military and economic aid to Cambodia which had begun under the French.

Simultaneously, Democrat supporters found themselves facing violent intimidation from Sihanouk's security forces. Voting procedures at the elections were flagrantly fixed. It is debatable who would have won free and fair elections - Sihanouk the national hero and now apparently a political progressive, or the Democrats—but, in the event, Sihanouk's Sangkum won every seat in the Assembly. After continuing harassment, the Democratic Party dissolved in 1957. Sihanouk, though technically no longer king, now truly seemed to be monarch of all he surveyed.

For over a decade after 1955 he continued to show great adroitness and energy. He personally oversaw all facets of government, controlled news and information, and regularly addressed the people. His rhetoric of "Buddhist Socialism", coming from the lips of a man who retained the aura of a semi-divine king, seemed to offer something for everyone. He bemused his critics of both the left and the right, leaving them unsure where he, or they, stood. Sihanouk enjoyed surprising people with sudden switches of policy, though whether these switches arose from calculation or whim was never clear. The sole constant of his rule was intolerance of opposition. Hundreds of dissidents "disappeared" during this period.

Stifling the discord which undoubtedly would have appeared in a more open political system was Sihanouk's main, if dubious, domestic achievement. He gave Cambodia a kind of peace, which, in later years, many Cambodians would remember fondly. Another domestic achievement was the expansion of education, on which Sihanouk spent as much as 20 per cent of the national budget. Large numbers of secondary- and tertiary-educated young people emerged. Crucially, however, Sihanouk was uninterested in economic matters, and under him the Cambodian economy, after initial growth, went into decline. The combination of stifled political life, an expanding educated class (many of whom were unemployed or underemployed) and a decaying economy would prove disastrous for Sihanouk and Cambodia's domestic peace.

Looming over that peace was the resumed conflict in neighbouring Vietnam. Sihanouk was anxious to save his country from involvement in the conflict, but he also wanted to position Cambodia and himself to be on good terms with the victor. To these ends he proclaimed Cambodia's neutrality but judged it expedient to tilt to the left in foreign and domestic policy. In 1963, he rejected United States aid and nationalised Cambodia's banks and import-export trade in the name of "socialism". In 1965, he broke off diplomatic relations with the United States. Secretly, meanwhile, he accepted the use of Cambodian territory by North Vietnamese forces and the southern Vietnamese NLF insurgents in their fight against the United States-backed Saigon regime. Openly, he established cordial relations with China, perhaps hoping that China might restrain any larger Vietnamese designs on Cambodia.

The rejection of US aid reduced Cambodia's income significantly and disgruntled Cambodia's conservatives, particularly in the military. Nationalisation disgruntled the business elite, heightened inefficiency and corruption, and led to hard times for the people. Sihanouk's toleration of Vietnamese forces on Cambodian soil (who received supplies via the Cambodian port of Sihanoukville) disturbed patriotic Cambodian sentiment.

Around 1966 Sihanouk seems to have tired of his political juggling. His "hands-on" control diminished and the power of the conservative forces in Sangkum and his administration increased. There was growing popular disillusionment with Sihanouk's policies and style, at least in urban areas. The countryside presented a mixed picture; Sihanouk's reputation remained high with many rural people, but in remoter areas a small but revivified communist insurgency was gaining ground. In 1967–68, government forces brutally crushed a peasant revolt in the north-west to which the communists had given leadership. (The revolt was caused by government seizures of rice at low prices under Sihanouk's nationalisation policies.)

In 1969, Sihanouk cautiously re-opened diplomatic relations with the United States, but this now seemed more a sign of indecisiveness than of his old political skills. In March 1970, while

Sihanouk was overseas, the predominantly conservative National Assembly withdrew confidence in Sihanouk as head of state. The principal force behind the move was Sihanouk's cousin and deputy prime minister Sisowath Sirik Matak. Sihanouk's prime minister and long-time associate, Lon Nol, went along with the move, and became head of the new government of the "Khmer Republic' declared in October 1970.

WAR AND REVOLUTION, 1970–1975

The coup against Sihanouk polarised the population. The Lon Nol government initially enjoyed significant support, but Sihanouk rallied anti-government opinion. In late March 1970, he broadcast from Beijing, appealing to people to "engage in guerilla warfare in the jungles against our enemies". The main beneficiaries of his appeal were the communist insurgents, who now enjoyed Sihanouk's blessing and prestige. Moving swiftly to capitalise on their windfall, by 1972 the communists had effectively ranged the countryside against Phnom Penh and other urban areas. Meanwhile, the Lon Nol government proved tragically inept. A series of drives by government forces against the Vietnamese forces in Cambodia in 1970–71 were repulsed with massive casualties, permanently weakening the government's military capabilities. Ironically, the Vietnamese would withdraw from Cambodia voluntarily in early 1973.

The United States backed the Lon Nol government, but resumed US aid served mainly to foster gross corruption in the administration and the military. Lon Nol suffered a stroke in 1971 and failed thereafter to give strong leadership to his factionalised and increasingly demoralised power base. US bombing of the countryside—massive in intensity and appallingly destructive—probably slowed the communist-led advance on Phnom Penh but also drove many of the population to support the insurgency and to regard the US-aligned urban areas with bitter hatred.

In the United States, dwindling confidence in President Nixon and growing opposition to his handling of the Indochina conflict led the US Congress to end the bombing of Cambodia. Thereafter it was a matter of time before the Lon Nol regime collapsed. The insurgents took Phnom Penh on 17 April, 1975.

'DEMOCRATIC KAMPUCHEA': KHMER ROUGE GOVERNMENT 1975–1979

The name "Khmer Rouge" (strictly "Khmers Rouges"—red Khmers) was popularised by Sihanouk in the 1960s as a term for leftist anti-government forces in the countryside. It has remained the name in general use for the forces who took power in 1975, set up a state they called "Democratic Kampuchea', and who, after their overthrow in 1979, resumed rural-based insurgency. In April 1975, however, these forces called themselves *angkar padevat* ("revolutionary organisation"). Their communist leadership was not made explicit until September 1977, when the existence of the CPK (Communist Party of Kampuchea) was announced.

The CPK had been set up in 1968 to resume the insurgency tactics abandoned by the former Khmer People's Revolutionary Party (KPRP) in 1954. In the intervening years the KPRP, based in Vietnam, had continued underground recruitment in Cambodia. Its most famous recruit in retrospect was a young middle-class, Paris-educated schoolteacher, Saloth Sar, who would take the name Pol Pot and rise to leadership of the CPK.

Under Pol Pot the CPK devised a ferociously radical programme of reform for Cambodia. In April 1975, the country was sealed off from the outside world. Phnom Penh and other urban centres were forcefully evacuated and left mostly to decay. All Cambodians were to become farmers under the direction of angkar. Markets, private trade and the use of money were abolished. Professional activity ceased. Books were forbidden and education was abandoned—except for propaganda sessions. Religion was proscribed and the *sangha* dispersed; many former places of worship were levelled. Angkar dictated people's movements, activities, food allowances and dress. Former upper- and middle-class people, former government employees, most professionals and most educated people were treated as expendable labour in the countryside. Many died.

Pol Pot's government glorified ancient Angkor but otherwise almost wholly repudiated Cambodia's past. A totally new "Kampuchea" was going to be built, starting in 1975—"Year Zero". The origins of this apocalyptic programme have been much debated by commentators. Influences on the CPK leadership may have included extreme left-wing theories fashionable in France in the 1950s and 1960s and Mao's "Great Leap Forward" and "Cultural Revolution" in China. But "Pol Potism" was distinctively Cambodian in making popular resentment of Cambodia's humiliating national history the main driving force of revolution. The revolution's enemies were not only the class enemies defined by Marx but any foreign peoples who had degraded Cambodia—led by the Vietnamese, Thais and Americans—and any Cambodians who had colluded with them, which to the CPK meant all city folk. The brutal simplicity of these doctrines, and the vision of building a new Khmer society untainted by foreigners and the old elite, appealed particularly to youth. The lower echelons of angkar were mainly made up of young people, many still teenagers.

The consequences of the CPK's programme were catastrophic. Conditions of life varied from province to province, but hardship was severe to extreme everywhere. While an estimated 500,000 Cambodians had died during the 1970–75 war, over one million more would die under Khmer Rouge rule, from brutality and callousness, mismanagement, malnutrition, disease and the virtual abolition of medical services.

The CPK leadership's particular hatred of the Vietnamese had several consequences. Firstly, the party began to repudiate its Vietnamese-sponsored background. The repudiation turned into a purge of CPK cadres and members who had been trained in Vietnam or who were thought to sympathise with Vietnam's communist government. Tens of thousands died, often after brutal torture, though some escaped to Vietnam. Secondly, Cambodian forces staged repeated incursions into Vietnam, seeking redefinition of the Viet-Cambodian border. Thirdly, Viet-Cambodian relations came to mirror the great split in the communist world—while Vietnam was closely aligned with the USSR, Cambodia moved under the protection of China.

Vietnam staged a warning offensive into Cambodia in late 1977, but subsequently withdrew its troops, massing them along the border. Provocation continued, however, and on Christmas Day 1978 the Vietnamese again invaded. Khmer Rouge forces collapsed before them and the Vietnamese entered a ghostly Phnom Penh on 7 January, 1979. Soon Vietnamese forces in Cambodia would number 250,000. They failed, however, to capture Pol Pot or his close colleagues.

CAMBODIA AS "VIETNAMESE PROTECTORATE", 1979–1991

Though initially welcomed by most Cambodians, the Vietnamese were aware of the centuries-old fear of Vietnam in the country. They also knew that their invasion of a sovereign nation, however repellent its government, could bring international condemnation. Thus, they rapidly established the People's Republic of Kampuchea (PRK) under a government headed by Cambodians, mostly former CPK members who had fled the party's purges. These included Heng Samrin, head of state, and Hun Sen, who would become premier in 1985. Although another one-party state, the new government was relatively laissez faire in the economic and social fields, dismantling the Khmer Rouge's collective farming and restoring the use of money and private trade.

However, Cambodian society was by now utterly destabilised. Before traditional farming could be restored, Cambodia suffered terrible famine. Only by the mid 1980s would the traditional subsistence economy regain equilibrium and the shops and markets of the towns return to precarious life. Meanwhile the PRK, like Vietnam, became an international pariah, supported only by the Soviet bloc and some neutral nations such as India. The United States, China, Thailand and the other ASEAN nations led international condemnation of the Vietnamese presence in Cambodia and of the PRK "puppet" government. Denied legitimacy, the PRK was also denied much international economic aid and trade.

The pawns in this stand-off, apart from the general Cambodian population, were hundreds of thousands of Cambodian refugees camped along the Thai-Cambodian border, who had fled war, famine, the Khmer Rouge or the Vietnamese occupation. Working amongst them were two Cambodian political organisations—the Khmer Rouge and the KPNLF (Khmer People's National Liberation Front), a non-communist, anti-Vietnamese body headed by Son Sann, a former prime minister. The Khmer Rouge enjoyed the staunch backing of China, then also at loggerheads with Vietnam, and received Chinese military aid funneled through Thailand. Despite its grotesque record, the Khmer Rouge also enjoyed international prestige as Cambodia's "legitimate" government, holding Cambodia's seat at the United Nations. Inside Cambodia the Khmer Rouge maintained a shadowy guerilla presence, despite every effort by Vietnamese and PRK forces to eliminate it.

In the early 1980s, Sihanouk and his son, Prince Norodom Ranariddh, also established an anti-PRK organisation, FUNCINPEC (the French acronym for National United Front for an Independent, Neutral, Peaceful and Co-operative Cambodia). Sihanouk had survived the years of Khmer Rouge government under virtual house arrest (he lost 14 children and grandchildren in those years) and was now based in Beijing or, sometimes in North Korea. In mid-1982 a shaky coalition was brokered between the three Cambodian anti-PRK organisations. The Khmer Rouge announced the abolition of the CPK and claimed to be abandoning its former policies. Few believed this.

The international impasse continued through the 1980s. In 1989, Vietnam withdrew its troops from Cambodia, partly because the PRK government now appeared self-sustaining but mainly because of Vietnam's loss of Soviet aid following the collapse of the USSR. In Cambodia, in 1990, the PRK transformed itself into the SOC (State of Cambodia) which effectively committed itself to a private enterprise economy, as Vietnam and China were doing. The SOC government also became active in restoring Cambodian Buddhism.

The ending of the Cold War and the changing economic goals of China and Vietnam opened the possibility of ending the stand-off over Cambodia. After much diplomacy in which Australia played a key role, 20 nations convened in Paris in October 1991. The conference persuaded the SOC government and the three opposition organisations to form a coalition administration pending national elections under United Nations supervision. The inclusion of the Khmer Rouge in this arrangement shocked many people, inside and outside Cambodia, but the move has been defended as the only means of breaking the deadlock, given China's inability to abandon the Khmer Rouge without losing international face. The assumption of responsibility for Cambodia by the UN and the promised elections gave China the chance to discard its ties with the Khmer Rouge.

UNTAC, THE 1993 ELECTIONS AND THE ROYAL GOVERNMENT OF CAMBODIA

The United Nations established UNTAC (United Nations Transitional Authority in Cambodia), which came to consist of 22,000 personnel, two-thirds of them military, from a number of nations. UNTAC's main tasks were to disarm the forces of all four Cambodian factions, repatriate the refugees, monitor the coalition administration of the country (in practice the SOC administration and security apparatus retained great power) and prepare the planned elections. UNTAC's achievements were mixed. The refugees were repatriated but the disarmament process collapsed in May 1992 when the Khmer Rouge, and then SOC, refused to participate. UNTAC also failed to deal with charges that the SOC security forces were using violence against their coalition partners, especially Sihanouk's FUNCINPEC. Sihanouk himself played an unnerving role in this period, appearing in Cambodia to warm popular acclaim but disappearing back to Beijing or Pyongyang with expressions of displeasure and foreboding.

UNTAC won plaudits, however, for its handling of the elections in May 1993. Nearly 90 per cent of enrolled voters (close to five million people) went to the polls, despite threats of Khmer Rouge violence. The Khmer Rouge had decided to boycott the elections, presumably fearing a dismal rebuff from the people. FUNCINPEC candidates won 58 of the available 120 assembly seats. Candidates from the former SOC government contested the election as the CPP (Cambodian People's Party) and won 51 seats. Son Sann's group, now the BLDP (Buddhist Liberal Democratic Party), took ten seats, and a minor party took the one remaining seat.

Elements of the CPP disputed these results but others man-oeuvred to retain a prominent role in government—a role they were virtually guaranteed anyway, given CPP's strength in the bureaucracy, military and police. The following months of deal-making seemed to many observers to decline into a scramble by all parties for the perks of office, a scramble complicated by factionalism within each of the parties. Two months after the election an interim coalition adminis-tration was formed which, in September, became the Royal Govern-ment of Cambodia—in the same month, the Assembly recognised Sihanouk as Cambodia's King once more. Heading the coalition government were Prince Norodom Ranariddh (FUNCINPEC) as "first" prime minister and Hun Sen (CPP) as "second" prime minister. Similar balances had been constructed throughout the ministry. King Sihanouk—technically now a constitutional monarch presiding over a pluralistic, democratic political system—continued to intervene in policy-making, despite reports that he was now ill with cancer. Some felt his meddling was destabilising while others saw them as constructive attempts to balance the antagonistic forces grouped within the government.

CAMBODIA IN THE 21st CENTURY

The coalition between Hun Sen and Ranariddh—fragile and acrimo-nious at the best of times—ruptured in 1997 following a violent power struggle that saw the latter forced to flee into temporary exile overseas. Following threats by foreign donors to withdraw aid and calls for reconciliation by King Sihanouk, Hun Sen and his CCP agreed to hold fresh elections in July 1998. These were marred by violence and accusations of vote-buying, and resulted in an easy victory for the CCP. Opposition leaders Ranariddh and Sam Rainsy (of the Sam Rainsy Party, formerly the Khmer Nation Party) dismissed the result as a fraud. However, their capacity to do anything about it was circumscribed by Hun Sen's control of the government and military, as well as the official media. In addition, foreign observers reported that although the CCP had marshalled these forces during the election to influence otherwise apathetic villagers in a way its opponents could not match, the poll was generally free and fair nonetheless, and the result an accurate reflection of the majority's wishes. Such was Hun Sen's dominance in the subsequent years that his party defeated the opposition to claim 47 per cent of all votes cast during general elections in July 2003. FUNCINPEC (which gained 21 per cent) and the Sam Rainsy Party (SRP, which gained 22 per cent) immediately claimed that the ballot was not free and fair and demanded that Hun Sen step down. Since the CCP had failed to obtain a two-thirds majority of National Assembly seats, which would have enabled it to form a single-party government, it was forced to negotiate. It was not until June 2004 that it was able to reach an agreement with FUNCINPEC. In general elections in July 2008, the CCP won a convincing victory with 58 per cent of the vote, entitling Hun Sen's party to 90 seats in the 123 seat National Assembly. This compared with SRP's 22 per cent (26 seats) and other parties, including FUNCINPEC, gaining only 20 per cent (seven seats).

One favourable development for the country lies in the fact that by the late 1990s the Khmer Rouge ceased to exist as a political or military threat. A succession of military defeats and defections due to a withdrawal of aid from their backers in Thailand and China, and a general decline in the organisation's political relevance in the post-Cold War era, all combined to undermine the Khmer Rouge's influence. Pol Pot died on 15 April 1998, and the movement's last commander at large, Ta Mok, was captured in March 1999. Unrepentant to the end, before his death Pol Pot blamed the "Year Zero" disaster on disloyal Cambodians and the Vietnamese.

Many human-rights observers have been critical of the government's seeming reluctance to prosecute those responsible for the killings committed by the Khmer Rouge. Even though King Sihanouk signed a new law in 2001 setting up a tribunal to try those accused, few former Khmer Rouge officials have been sent to trial. Hun Sen himself has been accused by human-rights observers and opposition parties of supporting increased repression against protesters, critics and members of rival political parties, especially in 2003 when he announced the formation of a "Central Bureau for Security" intelligence wing consisting mostly of high ranking CPP officials.

In November 2002, Cambodia hosted the eighth ASEAN Summit and in September 2003 received permission to join the World Trade Organization—the first "least developed" country to be invited to join. In October 2004, King Sihanouk announced he would abdicate, citing ill-health. His son, Prince Norodom Sihamoni, was announced as his successor.

The current government is heavily underwritten by foreign aid donors, especially Japan, the United States, the European Union and Australia. China has also recently emerged as an important aid donor, lender of "soft" (low or zero interest) loans and foreign investor. As Chinese assistance has tended to be free of the conditions accompanying western aid (especially regarding progress on human rights and corruption), it has been particularly welcomed by Hun Sen. He described China as Cambodia's "most trustworthy friend" during a visit by Chinese Premier Wen Jiabao in April 2006.

Dependence on foreign aid (which in the period 1993 to 2006 was estimated at over US$6 billion) is likely to lessen in the future as donor countries scale back their largesse and Cambodia develops alternative sources of revenue, such as the booming tourist industry. Indeed, the services sector now accounts for nearly half of GDP. Defence spending has also been pared back from 6.4 per cent of GDP in the mid 1990s to approximately one per cent today, though Cambodia still maintains a large standing army with a top-heavy command structure. International aid projects and foreign and domestic private enterprise have been encouraged by the "technocrats" who hold the economic portfolios, but face an often irresolute government, a still inadequate legal framework, and an unwieldy and often corrupt bureaucracy, customs service and police force. Law and order has also become a concern, with armed robbery and murder all too common occurrences in a society awash with weapons following decades of civil war.

These uncertainties pose many challenges for Cambodia's development. Over the centuries, the country's fortunes have risen and fallen, depending on the policies of its larger and more powerful neighbours. In this century, it is to be hoped that Cambodians may at long last be in command of their own economic and social development against a backdrop of peace, social cohesion and political stability—all elements tragically lacking in much of the last one.

3 EAST TIMOR

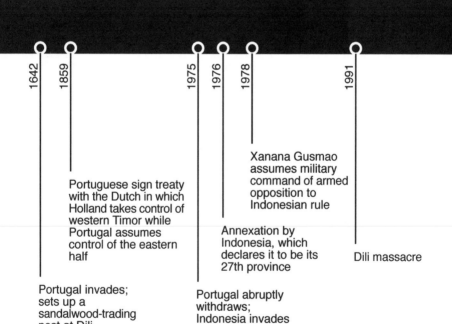

1642

1859

1975

1976

1978

1991

Portuguese sign treaty with the Dutch in which Holland takes control of western Timor while Portugal assumes control of the eastern half

Xanana Gusmao assumes military command of armed opposition to Indonesian rule

Annexation by Indonesia, which declares it to be its 27th province

Dili massacre

Portugal invades; sets up a sandalwood-trading post at Dili

Portugal abruptly withdraws; Indonesia invades

The Merdeka Monument in Dili City

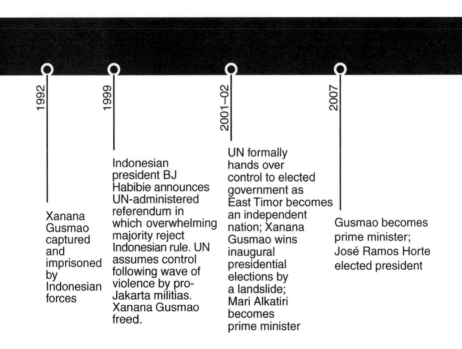

1992

Xanana Gusmao captured and imprisoned by Indonesian forces

1999

Indonesian president BJ Habibie announces UN-administered referendum in which overwhelming majority reject Indonesian rule. UN assumes control following wave of violence by pro-Jakarta militias. Xanana Gusmao freed.

2001–02

UN formally hands over control to elected government as East Timor becomes an independent nation; Xanana Gusmao wins inaugural presidential elections by a landslide; Mari Alkatiri becomes prime minister

2007

Gusmao becomes prime minister; José Ramos Horte elected president

3 EAST TIMOR

Little is known about Timor's pre-colonial history. However the opportunities to profit from its abundant sandalwood forests prompted the Portuguese to establish a trading post on the island in 1642, which was around the period the Dutch were consolidating their presence elsewhere across the archipelago and establishing what was to become the Dutch East Indies. Dutch expansion over the subsequent centuries led to a treaty between the two European trading powers which ceded the eastern half of Timor to Portugal while the Dutch took control of the western half.

Timor island assumed a strategic importance during World War II and its people endured a brutal wartime occupation in which 10 per cent of its population—approximately 50,000 people—are thought to have died. More tragedy was in store for East Timor in the post-war era when the Portuguese—who had resumed control in 1945—abruptly withdrew in 1975 as a result of decolonisation policies being pursued by the newly installed democratic government in Lisbon. Portuguese sovereignty had brought few tangible benefits to the East Timorese people and their sudden departure left East Timor totally unprepared for independence.

Indonesia's President Suharto became alarmed that a Marxist government seemed likely to take control in the ensuing chaos and, with tacit support from Australia and the United States, the

Indonesian armed forces invaded East Timor. In the following year, 1976, Indonesia announced its formal annexation and declared East Timor to be its 27th province, although few countries, or, indeed, and the United Nations, ever recognised these claims of sovereignty. The occupation was met by fierce resistance from armed guerillas, the main group of which was called Fretilin. During the period of Indonesian rule, a quarter of the population was estimated to have died from famine and disease.

The methods by which the occupying forces quelled dissent received huge international exposure during 1991 following what was to become known as the Dili massacre, in which Indonesian soldiers shot dead hundreds of unarmed protesters. Suharto's government was further embarrassed when two of the most internationally prominent anti-Indonesian figures, exiled Fretilin representative Jose Ramos Horta and Bishop Carlos Belo (spiritual head of East Timor's over-whelmingly Catholic population until his retirement in 2002) were jointly awarded the Nobel Peace Prize in 1996.

Following Suharto's resignation in 1998, his successor B. J. Habibie was keen to end the diplomatic running sore that more than 20 years of failed pacification programmes had come to represent. He announced that a UN-supervised referendum on greater autonomy would be held on 30 August, 1999 and gave assurances that if the East Timorese people rejected it, he would allow East Timor to cut itself loose from Indonesia. When 78 per cent of voters rejected Habibie's proposal, the way was clear for full independence.

In the months following the vote, a wave of violence in which over 2,000 people died was perpetuated by pro-Jakarta East Timorese militias with the covert backing of the Indonesian military, whose generals had been humiliated by the sudden volte-face shown by the politicians. During this chaotic period, thousands of refugees fled into West Timor and much of East Timor's infrastructure was razed by rampaging militiamen. When it became clear to Habibie that his army was unwilling to reign in the militias, he reluctantly allowed a UN multinational peace-keeping force to restore order in late 1999 and prepare the territory for full independence, which was formally granted at midnight on 20 May, 2002. Former Fretilin commander Xanana Gusmao (who had been captured and imprisoned by the Indonesians in 1992) was sworn in as East Timor's first president after winning 80 per cent of the popular vote in presidential elections the preceding month.

At the time of independence, Gusmao commanded tremendous respect both at home and abroad (and still does), with his stature and integrity earning him frequent comparisons with South Africa's

Nelson Mandela. But the problems he and Prime Minister Mari Alkatiri (who headed Fretilin's political wing, which won the biggest block of seats in the Constituent Assembly elections of 2001) faced in leading East Timor into a prosperous future were formidable. Tensions between the two men escalated in March 2006 when one third of the national army (mostly soldiers from the western regions of the country) mutinied amid claims by their commanders that the government had favoured units from the east, which had provided the bulk of anti-Indonesian rebels during Indonesian rule.

The mutineers demanded the government resign, and accompanying civil unrest and anarchy resulted in 150,000 people fleeing the capital for refugee camps. An international UN-sponsored peace keeping force, led by Australia and including soldiers and police from New Zealand, Malaysia and Portugal, eventually restored order. On 30 May President Gusmao declared a state of emergency and Prime Minister Alkatiri resigned on 26 June in favour of José Ramos-Horta. In February 2007, Ramos-Horta declared his candidacy for forthcoming presidential elections and Gusmao declared his candidacy for prime minister on behalf of a new political party, the Conselho Nacional de Reconstrução do Timor (CNRT), which was set up to oppose Fretilin's control of parliament. In 2007 presidential elections, Ramos-Horta defeated Fretilin's candidate Francisco Guterres to become president, while legislative elections in the same year resulted in a coalition government (excluding Fretilin, which nonetheless remained the largest single party in parliament) led by the CNRT. Gusmao became prime minister. Fretilin's failure to do as well as expected stemmed from widespread disillusionment at corruption by party functionaries and at the slow pace of reform.

The country was shocked in early 2008 by coordinated assassination attempts by rebel soldiers on both Gusmao and Ramos-Horta. On the morning of 11 February, Gusmao escaped an attempted ambush while Ramos-Horta was shot in the chest in a separate attack. He made a remarkable recovery in an Australian hospital and returned triumphant to Dili to resume official duties in April 2008. The rebel's leader, Alfredo Reinado, was killed in the attack on Ramos-Horta.

East Timor is one of the poorest countries in the region with more than 40 per cent of its 1.1 million people living below the poverty line. Unemployment in the urban areas remains stubbornly high while the rural sector, which comprises 90 per cent of the population, primarily consists of subsistence farmers (though it is hoped coffee may one day constitute a key export market). Illiteracy is estimated at 50 per cent and life expectancy is just 57 years.

The biggest hope for East Timor's economic development stems from its sovereignty over oil and gas reserves in the Timor Sea. In May 2005, Australia and East Timor jointly announced an agreement to carve up multi-billion dollar offshore oil and gas reserves, following talks which had commenced in 2002 over their disputed maritime boundary. Under the agreement (signed in 2006 and entered into force in 2007), the two countries deferred a decision on a permanent boundary for up to a century. In return, East Timor will derive several billion extra dollars from the most profitable Greater Sunrise field than it would have under an interim deal struck in 2002. In May 2002 Alkatiri set up a petroleum revenue reserve fund based on the Norwegian model in which interest accrued from the fund is used to fund national development. In 2009 Fretilin, then in opposition, bitterly opposed an attempt by Gusmao (as prime minister and leader of the CNRT) to draw on US$240 million of the fund (including its capital base) to generate employment and counter the causes of discontent that rocked the country in 2006. Fretilin accused the government of seeking to operate a slush fund. It is certain that in spite of access to petroleum revenues, the new country will remain heavily dependent for its development on foreign aid and expertise for the foreseeable future.

In July 2006 East Timor signed the ASEAN Treaty of Amity and Cooperation, the first step towards full membership. In September 2007 Ramos-Horta announced he had established a task force to prepare for the country's eventual accession to ASEAN, which he predicted would take place in approximately five years. Even though in many ways it has more in common with the constituent members of the Pacific Islands Forum, ASEAN would be a more logical choice given its greater political and economic clout. It would also provide a further forum for engagement with Indonesia. To this end East Timor's leaders have repeatedly signaled the government's priority is to ensure good relations with Indonesia in order that issues of trade and border demarcation are resolved in a spirit of cooperation.

4 INDONESIA

6th–8th centuries

13th century

16th century

1602

1796

1942

1945

1946–49

1950

VOC bankrupt:
Dutch government
assumes control

Netherlands United
East India
Company (VOC)
formed and attacks
Jayakarta in 1619

Portuguese first to
establish trading
posts

Islam spreads
throughout
archipelago

Borobudur and
Prambanan
temples built

President Sukarno
elected leader of
independent
Indonesia

Dutch resume
control and guerrilla
war starts

Independence
unilaterally declared
on 17 August

Japanese
occupation

Borobudor

1959–65

1965

1965

Late 1980s

1997

1998

1999

1999

2001

2004

Wahid impeached and vice-president Megawati Sukarnoputri becomes president

Non-oil exports exceed oil exports and Indonesian economy undergoes steady liberalisation and internationalisation

President Abdurrahman Wahid elected

New Order government under President Suharto

East Timor becomes independent

Unsuccessful coup attempt by some army officers

President Suharto steps down

Period of Guided Democracy

Asian economic crisis envelopes Indonesia

Susilo Bambang Yudhoyono elected president; tsunami kills over 164,000 people

4 INDONESIA

Indonesia's geography is an integral part of its history. A sprawling archipelago straddling the equator, Indonesia has more than 13,500 islands, ranging from tiny areas that not so long ago were merely atolls to the huge island of Sumatra. In 2009 it had 229 million people, spread very unevenly across these islands. At the one extreme, over 130 million live on densely populated Java; at the other extreme, the large, resource-rich island of Kalimantan is sparsely populated. Indonesia is a tropical country with a volcanic spine running through its archipelago. Many volcanoes are still active, every so often wreaking destruction on surrounding peoples and crops. But the volcanic soil and the tropical climate have made most of Indonesia extremely fertile, nowhere more so than the river valleys of Java, where prosperous kingdoms have waxed and waned over more than a thousand years.

The Indonesian coat of arms bears the inscription "Unity in Diversity". The diversity of Indonesia is apparent to even the most casual observer. There are over 300 socio-linguistic groups in Indonesia, each with a distinct culture and heritage. Only about one in six Indonesians speaks the national language at home. Even fewer speak Bahasa Indonesia as their first language. The mother tongue of the vast majority is a regional language; for example, Javanese, Balinese, Minangkabau or Acehnese. Nursery rhymes, childhood stories, myths, legends and cultural mores are as diverse as the languages. Not surprisingly, most Indonesians first develop a regional identity, only learning the national language, Bahasa Indonesia, and with it an Indonesian identity, when they begin school. Only in the major cities of Jakarta, Surabaya, Bandung and Medan are there significant numbers of people who speak Bahasa Indonesia in the home and identify themselves as Indonesians from childhood. The diversity of Indonesia is an enormous challenge to the modern State. Nation-building in Indonesia is no mere slogan, nor is it merely a euphemism for economic development. The Indonesian government is acutely aware that national unity and a national cultural identity have to be created. The regional identity that most Indonesians acquire automatically, together with the country's cultural and linguistic diversity, makes nation-building and the development of social cohesiveness a long-term and difficult task.

PRE-COLONIAL INDONESIA
South-East Asia lies astride the great trading routes from China to India. There are records stretching back over 2,000 years of traders sailing their ships between China and South-East Asia and between South-East Asia and India. South-East Asia, and especially the Indonesian archipelago, was a source of spices, gourmet foods, sandalwood, medicines and other tropical products. Chinese, Arabic and Indian traders were a common sight in the ports which dotted the archipelago.

There were two broad types of states in the Indonesian archipelago in the pre-modern period. First were the coastal states. Located at the mouths of rivers with good secure harbours, they were dependent on regional and international trade. The most prominent of these were on or close to the Straits of Melaka, through which shipping between China and India (and later Europe and China) had to pass—on the east and south coast of Sumatra and on the north Java coast. Second were the inland states. The wealth of these states was based on rich agricultural production from the volcanic soils of the alluvial plains. The most prominent of these were in Central and East Java and in Bali.

The earliest kingdoms in the Indonesian archipelago were Hindu/Buddhist states. Hinduism and Buddhism came to South-East Asia from India, spreading along the trade routes and being adopted by local rulers attracted by the Court ritual and religious/philosophical ideas. Today visitors to Indonesia flock to the central Javanese city of Yogyakarta. Together with its neighbouring city of

Solo, Yogyakarta is the heartland of the Javanese, the centre of their history, culture and philosophy. Within 30 kilometres of Yogyakarta are two great religious monuments: the Buddhist temple of Borobudor and the Hindu temple of Prambanan. Both were built out of local stone between the sixth and eighth centuries, hundreds of years before the medieval cathedrals of Europe even began. Restoration projects have revealed the stunning beauty of the temples, their sheer scale of construction and the intricate carved base-reliefs which adorn them from top to bottom. These are religious monuments, dating from a time when Hinduism and Buddhism were the predominant religions in Java. They are evidence of the prosperity of the kingdoms to which they belonged, the engineering knowledge of their people, their craftsmanship and their artistry. Borobudor and Prambanan temples are the finest in Indonesia, but hundreds of other smaller temples can be found throughout Java. The Balinese remain predominantly Hindu and there are many thousands of old and new temples in Bali.

Muslim traders are recorded in the Indonesian archipelago as early as the sixth century, but the Islamisation of Indonesia began in the 13th century with the conversion of the ruler of Aceh, at the northern tip of Sumatra. We know little about this early conversion but it is clear that the Islamisation process was very slow, with people absorbing Islamic beliefs into existing religious and philosophical systems as they adapted Islam to Indonesian soil. When the Dutch arrived in Indonesia at the beginning of the 17th century, the kingdoms they engaged with were almost all Islamic, with Hinduism restricted to Bali. But the nature of Indonesian Islam varied greatly, and still does. There is a broad spectrum of practices and intensities of belief, ranging from the Acehnese, who are generally more publicly Islamic and more strict adherents to the principles of the Koran than others in Indonesia, to the people of central and east Java, who have a more relaxed Islamic faith sustained alongside pre-Islamic beliefs and practices.

The inland kingdoms were prosperous agrarian states generating considerable agricultural surpluses. They were strongly hierarchical states, with taxation systems extracting agricultural products and labour from the peasants. They developed legal systems and bureaucratic structures. The agricultural surpluses supported large courts and the skilled workers needed to build the massive stone temples. The courts promoted high cultures of music, dance, philosophy and literature. The great Indian epic poems, the *Mahabharata* and the *Ramayana* were adapted by court musicians, dancers and master puppeteers as vehicles for the transmission of Javanese or Balinese ethics and cultural values. Writing systems were based on Sanskrit, with many Sanskrit words entering local languages.

When the Europeans arrived in South-East Asia in the middle of the 16th century, there were well-established states across the whole of South-East Asia. The early European visitors marvelled at the prosperity of the region, the health of its peoples and the sophistication of its high cultures. There were long-standing trading networks linking the South-East Asian states and a tradition of shipbuilding and maritime skills which saw traders from South-East Asia ply their wares as far afield as China and India. The major Indonesian states were at Aceh, on the northern tip of Sumatra; in Central Java; in Bali; in the Malukas and Sulawesi; and on the north coast of Java. They competed vigorously, sometimes waging war on each other. There was a constant flow of goods and people across the archipelago, using Malay as the medium of communication.

COLONIALISM

The Portuguese were the first Europeans to acquire outposts in Asia. In the 16th century they established trading posts and colonial outposts in places as disparate as Goa in India, Melaka in Malaysia, Ambon and Timor in Indonesia, and Macau in China. By the beginning of the 17th century the power of Catholic Portugal and Spain was waning in the face of the emerging Protestant nations of England and the Netherlands. The English East India Company and the Netherlands United East India Company (VOC) were established in 1600 and 1602, respectively. For nearly 200 years they were fierce commercial rivals in Asia. The VOC moved quickly to establish trading posts in India, Ceylon, Taiwan and China, seeking the produce of "the Orient". A major target was the Spice Islands, what is now Sulawesi and Maluku in eastern Indonesia. The VOC first became involved in the Indonesian archipelago through trading with local kingdoms, but its desire to monopolise the spice trade to Europe quickly caused it to expel the Portuguese from Ambon and then to destroy the local kingdoms. In 1619, the VOC launched an attack on Jayakarta, then a major fort and trading town of the West Java kingdom of Bantan where the VOC had been trading peacefully for a number of years. The Bantanese were driven out and on the ashes of the razed town the VOC established its headquarters for the archipelago. Jayakarta was re-named Batavia, a name which was retained for the capital of the Netherlands East Indies until the declaration of independence in August 1945, when it was again re-named, this time as Jakarta.

The VOC slowly extended its physical presence in the Indonesian archipelago. Throughout the 17th and 18th centuries it behaved much like a local kingdom, creating and breaking alliances with rival kingdoms to make war on its enemies and trading widely both within the archipelago and with China, India and Europe. But there were crucial differences which eventually enabled the Dutch to conquer the archipelago. First, the VOC had a power base outside the archipelago, with gunboats and troops stationed throughout Asia which it could use against indigenous rulers. Second, the VOC had a broader strategic framework and, against traditional ruling elites with little experience of the world outside the archipelago, they were able to take advantage of the rivalry between local kingdoms. Third, by the 18th century they had superior weaponry.

Nevertheless, it was not until 1756 that the VOC controlled the whole of Java, when it divided the Mataram Court of Central Java against itself. The VOC went bankrupt in 1796, wracked by corruption. It then controlled Java, Ambon and small nearby islands, and small enclaves in central and southern Sumatra. It was the biggest, most powerful State in the archipelago, but most of what is now Indonesia still lay outside its control. The Netherlands Crown took over the assets of the VOC and, after a brief interlude of British control of Java during the Napoleonic Wars, the East Indies reverted to Dutch rule. Through the 19th century, the Netherlands East Indies government gradually extended its control over Sumatra and eastern Indonesia. With the destruction of the Balinese kingdoms in 1905 and the defeat of the powerful kingdom of Aceh in 1911 the colony was complete. The Dutch often talked of their 300 years in the Netherlands East Indies but, for most people in the archipelago, incorporation into the Netherlands East Indies occurred towards the end of the 19th century or in the first decade of the 20th century. Local pride, regional political, cultural and personal loyalties and a sense of local history remained strong when the Japanese destroyed the Dutch empire in 1941.

By the beginning of the 20th century the Dutch had created the Netherlands East Indies as a centralised state, with power concentrated in the capital, Batavia, an efficient bureaucracy and a police and military service able to maintain social control. After the bitter experience of fighting the fiercely Islamic kingdom of Aceh for over 40 years, the colonial government maintained a careful watch on Islamic religious leaders. Its policy distinguished between Islam as a religion and Islam as a political force. Religious observance was interfered with as little as possible, though mosques, Islamic schools and religious teachers were carefully monitored to ensure that they did nothing to rally people against the colonial state. The involvement of Islamic leaders in political activities was carefully monitored and ruthlessly quashed if they appeared to be gathering local support. The Dutch promoted a Western-educated, secular elite built around the children of the pre-colonial elites and made every effort to prevent the development of a modernised Islamic elite.

The Dutch economic impact on the Indonesian archipelago was enormous. In their successful efforts to control the quantity and prices of the products of the archipelago, they gradually destroyed regional trading networks that had existed for hundreds of years, serviced in large part by indigenous traders who plied the archipelago and sailed as far as India to the east and China to the north. Indigenous traders were henceforth restricted to local trade. External trade became the exclusive preserve of European companies, and inter-regional trade the preserve of Chinese who were encouraged to immigrate from southern China.

Javanese agriculture in particular was transformed by the Dutch in the 19th century. They created what they called a "Cultivation System", by which Javanese farmers were compelled to produce designated crops for sale to the State at fixed prices. The crops—mainly sugar, indigo, coffee and tea—were then processed and transported for sale to European markets. By the end of the 19th century, Java was the world's largest sugar producer. Sugar mills were built throughout rural Java to process the raw cane and railways and ports constructed to take the export crops to market. Java, largely a subsistence economy before 1830, was transformed. The subsistence economy gave way to a much more diversified economy: the population steadily grew until, by the end of the 19th century, there was little uncultivated land left, and towns and cities expanded greatly to service the burgeoning export trade. By the beginning of the 20th century, most Javanese no longer owned land, working as tenant farmers, sharecroppers or wage labourers in the local area and nearby towns.

The economic transformation of Sumatra in the first 30 years of the 20th century was equally dramatic. Huge areas of virgin forest made way for tobacco and rubber plantations. Sumatra became one of the world's largest and finest suppliers of tobacco and, together with Malaya, its largest supplier of rubber. When oil was discovered in the 1920s, it became the springboard for what was to become the Royal Dutch Shell Oil Company.

Much of the labour which opened up Sumatra was Chinese. Chinese had long been resident in the Indonesian archipelago, predominantly as traders and merchants, and there had been a steady growth in their numbers in the 17th and 18th centuries. The great expansion, however, was part of the wider process of Chinese migration to South-East Asia, Australia, the Pacific and the United States after the acquisition of Hong Kong by Britain in 1842 and the forced opening of treaty ports on the South China coast. In the Netherlands East Indies, they became not only traders, shopkeepers and urban workers but labourers on plantations, in tin and coal mines and on wharves and ships. They were never a large proportion of the colony's population, less than 3 per cent, but by the 20th century were dominant in local trade and urban commerce.

The economic transformation of Indonesia led to an accelerating process of urbanisation. By the mid-1910s, the major cities in Java were already unable to cope with the migration from rural areas. The increasingly densely populated poorer parts of the towns and cities had low-quality houses, with no sanitation systems or piped water. They flooded badly during the annual monsoon season, with their people wracked by malaria and water-borne diseases such as cholera and typhoid. The colonial government lacked the political will to tackle these urban problems which, by the 1920s, were probably beyond its capacity to solve. Living conditions for most urban Indonesians steadily worsened from the 1920s through to the 1970s.

The Dutch introduced Western education in order to provide the skilled labour needed by the expanding colonial economy. Dutch was used as the medium of instruction by the best schools, graduation from which led to the better-paid administrative jobs or the possibility of entering a university in the Netherlands or the medical and law schools in the colony. But entry to these schools were very difficult and, those few on scholarships aside, in practice was restricted to children of the indigenous elites or government officials. It was easier to get a modicum of education in schools where the medium of instruction was the vernacular language. Even so, at the end of the Dutch colonial era, the literacy rate in Indonesia was lower than in that of any other European colony in Asia, with the exception of the Portuguese colony of East Timor.

NATIONALISM

The first people to regard themselves as Indonesian, rather than as Javanese, Acehnese or a member of one of the other ethnic groups, were young men and women who had received a Western education at local high schools and, subsequently at universities in the Netherlands. The term "Indonesia" was first used in the early 1920s, but by

1928 the idea of being Indonesian and the determination to create a modern Indonesian nation free from Dutch colonial rule was widely held. In that year, a national Youth Congress was held in Batavia, at which thousands of emotionally aroused youths witnessed the ceremonial raising of the red and white flag, recited a National Pledge and sang a newly composed national song. This was a public expression of their determination to create an independent Indonesia, with a common flag, language (Bahasa Indonesia, which was derived from Malay) and national identity which transcended regional and ethnic loyalties.

The first stirrings of nationalism in the 1910s were seen by the Dutch colonial government as potentially dangerous but not an immediate threat. As political parties enrolled thousands of members and as newspapers and propaganda handbills were widely distributed, the colonial laws were made more restrictive and political activists repeatedly jailed or exiled from the colony. The Dutch could never understand the intensity of nationalist feelings and had no plans for the colony's political development beyond vague references to the possibility of self-government eventually.

The Indonesian Communist Party (PKI) tried a revolutionary path to independence in badly planned uprisings in November 1926 and January 1927. The only result was that thousands of Indonesians, many of whom had only a marginal connection with the PKI, were either jailed or exiled to a political prison on the malaria-infested upper reaches of the Digul River, in what is now West Irian. There they stayed until taken to Australian jails in 1942 in the wake of the Japanese occupation of Indonesia. Ironically, they did not remain in jail long once Australian trade unionists realised that they were political prisoners. Many of them became leaders of a campaign to support Indonesian independence in 1945 and 1946. This resulted in Australian trade union blacklisting Dutch shipping and in the Australian government giving diplomatic support of the Indonesian Republic against the Dutch.

The most prominent Indonesian nationalist from the mid 1920s was a young engineering graduate named Sukarno. Before he was exiled in February 1934, Sukarno laid the basis for his dominant political position after 1945 as President of Indonesia. Sukarno alternatively charmed and irritated his fellow nationalists, but even his strongest opponents admired the brilliance of his oratory. Wherever he went, he drew large and enthusiastic crowds to his political rallies in both large cities and small towns.

More than any other person, Sukarno succeeded in spreading the simple message of freedom to a wider cross-section of urban and rural

Indonesians than ever before. He popularised the nationalist ideology—the simple idea that his people were Indonesians and must set aside their religious and ethnic differences to unite in opposition to colonial rule. Although he was exiled in 1934, his memory lingered on in the minds of ordinary Indonesians who had heard him speak or been charmed by his charismatic personality or had simply heard of his heroic qualities from others.

Two major issues were not resolved by the colonial nationalist movement but became major issues in Indonesian politics in the 1950s and 1960s. First there was the question of the role of Islam in Indonesia. The mainstream of the nationalist movement in the 1920s and 1930s was in agreement that an independent Indonesia should be a secular state. This position was adopted partly because of the religious diversity of Indonesia: although Muslims were in an overwhelming majority, only a minority of these were strict adherents to Islamic teachings and precepts. A secular state was seen as a way of avoiding conflict. Some Islamic political parties disagreed and, after independence, strengthened their demands for national laws to be based on Islamic teaching. In Indonesia today this is still one of the most sensitive issues.

A second major unresolved issue was whether Indonesia needed a social and economic revolution, or whether political independence was a sufficient goal. The advocates of major social and economic reforms were in a minority in the 1920s and 1930s. The dominant view was that Indonesians should concentrate on achieving independence and concern themselves with these potentially divisive issues after this was achieved. Those who wanted more fundamental social and economic reforms revived their activities in the 1950s. Their criticism was then directed at an Indonesian government in the hands of those who had led the nationalist movement since the late 1920s.

THE JAPANESE OCCUPATION

The Japanese occupied Indonesia in March 1942, with little resistance from the Dutch. Initially, they were welcomed by many Indonesians, who were glad to be freed from Dutch rule and impressed by Japanese propaganda slogans such as "Japan the Light of Asia" and the "East Asian Co-Prosperity Sphere". However, it did not take very long for the Japanese to alienate themselves from all levels of Indonesian society. The *romusha* programme on Java, whereby all able-bodied males were required to provide free labour for the war effort, affected almost every family. Most *romusha* labour was used within the colony, on projects such as building railway lines and ships and on infrastructure construction. But hundreds of thousands were sent overseas to work on the construction of the Thai-Burma railway and Japanese projects elsewhere in South-East Asia. Rice production on Java fell, through Japanese mismanagement as much as any other cause, and food and clothing were soon in desperately short supply. Indonesians quickly learnt that despite Japanese propaganda stressing Asian solidarity against Europeans, they were treated as distinctly inferior people by the Japanese.

However, Japanese occupation policies had some long-term benefits for Indonesia. First, in removing the Dutch from administrative functions the Japanese elevated Indonesians to positions they would not have been able to obtain under colonial rule. This administrative experience proved useful after 1945. Second, they prohibited the use of Dutch and, while promoting Japanese, were pragmatic enough to realise that few Indonesians would be able to master that language quickly. They therefore promoted the use of Indonesian in schools and in government administration. This proved to be of help to the infant Republic of Indonesia after 1945. Third, they mobilised young Indonesians to support the Japanese war effort. Various schemes were created to provide military training for young people. This military training proved invaluable when Indonesia had to confront the re-occupying Dutch forces between 1946 and 1949. Fourth, they freed nationalist leaders from jail, including Sukarno, on the condition that they supported the war effort. Sukarno and other nationalists used every opportunity to nurture a sense of being Indonesian, using all the propaganda tools placed at their disposal by the Japanese.

By the end of 1944 it was clear to the Japanese that they were losing the Pacific War. As a consequence, they determined to make it as difficult as possible for the Western powers to re-occupy their former colonies. In Indonesia, they began to promote moves towards independence, encouraging nationalists to work out a desirable constitutional framework. Some Indonesians were alarmed at the prospect of obtaining independence courtesy of the Japanese, believing that this would cause the Allied powers to view an independent Indonesia as a puppet regime, thereby playing into the hands of the Dutch whose Netherlands Indies Administration had spent the war years in Brisbane planning to reoccupy Indonesia as soon as the war was over. When the atomic bombs brought the Pacific War to an end, these people prevailed on Sukarno and his fellow nationalist leaders to declare independence unilaterally. On 17 August 1945, at a simple flag raising ceremony in Jakarta, the Republic of Indonesia was born.

THE REVOLUTION

The Netherlands rejected this declaration of independence, asserting that it was the legitimate government of Indonesia. It began its re-occupation of the country in the middle of 1946 and quickly gained control of most of the towns and cities. The government of the Republic of Indonesia retreated to the principality of Yogyakarta in Central Java. Over the next four years, the Indonesians fought the Dutch on two fronts: In a guerrilla war which quickly bogged down thousands of Dutch troops and prevented the Dutch from holding the countryside; and with a diplomatic offensive that focused on pressuring the United States to withdraw Marshall Plan aid from the Netherlands and on urging the newly created United Nations to support its independence. In December 1949, an agreement was finally reached between the Republic of Indonesia and the Netherlands, bringing the war to an end and formally recognising the end of Dutch colonial rule.

Many Western observers argued that Indonesia would not survive very long, in the face of regionalism and cultural and ethnic diversity. In retrospect, they greatly underestimated the enormous sense of being Indonesian which had been created among a broad cross-section of people by what Indonesians called their "Revolution". Having to fight for their independence gave the Indonesian elites a strong sense of nationalism. Above all, the Revolution saw the emergence of a strong Indonesian army, with a firm ideological commitment to maintaining national unity and to taking a leading role in the development of their society.

As a result of three years of Japanese occupation and four years of warfare with the Dutch, the Indonesian economy was devastated. The economic infrastructure was in tatters, most of the little industry that had existed in 1941 was in ruins and productivity in the plantations and on the farms had regressed to well below pre-war levels. Under-employment in the urban areas was a massive problem, essential services simply didn't work. In the countryside, growing population pressure on the land led to lower per-capita outputs and a steady stream of migrants to the already overcrowded towns and cities. Added to this was the problem of what to do with the hundreds of thousands of people who had given years of their lives as guerrillas fighting the Dutch. They feared demobilisation when there was little prospect of gainful employment. In 1950, revolutionary élan was high and expectations of the fruits of independence were even higher. The tragedy was that no government in the 1950s could possibly have satisfied these expectations.

INDONESIA AFTER INDEPENDENCE

On the eve of independence, Indonesian political elites were agreed that Indonesia should be a unitary state and should have Bahasa Indonesia as its national language. They were united on little else. The 20 years between 1945 and 1965 was a period of de-colonisation, where four broad groups struggled for control of the state. First, there were those who wanted a multi-party parliamentary democracy. Second, there were those who wanted some kind of consensus parliamentary system, arguing that Western liberal democracy was an imported idea not suited to Indonesian cultural and political values. Third, there were those who wanted some kind of Marxist state—the communists were the most visible and strongest but there were other groups who wanted a liberal Marxist state or a democratic socialist state. Fourth, those who wanted a state based in some way on Islam, ranging from those who wanted an Islamic state to those who wanted the state merely to reflect Islamic values. These broad divisions can be traced back to debates that had been going on within nationalist circles since the 1910s.

The Indonesian army generally supported the second group among the Indonesian elite—those who wanted a consensus political system. The army leadership consistently saw the army as the major force behind the Indonesian Republic's defeat of the Dutch and, because of this, believed it had a special role in post-independence Indonesia. From the early 1950s, its leaders spoke of the army's "dual function"—to defend the nation from external threats or internal subversion, and to be the engine of development and the protector of the Revolution. The army had always been suspicious of politicians. Its involvement in politics was very different from that of armies elsewhere in Asia, Africa and Latin America which, on seizing power, invariably promised to return to civilian rule as soon as possible. The Indonesian army made no such commitment. It venerated its origins as a people's army, was proud of its close ties with rural people during the guerrilla campaign against the Dutch, and believed that it was more able than any other group to generate and manage the transformation of Indonesian society.

While the army was an important force in Indonesian politics in the 1950s, it became the dominant force only after the events of 30 September, 1965—the so-called "coup". These events were a major turning-point in post-independence Indonesian history. There has been a great deal of debate as to what actually happened. The conflict between competing political groups in Indonesia since 1945 had become more intense by the 1960s. Many observers, both

Indonesian and foreign, believed that the Indonesian Communist Party was becoming dangerously strong and might shortly be in a position to take over the state. Others were concerned about the growing strength of the armed forces, which had become more centralised and united in purpose by the early 1960s. The political instability was heightened further in 1965 with rumours of Sukarno being terminally ill and of both the PKI and the armed forces preparing for a coup. On 30 September, a group of lower-level army officers declared the overthrow of the Indonesian Government. The next day, the PKI's official newspaper threw its support behind them. Within 24 hours, the strategic army reserve in Jakarta, under the command of General Suharto, had put down the coup and arrested its leaders. Over the next six months the army vigorously rooted out members of the Communist Party, whom it blamed for the failed coup and for the murder of six generals. At least 400,000 people were killed in that six-month period, mostly in rural Java and Bali. In the aftermath of the events of 30 September, the Communist Party, one of the principal political forces since 1945, was destroyed. After 1965, the military-dominated government led by President Suharto restructured Indonesian politics. It called itself the "New Order" government, as opposed to the "Old Order" of Sukarno's presidency.

Independent Indonesia began as a liberal democracy—with a multi-party parliamentary system, a free and diverse press and with freedom of organisation for voluntary groups, including labour unions. However, its populist president, Sukarno, had argued against Western-style multi-party parliamentary democracy (what he called "50 per cent plus one democracy") since the 1920s. He argued that it was not in accordance with Indonesian cultural values, which stressed harmony and consensus. Sukarno was a strong advocate of "democracy with leadership": so too was the army. When parliamentary democracy faltered in the mid 1950s—with widespread discontent at the failure of the revolution to produce prosperity for all—Sukarno marshalled like-minded forces. "Guided Democracy" between 1959 and 1965 balanced political party representation in parliament with representatives from "functional groups"—defined as the armed forces, workers, peasants, Muslim scholars and numerous minority groups. The armed forces functional group—Golkar—quickly became the strongest.

Suharto's New Order government openly fostered Golkar. Elections were held every five years since 1971, but they were carefully managed. Golkar was provided with government funds and the bureaucratic and military apparatus swung behind it. Candidates put forward by all political parties were vetted by a government committee and tough electoral rules applied. Not surprisingly, Golkar won two-thirds or more of the votes in each of the elections through to 1997.

Suharto's government insisted that *pancasila* become the sole ideological basis of all political and social organisations. *Pancasila* was the five principles first enunciated by Sukarno in 1945 as the basis for Indonesian public life: belief in one God; national unity; humanitarianism; democracy based on consensus and representation; and social justice. It was a vague, syncretic philosophy, but its very obtuseness allowed for many interpretations. With the Communist Party destroyed, the army, the government and much of the Western-educated elite saw a revitalised Islam as the greatest threat to their control of the State. Suharto's government was determined to inculcate *pancasila* philosophy throughout the country. The consensus political system, for example, was called "*pancasila* democracy". All school and university students had to pass examinations in *pancasila*, as did civil servants and members of the armed forces. The intention was to remove from the Indonesian political agenda what the government saw as the evils of liberal democracy, Marxism and militant Islam.

The debate over *pancasila* from the early 1970s was not the first time the issue had been heatedly discussed. In mid 1945 the committee of politicians preparing the way for independence after the defeat of Japan were most strongly divided on the role of Islam in independent Indonesia. Many Muslim politicians demanded that Islam be the official religion while others demanded an Islamic state. However, the majority of Western-educated Indonesians, who dominated the nationalist movement from the 1920s, were philosophically committed to a secular state, a commitment strengthened by their understanding of the religious diversity in Indonesia. Not only is there a significant Christian minority and a small number of Buddhists and Hindus, but many of the 90 per cent who are Muslims hold eclectic beliefs and even orthodox Muslims are divided by different theological positions and political affiliations.

However, some Muslims have never abandoned their desire for Islam to be the basis of the Indonesian State. Others, while not wanting an Islamic state, have been increasingly critical of what they have seen as the moral pollution of Westernisation. There was an Islamic revival in the 1970s and 1980s which, in part, reflected the impact of the Iranian revolution and the general resurgence of revivalist Islam in the Middle East on Muslims throughout the world.

Many tens of thousands of Indonesians make the pilgrimage to Mecca each year and, while there, are influenced by these revivalist ideas. It is important to see the great diversity of thinking within those Indonesians who identify themselves as part of an Islamic community. The vast majority accept that because of its religious diversity Indonesia can never be an Islamic state and, within this overall philosophical framework, strive to develop political, social and economic policies which reflect their religious values.

Suharto's government steadily de-politicised Indonesian society. The press was subject to formal and informal controls and the state-operated television network was under firm control, its bland news and information services reflecting government views. Magazine publishing was licensed and books could not be published without a government permit. The result was a system of self-censorship whereby editors and publishers erred on the side of caution in order to avoid the risk of being closed down or having their books and magazines seized. On many occasions, the government withdrew right to publish for lengthy periods or permanently closed down publications.

Despite this authoritarianism, Suharto was unable to close down debate on major social, economic and political issues entirely. Writers and editors learned the art of subtlety and innuendo and of pushing criticism just so far. The carefully worded editorial or commentary in daily newspapers was a major method of airing sensitive topics. Cartoonists frequently made critical comments in pictures that could not be made in words—indeed, Indonesian newspapers and magazines fostered talented cartoonists able to make subtle but telling social comment. In the world of literature, critics of Indonesian society were also by no means silent.

When the New Order government came to power in 1965, the Indonesian economy was in chaos, inflation was rampant and the social and economic infrastructure had just about collapsed. Much was achieved in over three decades. Until the financial crisis of 1997, there was continuous economic growth, inflation was brought under control, the economic infrastructure was enormously improved and sustained efforts were made to tackle some of the long-standing fundamental problems of the economy.

For example, rice is the staple food in the Indonesian diet, yet Indonesia was a net importer of rice from the late 19th century until the 1980s. Despite the intricate rice terraces, large-scale irrigation and enormous labour inputs, the productivity of Indonesian rice farmers steadily declined in the 1950s and 1960s. With a relentlessly increasing population, the result was a reduction in rice consumption per person and the substitution of less nutritious foods such as cassava.

All this has changed since 1979, with dramatic improvements in crop yields and per-capita output. In 1983, Indonesia produced its first rice surplus for perhaps 100 years. The dramatic turnaround in rice production was a result of the Indonesian government's successful agricultural policies. While many developing countries ignored agriculture in favour of industrial and urban development, the Indonesian government poured money and expertise into improving agricultural output. The result was considerably increased productivity and the development of agro-businesses for the export of primary products and processed foods.

Successful agricultural policies were the base on which resource development and industrial policies were constructed. With the gradual opening of huge coal mines in eastern Kalimantan in the 1990s, Indonesia became a major coal exporter. In the 1970s and early 1980s, economic development depended on revenue derived from the export of oil, which was boosted by the price hikes imposed by OPEC. As the price of oil fell in the 1980s, Indonesia was forced to review its economic policies. The result was a steady liberalisation and internationalisation of the economy, with the emphasis on securing international investment and developing export-oriented manufacturing industries. By the late 1980s, Indonesia became a major textile, footwear and clothing exporter and a growing exporter of consumer products.

THE END OF SUHARTO'S RULE

Authoritarianism, corruption and nepotism were increasingly the hallmarks of the Suharto era. Despite this, Suharto's government brought stability to Indonesia after the chaos of the late 1950s and early 1960s and for 30 years delivered steady economic growth. Many of those who benefited most owed their new wealth more to political connections and privileges than to entrepreneurial skills or sheer hard work. And the gap between the political, military and economic elites and the mass of urban and rural people had become obscenely wide by the mid 1990s. Nonetheless, ordinary Indonesians enjoyed basic amenities they had never had before: enough to eat and a steadily improving diet; better clothing and housing; subsidised neighbourhood clinics that provided basic health care; and educational opportunities for their children. Development funds were spread to the rural areas, resulting in strong growth in agricultural production. There was a rapid growth in the urban middle class which developed modern consumer demands and, through vastly improved communications, was linked into the global network of ideas. As long as the national economic cake was increasing in size and the fruits of economic development trickled down from the favoured few to the newly emerging middle classes and to ordinary urban and rural workers, the majority of the population, while resenting the growing corruption and nepotism of the government, was not prepared to challenge the strong military and institutional control emanating from Jakarta.

In the 1990s, speculation about a replacement for the aging Suharto grew, particularly among the urban middle classes. Suharto might have responded to this disquiet—and the increasingly open critiques of his rule—by slowly loosening state controls and encouraging the emergence of a new political consensus. Instead, he turned even more to his family and cronies, played one group off against another and used force to punish dissidents and dissuade others from questioning the state. The closed political system prevented open debate, let alone the emergence of experienced politicians as potential presidential successors. It also obscured the disastrous direction in which Suharto's family and associates—using their political connections to amass personal fortunes—were taking the economy by the early 1990s.

The succession problem turned into a crisis of legitimacy in late 1997, when it became obvious that there was a speculative bubble, and capital flight occurred. The currency quickly crashed from around 4,000 rupiah to more than 12,000 rupiah to the US dollar. Suharto's claim to legitimacy collapsed with it. In May 1998, just weeks after another carefully controlled election had again appointed him president, Suharto was forced to resign by the pressure of street demonstrations led by university students. The genie of popular protest was out of the bottle and with it the ethnic, religious and class divisions which for 30 years had been papered over by authoritarian means.

Since independence, successive Indonesian governments have been involved in a process of nation building—both literally and symbolically. National identity could never be taken for granted. Indonesia is a very diverse country. It is also a fragile country. One of the tragedies of recent Indonesian history is that the lack of open political debate for most of the five decades since independence has prevented the emergence of a consensus on what Indonesia should be. Suharto tried to impose his vision, but received only grudging and formal assent. This formal assent collapsed with the social and economic catastrophe of Indonesia's financial collapse in late 1997.

With the dramatic resignation of Suharto after months of street protests, urban riots and army violence, the demand for greater openness and a return to a democratic society has dominated Indonesian public discourse. However, few countries that have had long-standing authoritarian regimes have found the transition to democracy easy and Indonesia is no exception. Suharto may have gone, but others who held power under him were reluctant to give it up. Much of the rioting and violence that wracked Indonesia through 1998 and 1999 was alleged to have been organised by shadowy groups aligned to factions within the military and to old civilian elites who saw more advantage in instigating an atmosphere of chaos than in assisting a transition to a more open society.

The Indonesian Constitution stipulates that in the event of death or resignation of the president, the vice-president assumes the position for the remainder of the term. The Sulawesi-born vice-president, Dr B.J. Habibie, duly took over as president, though continued popular protest and urban violence quickly forced him to concede the need for new elections as soon as possible. He had, after all, been installed as vice-president by Suharto, despite widespread opposition and rumblings from Indonesia's normally silent neighbours that it was not a good idea.

In December 1998, the Indonesian parliament, under pressure from street demonstrations and sensing the mood for greater openness, passed new electoral laws that opened the way for elections in June 1999. The June elections passed remarkably peacefully. For most Indonesians, this was their first experience of a real election. As expected, no one political party obtained a majority of the votes. The Indonesian Democratic Struggle Party, led by Megawati Sukarnoputri—the daughter of former President Sukarno—gained the largest block of seats in the parliament, followed by the Party of National Awakening, a modernist Muslim party led by Abdurrahman Wahid, with Golkar a distant third. Megawati's popularity among ordinary Indonesians, particularly in the cities and towns of Java, was clear. She was the symbol of opposition to Suharto and the corruption, nepotism and repression of the New Order government.

The election of June 1999 created a new House of Representatives which, together with government and military appointees and representatives of the regional parliaments, formed the People's Consultative Assembly (MPR) which met in October 1999 to hear a report from the outgoing president, Dr Habibie, and to elect a new president and vice-president. Leading up to the votes, the contest was seen as between Habibie (Golkar's nominee) and Megawati (nominee of the Indonesian Democratic Struggle Party). However, the MPR rejected Habibie's Accountability Speech of his period in office, effectively delivering a vote of no-confidence, which caused him to withdraw from the presidential race. To the surprise of most observers, Abdurrahman Wahid was elected as president by a clear majority, with Megawati later elected as vice-president. Though Megawati lost the race because of her poor political skills in the jockeying for power between the general elections of June and the presidential election of October, her defeat was also partly attributable to the fact that she was not supported by the Muslim-based parties. As the long-time leader of the largest Islamic organisation, Nahdlatul Ulama, Abdurrahman Wahid's Islamic credentials were the deciding factor.

One of President Habibie's most profound decisions during his short term was to announce that a UN-supervised referendum on greater autonomy for East Timor would be held on 30 August, 1999. He also gave assurances that if the East Timorese people rejected it, he would allow East Timor to cut itself loose from Indonesia. 78 per cent of voters rejected Habibie's proposal, the way was clear for full independence.

However, in the months following the vote, a wave of violence in which more than 2,000 people died was perpetuated by pro-Jakarta East Timorese militias with the covert backing of the Indonesian military, whose generals had been humiliated by the sudden volte-face shown by the politicians. During this chaotic period, thousands of refugees fled into West Timor and much of East Timor's infrastructure was razed by rampaging militiamen. When it became clear to Habibie that his army was unwilling to reign in the militias, he reluctantly allowed a UN multinational peace-keeping force to restore order in late 1999 and prepare the territory for full independence, which was formally granted at midnight on 20 May, 2002 (see Chapter 3).

Hopes were great among Indonesians that Wahid would prove to be the unifying force capable of reconciling the disparate interests and the guiding hand able to stabilise and develop the moribund economy. *Reformasi*—the slogan heard repeatedly on the streets, on public platforms and in the press during this period—was a clarion call for change rather than a detailed programme. But clearly, large numbers of students and the urban middle class, as well as ordinary Indonesians throughout the vast archipelago, wanted greater social and economic justice and a real say in the decisions affecting their lives. People wanted jobs, lower inflation and a return to the economic growth that prevailed before the financial collapse of 1997, but they would no longer tolerate the corruption, the nepotism and the ostentatious display of wealth by a small economic and political elite that were so much in evidence during the New Order.

The road to a permanently more open society was strewn with difficulties. To continue the process of greater openness and in order to develop a strong civil society, the government needed to achieve a number of delicate balances. It needed to reduce ethnic and religious tensions while encouraging open debate on Indonesia's future. It needed to find ways to balance the economic interests of indigenous Indonesians and Indonesians of Chinese ethnic backgrounds. It also needed to satisfy the demands of people outside Java for greater local autonomy while holding the diverse nation together and continuing social, economic and political reforms.

Unfortunately Wahid proved to be a president incapable of addressing these issues. While it is partly true that such lofty expectations could never have been satisfied by any leader given the extent of the problems at hand, it is also a fact that Wahid was undermined by his own failures of leadership. He antagonised the MPR and Vice President Megawati, and seemed unwilling to tackle a troubled economy, communal and separatist unrest and a political climate that had moved on since the twilight years of Suharto.

Wahid had once been almost revered by many Indonesians, spanning the entire gamut of the ethnic, social and religious divide as a man of proven wisdom, pragmatism and moderation. Yet after 20 months of his weak, ineffectual and sometimes erratic rule, many of his erstwhile supporters became disillusioned and he seemed oblivious to new political power blocs congealing around him and determined to see him ousted.

He was removed from office by the People's Consultative Assembly following a censure motion stemming from allegations of his involvement in graft. Defiant to the last, he threatened to impose a military-enforced state of emergency and dissolve parliament, a move rejected as unconstitutional by the chief of army. Vice-President Megawati Sukarnoputri became president on 23 July 2001.

Megawati set about trying to dispel popular perceptions of her as indecisive and blinkered by the strident nationalism that had so dominated her father, Sukarno, but which had less of a place in the Indonesia of the 21st century. Perhaps the weight of popular expectations would have been too great for any one person seeking to navigate a course between stability and change, but by 2003 she had lost the confidence of many of her supporters, both within the MPR and out on the streets. One of her key cabinet appointments was a popular retired general named Susilo Bambang Yudhoyono, who held the position of Coordinating Minister for Political Affairs, Security and Social Welfare. In 2002, the MPR approved legislation allowing for the direct election of the president and, in March 2004, Yudhoyono resigned his cabinet post, claiming Megawati had failed to include him in her decision making. This paved the way for him to stand as a presidential candidate against her.

In October 2004, Yudhoyono was declared the winner of the country's first direct presidential election, having defeated Megawati and securing 61 per cent of votes cast. His initial promise to enact sweeping reform was undermined by the massive social upheaval and loss of life resulting from the 2004 Boxing Day tsunami, which claimed the lives of at least 164,000 Indonesians, mainly in the northern Sumatran province of Aceh. The international community responded with promises of multi-billion dollar aid packages but the trauma and economic consequences affected many Indonesians beyond the provinces immediately hit. Nonetheless, Yudhoyono projected an image of confidence and competence which reassured the investment community after the indecisive leadership of Wahid and Megawati.

Terrorist bombings carried out by al-Qaeda (AQ)-backed operatives of the Jemaah Islamiah (JI) group in Kuta, Bali on 12 October, 2002 killed 202 people—including 88 Australian and 26 British tourists—and provided a major test of the government's commitment to respond vigorously by cooperating with the West in a sustained campaign against regional terrorists while still pursuing a reformist agenda. The short-term economic consequences of the attacks were evident in figures which estimated financial losses as a result of foreign tourist cancellations on Bali alone to be in excess of US$2 billion, with flow-on effects to all other parts of the national economy. Australian government travel warnings advising against non-essential travel to Indonesia by its citizens remain a source of contention between the two countries, since they restrict tourism and business investment. On the other hand, ongoing law enforcement cooperation, capacity building and intelligence sharing between Indonesian and foreign security services (especially Australia and the United States) in tracking down those responsible for terrorist acts indicated a renewed effort to addressing the issue of foreign-backed hardline Islamic groups operating within the country. Three of four of those found guilty of the attacks in Bali were sentenced to death in 2003 and executed in 2008, with a fourth receiving a life sentence. JI's spiritual leader, Abu Bakar Bashir, was not charged in relation to the bombings due to a lack of admissible evidence but was found guilty of subversion in 2003 and served two years in prison. Bashir's sentence was later overturned following an appeal to the Supreme Court, but he had already served his term. JI and loosely-aligned splinter groups are believed to have been behind a number of anti-Western bombings in Indonesia between 2003 and 2005, including attacks targeting Jakarta's Marriott Hotel (2003), the Australian Embassy (2004), and a second attack in Bali (2005). Initially, many Indonesians remained unconvinced of the existence of Islamic terrorist organisations in the country but testimony from several convicted terrorists during their trials dispelled most doubts. Today few Indonesians support the terrorist groups or their methods and a string of successes by Indonesian police has left terrorist groups such as JI splintered and operationally incapable of launching large-scale attacks on the scale of the first Bali bombing. Links between JI and AQ have also been severed.

Nonetheless, Yudhoyono needed to tread carefully to ensure the crackdown on Islamic fundamentalism was not perceived to be an attack on Islam itself. Sometimes this meant pandering to the wishes of Islamist parliamentarians to ensure their continued political support. In 2008 he endorsed a law preventing members of the breakaway Islamic sect Ahmadiyah from proselytising following a violent campaign by hardline Islamic groups to have the sect completely banned. Ahmadiyah had enjoyed a peaceful presence in Indonesia for nearly a century and restrictions on its activities were criticised by many commentators at home and abroad for being opportunistic and contrary to the pluralist state ideology of *pancasila*. In the same vein, his support in the same year for an anti-pornography bill proposed by some Islamic political parties infuriated many liberals and non-Muslims from places such as Bali and the eastern provinces, where celebration of the naked form is seen as an intrinsic part of local culture.

Some of the issues facing Indonesia today are disturbingly similar to those faced in the 1950s, when the first attempt at democracy was derailed by Sukarno's declaration of Guided Democracy in 1959. However, Indonesia in the new millennium is very different from Indonesia in 1959. It has a much stronger institutional and physical infrastructure and a larger, better-educated and more assertive middle class linked to the ideas and institutions of the outside world in ways unimaginable in the 1950s. Indonesians are far more internationally oriented—the communications revolution has had a massive impact—and the economy is much more tightly enmeshed with the global economy. There are considerable domestic and international pressures for this second attempt to create a more democratic and open society to be successful.

Immediately following Suharto's departure from office, some commentators speculated on the possible break-up of the Indonesian state as waves of ethnic and religious unrest swept the archipelago. In the decade since then, commentators have noted with concern in particular East Timor's succession and independence (see Chapter 3), separatism in Aceh and Papua (as Irian Jaya is now known) and communal violence in central Sulawesi and Maluku. The 2004 tsunami hit the Acehnese separatist movement (GAM) hard, but succeeded in focusing world attention on their plight and proved to be a catalyst in a comprehensive agreement negotiated in Finland in 2005 in which GAM agreed to abandon its armed independence struggle, disarm its fighters and accept the integrity of the Indonesian state. In return, the province was granted "self rule" and much greater control in keeping and disbursing locally-raised revenues (including oil and gas royalties). GAM was legalised and could freely operate as a political party. Its former fighters were granted an amnesty and foreign observers oversaw the phased withdrawal of the Indonesian army from the province. Both sides have largely complied with the terms of the agreement. In 2006, provincial and district elections—pronounced free and fair by international observers—resulted in GAM-backed candidates winning a convincing majority of positions, including governor and vice-governor. Peace agreements were also reached with warring communal groups in central Sulawesi in 2001 and with those in Maluku in 2002. At times sporadic outbreaks of violence still occur, but these are usually quickly contained by local security forces before they have a chance to spread. Also too much should not be read into the case of East Timor. Its independence is highly unlikely to threaten the future unity of the Indonesian state as East Timor was, for most Indonesians, a special case, since the UN and most countries never formally recognised Indonesia's annexation.

Elsewhere in Indonesia the idea of being Indonesian is still strong among the elites, not only in Java but throughout the other provinces. Few want to break up the nation. The hostility of non-Java elites, until recently most obvious in Aceh, is directed not at the idea of Indonesia but at what they see as the Javanisation of Indonesia and the unfair drainage of revenue to Java under Suharto's rule. A less centralised state, begun under Habibie and continued by his successors, has dissipated much of this tension. Nevertheless, the structure of the Indonesian state will continue to undergo change. In the decade after Suharto's resignation, the most pessimistic scenario—that Indonesia would revert to an authoritarian state where the fundamental unresolved issues remain unresolved—did not eventuate. The most optimistic scenario—that a more open and democratic Indonesia will at last be able to debate the fundamental questions of national identity and vision—is now occurring. It will take time—and there may well be many difficulties which will test the unity of the nation—but if the more optimistic scenario is fully realised, then Indonesians may soon boast of possessing arguably the most open and democratic civil society in the whole of South-East Asia.

5 LAO PDR

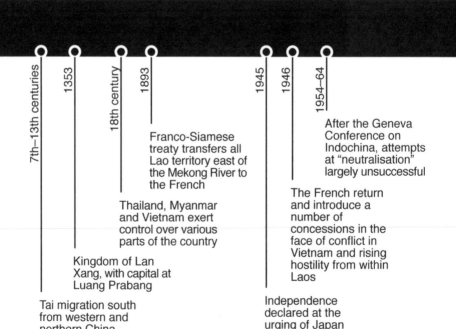

7th–13th centuries

1353

18th century

1893

1945

1946

1954–64

Franco-Siamese
treaty transfers all
Lao territory east of
the Mekong River to
the French

Thailand, Myanmar
and Vietnam exert
control over various
parts of the country

Kingdom of Lan
Xang, with capital at
Luang Prabang

Tai migration south
from western and
northern China

After the Geneva
Conference on
Indochina, attempts
at "neutralisation"
largely unsuccessful

The French return
and introduce a
number of
concessions in the
face of conflict in
Vietnam and rising
hostility from within
Laos

Independence
declared at the
urging of Japan

Exterior View of That Makmo at Wat Wisunalat

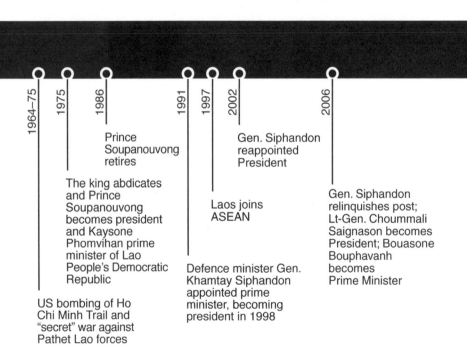

1964–75

1975

1986

1991

1997

2002

2006

Prince
Soupanouvong
retires

Gen. Siphandon
reappointed
President

The king abdicates
and Prince
Soupanouvong
becomes president
and Kaysone
Phomvihan prime
minister of Lao
People's Democratic
Republic

Laos joins
ASEAN

Gen. Siphandon
relinquishes post;
Lt-Gen. Choummali
Saignason becomes
President; Bouasone
Bouphavanh
becomes
Prime Minister

US bombing of Ho
Chi Minh Trail and
"secret" war against
Pathet Lao forces

Defence minister Gen.
Khamtay Siphandon
appointed prime
minister, becoming
president in 1998

5 LAO PDR

The Lao People's Democratic Republic or Lao PDR (previously Laos) occupies an area of some 237,000 square kilometres but has a small population of 5.9 million in 2009. It is a land-locked country, sharing borders with Thailand, Burma, China, Vietnam and Cambodia. Much of it is mountainous, and only about five per cent of the land is under continuous cultivation. Primary or secondary jungle (the latter resulting from transient slash-and-burn farming) covers 75 per cent of land area.

As a nation, Laos is a semi-artificial creation of the colonial era. The French devised its borders, cutting through many diverse ethno-linguistic groups. The preponderant Lao lowlanders brought to the emerging nation a long history of bitter division amongst themselves. Laos, as a neighbour of Vietnam, would also be wracked by ideological division and war for 30 years after World War II.

In 1975, the area of Laos was united under one indigenous government for the first time in almost 300 years. The doctrinaire socialism of this government led, however, to economic stagnation and the flight of almost ten per cent of the country's population across the Mekong river into Thailand. Today, the government, at least ostensibly, pursues "market socialism", welcoming domestic and foreign private enterprise and aid from the capitalist world. But the country's geography, ethnic complexity and turbulent history mean that Laos is starting from far behind most South-East Asian countries in nation-building and economic development. Even by official figures, by 2002 a quarter of the urban and a half of the rural population were living below the poverty line, and the UN estimated that nearly half of all children were stunted as a result of having an inadequate diet. The same proportion of adults were illiterate.

THE CREATION OF LAOS AND ITS EARLIER HISTORY
The borders of the modern state of Laos were established by the French colonial government in the late 19th and early 20th centuries. They were based primarily on French strategic and administrative considerations, paying regard to the region's human geography and traditional political relationships where it suited the French to do so. They sliced through ethnic groupings and historic socio-political ties, arbitrarily determining the future population of the country.

The population of the newly defined territory was relatively sparse - about 819,000 people were counted in 1921 - but nevertheless ethnically and culturally complex. A little over half the population were of Tai ethno-linguistic origin, one result of the great migration which scholars believe brought Tai peoples out of western China into mainland South-East Asia between the seventh and 13th centuries, and ultimately located Tai stock not only in modern Thailand, but also in eastern Burma, in Laos and in north-west Vietnam. People of Tai stock in Laos included both the lowland-dwelling Lao and a number of upland-dwelling groups of the northern provinces, such as the Lu, Tai Neua and Black, Red and White Tai (so named for the principal colours in their women's traditional costumes). Today all these people are grouped as "lowlander Lao" (*Lao Loum*).

The lowlander Lao became the dominant force in the region, politically, culturally and economically, but their political structures were not strongly integrated. In the mountainous terrain, rivalries of family and clan flourished. Four series of rapids on the Mekong river, with lengthy stretches of water between them, tended to focus Lao society around three distinct centres; from north to south, Luang Prabang, Vientiane (Vieng Chan) and Champassak. The Tai people of the uplands were even less politically integrated, although the villages of each group were organised into small principalities (*muong*) presided over by leaders of dominant clans.

The second-most substantial ethno-linguistic grouping was upland-dwellers of Mon-Khmer origin, presumably descendants of the peoples who had settled in the region before Tai immigration.

The Tai-speakers referred to them disparagingly as '*Kha*' (slaves); today they are grouped as "upland Lao" or (*Lao Theung*). Both terms encompass many self-consciously distinct communities with their own names for themselves. Political organisation beyond village level was rare in these communities, but occasionally they could unite, under particularly charismatic chieftains, to oppose lowlander exploitation.

Amongst the smaller ethno-linguistic groupings, the most notable by the time of French boundary-drawing were people with languages of Tibeto-Burman origin, today grouped as *Lao Soung* and including the Hmong and Yao, or Man. (The Hmong resented the lowlander term for them, *Meo*, which means "savage".) These people began to migrate into the area as recently as the late 18th or early 19th centuries and settled on upper mountain slopes, where amongst other crops, they grew the opium poppy. The Hmong shared a myth of a future Hmong kingdom, but for most practical purposes political organisation was rare beyond the level of village chief.

Human settlement in the region is known to date back many centuries BC. The most famous evidence of the region's pre-history consists of the huge stone mortuary jars found on the north-central Xieng Khouang plateau, which have given the area the name "Plain of Jars". Little is known about the society which created the jars, which date from the last centuries BC into the early Christian era. The known history of the region follows from the Tai migrations mentioned above. In the 13th century, Tai people constructed their first states, drawing together hitherto tribal communities under rulers claiming quasi-divine authority and kingly status. Examples of such states were Chiang Mai and Sukhotai (both located in what is now Thailand) and Luang Prabang.

The exact origins of Luang Prabang are shrouded in myth but there, in 1316, a royal prince, Fa Ngum, was born. He was brought up in the royal court of the great kingdom of Angkor, which then claimed an empire extending over much of modern Thailand, central and southern Laos, Cambodia and southern Vietnam. Fa Ngum married a Khmer princess and became a devout Theravada Buddhist. With Khmer forces he brought under his control large areas to Angkor's north and in 1353 established the kingdom of Lan Xang ("a million elephants"), with his capital at Luang Prabang.

Initially a tributary of Angkor, Lan Xang, became an autonomous kingdom as Angkor declined. For several centuries its power was arguably as significant as the growing Thai state (based on the city of Ayudhya) to its west, and the growing Vietnamese state to its east. At its height, Lan Xang controlled, at least in loose, tributary fashion, territories considerably more extensive than those of modern Laos, including much of modern Thailand's north and east and reaching into the south of modern China and the north-west of modern Vietnam.

Lan Xang was a Buddhist kingdom and, for long periods, a renowned centre of Buddhist scholarship. However, its Buddhist practices took on a distinctively Lao identity as the religion assimilated the traditional animist beliefs and rituals of the region. Buddhism also acted as a conduit for ideas, Indian in origin, of society as divinely-ordained hierarchy. Lan Xang's polity came broadly to resemble those of its Theravada Buddhist neighbours, the Burmese, Thai and Cambodian states. The king and aristocracy deserved reverence, taxes and services from their subjects because of their superior "merit" and pious support of Buddhism. Such politico-religious social integration extended only to the lowlander Lao, however. The "Kha" (uplanders) mostly resisted Buddhism, clinging to their diverse animist beliefs and local independence. And even among the lowlanders, Lan Xang's rugged geography and necessarily decentralised administration by regional overlords militated against a lastingly strong state.

Nevertheless, Lan Xang weathered internal rivalries, wars with the Thais and Vietnamese, and a generation of Burmese overlordship in the late 16th century. In the 17th century, now with Vientiane as its capital, Lan Xang reached its height under King Souligna Vongsa, who came to the throne in 1637 after defeating four rival claimants and reigned for a remarkable 57 years. He negotiated good relations with the neighbouring states, and within the kingdom gained a reputation for firm, just rule. The first European visitors to Vientiane reported on the city's prosperity and imposing religious buildings.

But, in an act worthy of epic tragedy, Souligna Vongsa refused to intervene when his only son seduced the wife of a senior court official and, under the prevailing law on such matters, was sentenced to death. Souligna Vongsa died in 1694 without a direct heir, and the subsequent rivalries for the throne, exploited by the Vietnamese and Thais, led to the kingdom's irrevocable break up.

In the early 18th century the cities of Luang Prabang and Vientiane became the capitals of antagonistic states, the latter under Vietnamese patronage. In the south, Champassak fell under Thai patronage. In the mid 18th century the Burmese became predatory again, reducing Luang Prabang to subjection and menacing Vientiane. Rather than supporting one another, the mutually hostile Lao states encouraged these outside powers to subdue their Lao rivals. The unhappy century closed with Vientiane under Thai overlordship, although Vientiane independently attacked and sacked Luang Prabang in 1791.

In 1805, the Lao prince Chao Anou became ruler at Vientiane, and won Thai and Vietnamese approval to reintegrate the central and southern provinces. In 1826, however, Chao Anou acted on a rumour (which proved false) that the British were attacking Bangkok. Chao Anou and his forces, eager to join in the humbling of the Thais, almost reached Bangkok before being repelled. Chao Anou fled, ultimately taking shelter from Thai vengeance in Vietnam.

These events opened a decade of devastation for the Vientiane state. In 1828, Thai forces sacked Vientiane and drove many thousands of the population westward into territory under Bangkok control. Vientiane and Champassak became minor Thai provinces. Chao Anou was captured by the Thais when he returned to his territory with ineffective Vietnamese backing; he died in Bangkok in 1835, bringing the Vientiane monarchy to an end.

Meanwhile, Vietnam was forcefully asserting its claims in the eastern provinces, particularly in Xieng Khouang. The Vietnamese were probably content to take the east while the Thais took the west and south, but in 1833, simultaneously with a Thai-Vietnamese clash in Cambodia, the Thais sent a force against the Vietnamese garrison in Xieng Khouang. The Thais were helped by forces from Luang Prabang, and by a local uprising in Xieng Khouang against the Vietnamese. As with Vientiane, the Thais adopted a "scorched-earth" policy in Xieng Khouang, deporting westward up to 80 per cent of the population (although some were able to return later). Thai-Vietnamese warfare continued until 1835, and concluded with the Vietnamese dominant in the east, as they had wished, and the Thais dominant in the western and southern provinces. The surviving northerly kingdom of Luang Prabang prudently acknowledged the overlordship of both its neighbours, though for practical purposes it, too, was within the Thai orbit.

FRENCH CONQUEST AND RULE TO 1940

The French takeover of Cambodia and Vietnam between the 1860s and 1885 led to keen French interest in the Lao territories for several reasons. They saw (wrongly) the Mekong as a potentially major trade route with China. They feared Thai interests in the territories, which they believed might be championed (also wrongly, as it transpired) by their imperial rival, Britain. From the 1870s, northern Laos and Vietnam were disturbed by armed bands of renegade Chinese (collectively referred to by the Thai term "*Ho*") and the French were anxious to pacify these areas. Finally, by 1885, the French controlled the Vietnamese emperor's claims to overlordship in the Lao territories.

The Thais had been sending armed forces to Luang Prabang and other areas in an attempt to subdue the Ho and confront possible French intervention. But in 1887 they were dramatically outmanoeuvred by the French explorer Auguste Pavie, who rescued the king of Luang Prabang when the Ho attacked and sacked his city. King Un Kham gratefully accepted French protection for his kingdom. Pavie went on to negotiate similar protection for other regional overlords.

In 1893 (with French gunboats menacing Bangkok) Thailand reluctantly signed a Franco-Siamese treaty which transferred to the French all Lao territories east of the Mekong. Further agreements in 1904 and 1907 added to "Laos" the parts of Sayaboury and Champassak provinces west of the Mekong. However, for most of its course through historically Lao territory the Mekong had now become an international frontier. The agreements on other borders with British Burma, China and with French-controlled Vietnam similarly conflicted with the historic settlement patterns and movements of Lao and other people of the region.

The French soon came to regard Laos as a quiet backwater, when they realised that it could offer no rapid economic return of any significance. Most people of the region continued as subsistence farmers, the lowlanders growing wet rice and the uplanders pursuing slash-and-burn cultivation. The colony's most important products became tin, mined by Vietnamese workers, and opium, grown by the Hmong and other mountain-dwellers. The tin contributed only a tiny percentage of the total exports of French Indochina (Laos, Vietnam and Cambodia). Opium, on the other hand, became Laos' single greatest revenue earner when purveyed by a French state monopoly throughout Indochina. An illegal opium trade also flourished with China, despite official French efforts to control it.

The French administration of Laos (technically now the protected kingdom of Luang Prabang plus nine Lao provinces) was lightly staffed. Much administration was carried out using traditional authority structures and Vietnamese minor officials. Vietnamese public servants, traders and professionals came to predominate in Laos' small urban population. Chinese also came to play a significant role in Laos' trade. Generally the Lao lowlanders accepted the French and other outsiders, but mountain-dwelling groups rose in revolt on several occasions. They were protesting against taxation and corvée demands possibly imposed inequitably, even corruptly, by officials from the traditionally resented lowlands.

Prior to World War II, modernisation in Laos was extremely limited. The telegraph and around 5,000 kilometres of roads (mostly unpaved) eased communications, but 90 per cent of the population remained in subsistence agriculture. Health care and other social services were confined to the towns, and no Western-style education was available in Laos beyond primary level (most primary education was conducted in the Buddhist temple schools). The Lao elite went to Vietnam or France to acquire an education, returning to form a small royal and aristocratic upper class, and a fledgling Lao middle class composed of public servants, policemen and soldiers, primary teachers and the like.

WORLD WAR II AND THE FIRST INDOCHINA WAR, 1940-1954

In 1940 the Thais, taking advantage of Japanese pressures on the French and with Japanese support, occupied the Lao provinces west of the Mekong. (These would be returned to the French in 1947.) However, the French retained administrative control in most of Indochina, under an agreement with the Japanese which allowed the free movement of Japanese forces. Thus, most of Laos stayed under French supervision until 9 March, 1945, when the Japanese interned all French personnel in Indochina.

The war years before March 1945 nevertheless brought significant change. The French, seeking to buttress Lao popular support, began to stimulate Lao nationalist pride. A "national renovation movement" staged rallies and parades, built schools and other amenities, fostered Lao music, dance and literature, and led to the first Lao newspaper. The first explicitly Lao infantry battalion was formed, under French control, in 1943. As elsewhere in South-East Asia, therefore, nationalist politicisation was a feature of the war years in Laos, although the Lao movement focussed only on the Lao lowlanders.

After March 1945 the pace quickened. In April, the king of Luang Prabang was obliged by the Japanese to repudiate the French and declare Laos "independent". In August, when the Japanese surrendered to the Allies, politicised Lao people were split between those who acquiesced in a French return and those who saw the opportunity to set up a genuinely independent state. The latter formed the Lao Issara (Free Laos) and set up a provisional government.

By now, however, an additional complication for Lao nationalism was taking shape. Between August and September 1945, Ho Chi Minh's communists seized control in northern Vietnam and set up the Democratic Republic of Vietnam (DRV). Some Lao Issara, seeking allies, established ties with the DRV, which eagerly backed the anti-French movement in Laos. The political contenders in Laos - and the entire population - were about to be sucked into the maelstrom created by the advent of communism in the region and by French - and later American - efforts to eliminate or contain it.

The French recaptured Laos by May 1946, and leading Lao Issara figures fled, some to Bangkok and some to link up with the DRV guerilla forces (the Vietminh) battling the French in Vietnam. In the late 1940s, Lao guerilla groups developed along the mountainous Laos-Vietnam border, aided by Vietminh know-how and supplies. Significantly, these groups won the support of some uplander communities hitherto alienated from the Lao nationalist movement. The uplanders may have been recruited with some cynicism by the Lao and Vietminh - who primarily viewed the uplanders as important for their strategically valuable territory and local knowledge - but trans-communal nationalist cooperation had at last made a start.

Meanwhile, the Lao Issara group in Bangkok was disintegrating. The French, anxious to pacify Laos in order to focus on the conflict in Vietnam, made a series of concessions to Lao feelings which undercut the hostility of many Lao Issara towards the restored French presence. In 1946, the French appointed the Luang Prabang monarch as king of all Laos, and also permitted an elected national assembly, leading to a national government. In 1949, they declared Laos "independent", though they retained ultimate control of the kingdom's armed forces, foreign policy and finances. The concessions were enough, nevertheless, to woo many Lao Issara back to Laos under amnesty.

Notable amongst the returnees was the royal Prince Souvanna Phouma, who became prime minister following elections in 1951. However, his half-brother, Prince Souphanouvong, in an echo of the country's history of ruling-class dissension, threw in his lot with the Vietminh-backed guerilla forces. In August 1950, Souphanouvong became prime minister of the newly formed Pathet Lao ("Land of the Lao"), a front organisation open to all Lao patriots though tightly controlled by committed communists. Another key pioneer Pathet Lao figure, as defence minister, was the Lao-Viet communist Kaysone Phomvihan, who was destined to become Laos' first and long-lasting communist prime minister.

By early 1954, Pathet Lao forces controlled large areas of the north and north-east of Laos, including the Plain of Jars and the provincial town of Sam Neua. They had been significantly helped in their advance by major Vietminh incursions into Laos in April 1953 and January 1954. The Pathet Lao was not invited to the Geneva Conference, convened by the great powers in May 1954 in the hope of settling the Indochina conflicts, but the Conference recognised Pathet Lao strength and acknowledged its right to administer the territory it held. The conference called, however, for the integration of the Pathet Lao with the Royal Lao government and armed forces, and for the neutralisation of Laos.

THE FAILURE OF "NEUTRALISATION", 1954-1964
Following the Geneva Conference, the French speedily withdrew from Indochina. In Laos the negotiations for a new, integrated national government would prove tortuous and long. The Pathet Lao was determined to enter a coalition only on strong terms, and was wary of growing American influence in Laos. In Vientiane, the moderate Souvanna Phouma was swept aside by US-supported right-wingers, who had gained the upper hand in the national assembly and Royal Lao armed forces.

Elections in December 1955 led, however, to Souvanna's return to the prime ministership on a platform of national reconciliation. In August 1956, Souvanna and the Pathet Lao leadership agreed on broad proposals for a "government of national union". Elections for 21 extra assembly seats were finally held in May 1958, with parties aligned with the Pathet Lao acquiring 13 of these. Souphanouvong entered the government as a senior economic minister. Another Pathet Lao leader, Phoumi Vongvichit, also acquired a ministry.

The arrangements were a dubious recipe for stability. In June 1958, Souvanna was again forced from office by the rightists, and the succeeding government went on to rule by decree. Souphanouvong and the other leftist deputies were arrested, although they later escaped with the aid of their guards and returned to Pathet Lao territory in the east. Pathet Lao troops who had been awaiting integration with the Royal Lao forces were disarmed, but many of them too escaped back to Pathet Lao territory. By July 1959 guerilla warfare was again in full swing in the north and north-east. United States aid to the Royal Lao forces sharply increased. Simultaneously, CIA personnel began to form "special forces" in Laos, attracting support among the Hmong in particular. With CIA assistance,

Hmong opium output began to find vast new markets in South Vietnam, Thailand and beyond.

The conflict increased in complexity in August 1960, when forces led by a young paratroop captain, Kong Le, seized Vientiane and demanded a restoration of neutrality. Souvanna Phouma agreed to return as prime minister, and subsequently reached an agreement with Souphanouvong on behalf of the Pathet Lao. In December 1960, however, Royal Lao troops under rightist command stormed Vientiane. Kong Le, his troops and Souvanna fled to the Pathet Lao-controlled Plain of Jars. The communist world and some non-aligned nations (such as India) now upheld Souvanna as Laos' rightful prime minister. The United States and the West recognised a new military-controlled Vientiane government, technically under another prince, Boun Oum, as prime minister.

Despite American intrigue in Laos up to this point, the incoming United States president in January 1961, John Kennedy, concluded that a neutral Laos was desirable. Neutrality, it was hoped, would exclude DRV forces from using the "Ho Chi Minh Trail", much of which ran through Laos, to reinforce and supply NLF ("Vietcong") forces now fighting the regime in South Vietnam. In May 1961, another Geneva Conference called once more for the neutralisation of Laos. In June, the three Lao princes, Boun Oum, Souvanna Phouma, and Souphanouvong, agreed to a second attempt at coalition government.

The new government came into existence in July 1962, with Souvanna as prime minister. The coalition led a tenuous existence, beset by tension, provocation and assassination, until mid 1964 when its Pathet Lao component effectively abandoned it, later dismissing it as a "US puppet". Souvanna held on as prime minister, but he and other neutralists were now reduced to irrelevance. Laos was becoming one of the key theatres of war in the sharply escalating conflict in Vietnam.

LAOS AND THE VIETNAM CONFLICT, 1964-1975

Secret United States bombing of Pathet Lao areas began in May 1964. By the late 1960s, and into the early 1970s, the bombing was massive, attempting 'saturation' destruction of the manifold branches of the Ho Chi Minh Trail. It created an estimated 750,000 refugees in Laos, and nightmarish conditions for Pathet Lao forces, but it never closed the Trail, or eliminated Pathet Lao headquarters and networks. On the ground, the Royal Lao and "secret" forces (and also substantial Thai forces) engaged each year in a "dry season" war with the Pathet

Lao. For many years the pattern of territories held by the opposing forces did not alter significantly. By 1972, however, the Pathet Lao was beginning to gain ground, backed by an increasingly optimistic and well-armed DRV.

In Paris, the DRV was engaged in serious peace talks with the United States, which would lead to the January 1973 agreements under which the United States withdrew its ground troops from Vietnam. The Pathet Lao, pursuing a policy parallel to that of the DRV, offered in 1972 to talk with the Vientiane government "without preconditions". In February 1973, the two sides reached an Agreement on the Restoration of Peace and Reconciliation in Laos.

The agreement provided for cessation of hostilities, after which the two sides would administer their respective territories, and for the withdrawal of foreign troops. The United States and Thailand withdrew their military personnel, though the DRV continued to use the Ho Chi Minh Trail. Further detailed agreements led to the formation of two bodies on which both the Vientiane government and the Pathet Lao were represented. These were the Provisional Government of National Union, in which Souvanna Phouma became prime minister, and a National Political Consultative Council (NPCC), of which Souphanouvong became chairman.

The NPCC subsequently committed itself to the retention of the monarchy and to generally liberal political and economic principles. Pathet Lao government ministers also acted moderately, reassuring many Lao people. The Pathet Lao goal of taking over the government remained, however, and the circumstances seemed to be favouring the achievement of that goal. Rightist morale was sinking as the United States, step by step, wound back its commitments in Indochina. Corruption and self-seeking - which had long been debilitating factors in the Royal Lao government area - intensified as fears grew that the US aid bonanza was coming to an end.

Even so, the Pathet Lao moved cautiously when, in April 1975, communist forces toppled the regimes in Saigon and Phnom Penh. Pathet Lao troops engaged the Hmong "secret army", but in the lowlands the Pathet Lao relied on staging a "popular revolution". In April and May, mass demonstrations against US properties and Lao rightists led to the wind-back of all American activity other than diplomatic representation, and propelled the flight from Laos of people identified with the former Vientiane government. The flight intensified when the Royal Lao forces were taken over by a pro-Pathet Lao commander in August. In November, following further demonstrations, the King abdicated and Souvanna Phouma stepped down as prime minister.

On 1 and 2 December, 1975, a "National Congress of People's Representatives" voted unanimously to establish the Lao People's Democratic Republic, to be governed by the Lao People's Revolutionary Party. Prince Souphanouvong became the new republic's first president, a position he held until his retirement in 1986. Kaysone Phomvihan became prime minister, a position he retained until 1991, when Khamtay Siphandon succeeded him and later became president in 1998.

LAOS SINCE 1975

After 1975, the new government imposed doctrinaire socialist policies on Laos. State trading organisations replaced private trade, and Laos' small industries were nationalised. The properties of "traitors" were expropriated. Political and social discourse became rigidly controlled, and those perceived to be opponents of the regime were eliminated or consigned to "re-education" centres. In 1978, the reorganisation of agriculture into cooperatives began. These policies aggravated the conditions created by 30 years of political upheaval and war, the withdrawal of US aid and an economic blockade imposed by Thailand. The declining economic situation and the political oppression led to the exodus as refugees of as much as ten per cent of the population. By 1979, Laos had lost the majority of its educated and skilled people.

The introduction of cooperatives – the policy which most directly affected the majority of the peasant population – met with passive but intense opposition. Harvest yields were catastrophically less than hoped for, and, in mid-1979, the policy was abruptly dropped. This about-turn heralded a series of measures which would gradually free up the country's economy. In November 1979, private production was again encouraged, and state enterprises were obliged to include in their goals efficiency, productivity and profit. In 1982, a reorganisation of government left the old guard in supreme control but introduced "technocrats" at vice-ministerial level, decentralised some decision-making, and liberalised foreign trade, private investment and joint state-private enterprise.

These and later changes to the command economy provoked some tensions within the ruling group. But in the late 1980s and early 1990s, the collapse of Soviet and European communism, the resulting loss of aid, and the growing economic liberalisation in Vietnam and China, produced decisive moves towards a market economy. However, Laos remains a one-party, theoretically socialist, state. Party diktat can override law and institutionalised procedures. Corruption, and the building of power bases through nepotism and "personal favours", also complicate economic development. This was a theme addressed with unusual candour by Vice-President Xaysomphone Phomvihane (son of the late President Kaysone) in 2007. He declared that corruption by party and state officials had become the country's principal social ill, followed by crime and drug abuse. He admitted that anti-corruption legislation endorsed in 2005 had done little to address this. That legislation was designed to augment a 1999 anti-corruption decree and the establishment of a counter-corruption committee under the Office of the Prime Minister. Unlike Vietnam and China, where dishonest senior officials have been routinely made an example of and prosecuted, this is still seldom the case in Laos. In fact the US State Department has assessed that corruption is on the increase.

With its small population, lack of infrastructure and land-locked position, Laos is unlikely to shake off quickly its status as one of South-East Asia's poorest countries, in spite of its liberal policies on foreign investment. Subsistence farming is likely to remain the chief user of labour for some time, and the chief means of survival for most Lao people. As mentioned in the introduction, the "dual economy", whereby an economically undeveloped rural backwater exists uneasily alongside the more advanced capital city, has led to internal migration and some social upheaval as rural people seek to improve their prospects. By the government's own figures, in 2001 a quarter of Vientiane's inhabitants and over half the people living outside the capital lived below the poverty line. However, Laos does have the potential for sustained economic growth. By the turn of the century, foreign enterprises were heavily involved in developing a number of hydro-electric projects, principally to sell power to Thailand and Vietnam. Other areas of potential development are mining, commercial agriculture, tourism and limited areas of manufacturing.

Meanwhile Laos' infrastructure is improving with various forms of international assistance. An Australian-financed bridge across the Mekong, which linked Laos and Thailand by road in 1994, and the expansion and upgrading of roads within Laos mean that it is becoming possible to drive from Singapore to Beijing, via Laos. In 2001, the Lao and Thai governments jointly announced an additional 1.5-kilometre bridge would be built to promote cross-border trade. Some Lao see their country's future as a transport hub, linking north-east Thailand with the Vietnamese port of Da Nang on an east-west axis and southern China with Thailand, Malaysia and Singapore on the north-south axis. Fears of social and environmental – not to mention political – consequences of Lao development have been at the forefront of national debate in the last few years. In 1995, the government launched a crackdown on "counter-revolutionary activities": a clear message that economic liberalisation should not be interpreted as leading to an end of the ruling party's monopoly on power. Such themes were unambiguously restated in 1997 when the country was admitted to ASEAN and was buffeted in the same year by the flow-on effects of the Asian economic crisis which originated in Thailand. Although 2.5 million registered voters were encouraged to vote in nationwide elections held in 2002, the ruling Lao People's Revolutionary Party was assured a sweeping victory as all but one of the candidates permitted to stand were party members. At the Seventh Party Congress in 2001, foreign aid donors - whose contributions provide a third of national income - were disappointed by a failure to commit to reform of the unwieldy state sector. Indeed, the private sector was not even mentioned. At the Eighth Party Congress in 2006, President Khamtay Siphandon stood aside in favour of Lt-Gen. Choummali Siagnason. Bouasone Bouphavanh was endorsed as the new Prime Minister. Six out of 11 of the key politburo positions (including five of the six most senior roles among these) continued to be occupied by former military officers. The influence of the military on government has therefore not lessened.

The government has yet to match its somewhat limited economic reform with much tangible political reform. It may have to, however, as Laos is drawn inexorably into the economic and social currents sweeping the rest of the region.

6 MALAYSIA

7th–14th centuries

1400

1641

Johore, with
assistance
from the Dutch
in Java, ousts
Portuguese

Melaka established
by refugees from Sri
Vijaya, which was
under seige from the
Javanese kingdom of
Majapahit

Sri Vijaya imperial state,
encompassing
Peninsular Malaysia,
Sumatra, western Java
and western Borneo

1824

1843–1917

1874

1941–45

1948

British acquire
Melaka and form
Straits Settlements
with Penang and
Singapore

"White Rajah"s
period in Sarawak

Pangkor Treaty with
Perak sets scene
for British to extend
control throughout
peninsular

Japanese
occupation

Federation of Malaya
formed and state of
emergency declared
after Communist
Party of Malaya
attempts revolution

1957

Independence

Porta de Santiago

1963
1969
1971
1981
1993
1998–99
2003
2004
2008

Dr Mahathir elected Prime Minister and adopts "Look East" policy

Mahathir resigns; replaced by Abdullah Ahmad Badawi

Tun Abdul Razak elected prime minister and New Economic Policy period begins

UMNO wins landslide election with Badawi as Prime Minister

UMNO re-elected with significantly reduced majority. Anwar Ibrahim re-enters parliament. Prime Minister Badawi announces he will stand aside in early 2009

Deputy prime minister Anwar Ibrahim dismissed, charged and convicted of corruption and further charged with sexual offences (later overturned). Released in 2004 and re-elected to parliament in 2008

Riots between Chinese and Malays

Malaysia formed; Tunku Abdul Rahman elected first prime minister

Government challenges power and privileges of royal state rulers and their families

6 MALAYSIA

More than 60 ethnic or culturally differentiated groups can be enumerated in Malaysia's population of 27 million, but the most crucial population division is that between Bumiputera and non-Bumiputera people. The Bumiputeras are those with cultural affinities indigenous to peninsular and Bornean Malaysia and the region. Malays constitute the principal Bumiputera group and account for around 64 per cent of Malaysia's population. Non-Bumiputeras are people whose cultural affinities lie outside Malaysia and its region – principally people of Chinese and Indian descent. Chinese constitute about 27 per cent of Malaysia's population, Indians about eight per cent.

The Malays have a long history and, since the 15th century, an Islamic culture in which they take pride. In the colonial era, however, their cultural world – extending across the Malay Peninsula and Indonesian Archipelago – was divided by Western colonial powers. In British Malaya and northern Borneo, Malays were relegated to minor social roles and virtually excluded from the foreign-financed modernising economy, which utilised immigrant labour. Malaysia's history since World War II has been primarily the story of the reassertion of Malay primacy without precipitating serious racial discord.

Malaysia's stability has enabled vast economic growth since the 1970s. The stability has, however, been at the expense of some elements of the democratic system with which Malaysia began as an independent nation. Malay advancement has also had an ironic political consequence – nowadays rifts and rivalries within the Malay community need as much adroit political management as the differences between Malaysia's ethnic groups.

EARLY HISTORY

The early history of the territories which now form Malaysia is shadowy, a matter of cryptic archaeological clues and obscure references in Chinese and other written sources. The limited evidence suggests, however, that in the first millennium AD both the Malay Peninsula and the northern Borneo coast were important landfalls for merchant vessels involved in the great maritime trading networks that linked South-East Asia with Africa, the Middle East, India and China. Port cities arose on the Peninsula and on Borneo as they did elsewhere in South-East Asia, offering merchants safe harbourage, transhipment facilities and collection points for the region's prized commodities: gold, tin and other minerals, rare woods, resins and other jungle produce, tortoiseshell, cowries and other marine produce, and – supremely – spices.

Malay history is often seen as beginning, however, in southern Sumatra, scholars believe that between the seventh and 14th centuries the Palembang region of southern Sumatra was the focus of a major maritime empire. They have called the central imperial state Sri Vijaya, though evidence about it is fragmentary and inconclusive. Near Sri Vijaya, and at times possibly its capital, was a place called Melayu, perhaps the cradle of Malay culture. The Sri Vijayan empire at its height probably dominated the trade of most of Sumatra, the Malay Peninsula, western Java and western Borneo. It enjoyed Chinese and Indian patronage, and, like most of South-East Asia in the first millennium AD, it borrowed and adapted Indian culture and religion. Its religion was probably a variant of Mahayana Buddhism.

MELAKA AND MALAY CULTURE: THE 15TH CENTURY

In the 14th century, Sri Vijaya was suppressed by the Javanese kingdom of Majapahit, a rival for control of archipelago trade. Refugees from Sri Vijaya moved north to the Riau-Lingga islands, then on to Singapore island and other locations before eventually founding the city of Melaka (Malacca). The *Sejarah Melayu* (the "Malay Annals") has it that their leader, Sultan Iskandar, was out hunting one day when one of his dogs was kicked by a mousedeer, normally the most timid and tremulous of animals. He took the mousedeer's courage as a fine omen for the founding of a new city.

Founded about 1400, Melaka would enjoy a century of greatness, both as a major trade centre and as a great cultural centre. Melakan Malay culture would be admired and adopted in many parts of the peninsula and archipelago, including northern Borneo. Tales of Melaka's wealth and influence would reach even Europe, making it a prime target for conquest when Westerners sailed into the Eastern seas.

Melaka's trading prowess was based on a number of factors. Its position was excellent, commanding the busy strait which took its name. Its rulers established efficient and secure conditions for traders, on land and on nearby sea lanes. Potential rival ports were brought into a tributary relationship to Melaka. At the height of its power Melaka probably dominated the Peninsula as far north as Perak, the Riau-Lingga archipelago and most of Sumatra's east coast.

At the same time, Melaka took care to become a tributary of powers greater than itself – most importantly China, but also Majapahit and the Thai state of Ayudhya. Sending tribute to such powers meant no loss of independence in practical terms, but did encourage such powers to send their traders to Melaka. A Chinese community quickly settled and became a feature of Melakan society, making Chinese people a part of Malaysian history effectively from its beginning.

At some time early in the 15th century Melaka's rulers adopted Islam, and this too contributed to the city's success, making it a favoured destination for Arab and Indian Muslim traders. Although some smaller ports in northern Sumatra preceded Melaka in turning to Islam, Melaka's conversion triggered the Islamisation of the peninsula and archipelago. Over the next century port city after port city would adopt the religion of the most powerful, prestigious and culturally dynamic of their number. Along with its religion, the port cities also tended to adopt the Melakan form of government – a blend of Middle Eastern Islamic forms with Indian forms brought from Sri Vijaya – and the language of Melaka, Malay. Malay thus became the most widely understood language in the region. In the 20th century, Malay would become not only the language of Malaysia and Brunei but, as the language of trade in the archipelago for centuries, it would form the basis of the Indonesian national language.

The golden age of Melaka ended abruptly in August 1511 when, after a month's siege, the city fell to the superior guns of the Portuguese. The Portuguese hoped to take command of Melaka's trading networks, particularly its control over spices from the

Moluccas. However, while the European newcomers had the power to take control of the city and the strait it overlooked, they lacked the resources to control the entire region and compel trade to continue at Melaka. Their posture as enemies of Islam scarcely helped. The Portuguese coup probably only stimulated the Malay trading world, as other port cities vied to take the fallen city's place, championing with new urgency Melaka's former religion and culture.

One state exemplifying this effect was Brunei, a port city dominating Borneo's north coast (today incorporating not only modern Brunei but also the Malaysian states of Sarawak and Sabah). Chinese records suggest that a port state, "P'o-ni", existed in the region from the fifth century. Now, around 1514, Brunei's rulers accepted Islam, emphasised their connections with Melaka's former ruling dynasty, and began to develop a "Brunei-Malay" culture.

A THREATENING WORLD: THE 16TH TO 18TH CENTURIES

Following the loss of Melaka, its ruling elite and their followers eventually established the sultanate of Johor, commanding the southern Peninsula and Riau islands. Elsewhere on the Peninsula, other states flourished, usually claiming legitimacy through connection with the former Melaka and paying tribute to Johor.

In spite of Portuguese attempts to subdue Johor, it prospered in the later 16th and early 17th centuries, especially when the Dutch arrived on the scene. Basing themselves in Java, the Dutch saw Johor as a useful counterweight to the Portuguese at Melaka and developed trading arrangements with the sultanate. In 1641, Johor helped the Dutch oust the Portuguese from Melaka, which then became a minor, outlying base in a growing Dutch empire.

The Dutch had considerably greater resources than the Portuguese had been able to deploy – and also, by the 17th century, greater resources than another Western power, the Spanish, who had established themselves in the Philippine archipelago in the previous century. But Dutch resources were not sufficient to fulfil their intended goal of trade dominance over the region. The Malay-Muslim trading world of the peninsula and archipelago thus persisted with considerable vigour after the advent of the Dutch.

The Dutch did attempt, however, to monopolise the region's most lucrative products, particularly the spices. They also took care to concentrate their naval and military resources against any state which emerged as a major threat to their monopolising strategies. No Malay state could ever hope now, therefore, to recreate the commercial power of 15th-century Melaka. Johor and other Malay states were now narrowly restricted in their trading and political potential.

One consequence of this was heightened, and in the end mutually destructive, competition between states. Johor, for example, long regarded Aceh and other Sumatran trading states as more serious opponents than any Western power. In northern Borneo, Brunei, which had suffered Spanish attacks in 1578, saw as its most serious opponent the slave-trading sultanate of Sulu (located in what is today the southern Philippines). In the 17th century, Sulu acquired from Brunei sovereignty over most of the area which today constitutes the Malaysian state of Sabah.

The scramble for diminishing trade share may account for the internal instability for which many Malay states would become notorious. A Malay sultan was, in theory, an awesome figure. Both South-East Asia's pre-Muslim Hindu-Buddhist traditions and Muslim thought invested him with divinely ordained power, making him temporal and spiritual supremo in his realm. Most Malay commoners existed in debt-bondage relationships with their royal and noble superiors, and trembled before their authority, but the Malay ruling classes competed vigorously amongst themselves for power and control of the material and human resources of their states. This could mean merely that sultans were often weak, ineffectual rulers. More damagingly, it could mean lengthy periods of civil strife. In one such episode, Sultan Mahmud of Johor was murdered in 1699; he was the last direct descendant of the Melakan royal house. His death foreshadowed more than a century of unstable authority in the sultanate and in other Peninsular states.

The politics of the Malay states were further complicated in the 18th century by a number of regional migrations. Bugis groups, originating in Sulawesi, established themselves in many states of the peninsula and archipelago. Skilled sailor-navigators, fighters and traders, the Bugis often became the dominant force in states where they settled. On the peninsula, Selangor became effectively a Bugis state. Meanwhile, Minangkabau groups from the west Sumatra highlands were also colonising Sumatra's east coast and crossing the Melaka Strait to the peninsula, where they established communities which ultimately would form the basis of the state of Negeri Sembilan.

In north-western Borneo, the sultanate of Brunei had to come to terms with the adventurous and fearsome "head-hunter" warriors who spearheaded the migrations of Dayak (Iban) communities. Rival Brunei chiefs often struck up alliances with rival Dayak groups, sharpening conflict in the sultanate. Both the Bugis and Minangkabau migrants of the 18th century would, over time, adopt Malay-Muslim custom and to all intents and purposes merge with Malay society. The Dayaks would be tamed under British colonial rule but would always retain their distinctive, non-Muslim, cultures.

Other factors would also increase instability in the 18th-century Malay world. The growing power of the British in India reoriented the trading patterns of the sub-continent. British traders in South-East Asia were often welcomed as potential allies against other Western or local powers, but their cargoes, featuring opium and firearms, were deadly. Meanwhile, Chinese doing business in the region tended increasingly to favour linkages with Westerners rather than local governments. They were thus heralding the "middleman" role which Chinese would hold between the indigenous peoples and the Western colonial regimes of the 19th and 20th centuries.

On the peninsula, the Thais also became a major intrusive force in the later 18th century. The Thai kingdom of Ayudhya had claimed sovereignty on the peninsula since the 14th century, and often exacted tribute from the more northerly states. In 1767, the city of Ayudhya was destroyed by the Burmese but, from 1782, a new Thai dynasty arose – the Chakri (still Thailand's royal house) – with a new capital, Bangkok. The early Chakri monarchs were determined to assert Thai royal authority more firmly than ever before. In the late 18th and early 19th centuries the northern Malay states of Patani, Kelantan, Kedah, Perak and, to a lesser extent, Trengganu, all experienced Thai pressures.

Patani effectively lost its independence and was absorbed within the Thai administrative sphere, thus creating a permanent Malay-Muslim minority in Buddhist Thailand. The other states continued as tributaries, running their own affairs, but Bangkok's enforcement of tribute payments and other decrees could be brutal and destructive.

In 1786, the ruler of Kedah, hoping to win an ally against the Thais, ceded Penang island to the (British) East India Company, which was looking for a safe harbour and trading base in the region. In 1800 a strip of territory on the mainland opposite the island was also ceded. The Kedah rulers merely acquired an annual pension for the ceded territory and, to their chagrin, the Company firmly refused to become involved in their struggles with the Thais. However, the first step had been taken towards British occupation of the peninsula.

THE BRITISH ADVANCE: THE 19TH CENTURY

In 1819, the East India Company acquired Singapore island from Johor. In 1824, an Anglo-Dutch treaty delivered Melaka into British hands, too, as part of a delineation by the two European powers of their respective spheres of influence in maritime South-East Asia. Making the Melaka Strait a frontier, the British took the Peninsula as their preserve, while the Dutch took Sumatra and all islands to the south of Singapore. Northern Borneo was not mentioned, though British interests would claim later, in the face of Dutch protests, that the terms of the 1824 treaty made that area a British sphere of influence too.

The 1824 treaty effectively determined the future boundaries of the British and Dutch colonial possessions in the region, and also of the nation-states which would emerge from the colonial era, Malaysia and Indonesia. In the 1820s, however, the British had no intention of entangling themselves in the Peninsula. They were satisfied with the Straits Settlements, as Singapore, Melaka and Penang became known from 1826. (The Straits Settlements remained under the East India Company until 1858, when the government of British India took over. In 1867, they were transferred to the control of the British Colonial Office.)

The Straits Settlements boomed and, inevitably, business interests there, Western and Chinese, became interested in exploiting the Peninsular states. The question arose of whether the states' traditional administrative structures would be able to cope with the pressures arising from the new economic ventures. The rulers of Johor, closest to Singapore, proved fully equal to a major expansion of Chinese commercial agriculture in their state, principally in pepper and gambier. Kedah was also well governed and able to cope with spillover pressures from Penang. The ruling groups of other states proved less adroit.

Pahang experienced civil war between 1858 and 1863, partly over the spoils arising from expanding ventures in mining and jungle produce. More seriously, endemic feuding developed within the ruling classes of the western Peninsular states of Perak, Selangor and Negeri Sembilan over the control of vast tin deposits, which had been worked in the 1840s. The tin was mined by Chinese labourers controlled by secret societies. Rival Malay chiefs aligned themselves and their followers with the forces of rival secret societies. Rival business houses in the Straits Settlements backed one side or the other with money and guns. By the 1860s these states were in anarchy and demands for official British intervention grew.

In 1874, one of the leading Malay disputants in Perak and the Governor of the Straits Settlements put their names to the Pangkor Treaty. The treaty recognised the former as sultan, but insisted, crucially, that he should accept a British Resident in his state, whose advice "must be asked and acted upon on all questions other than those touching Malay religion and custom". The British interpreted broadly which matters were unrelated to "Malay religion and custom", so taking effective control of most financial and administrative matters.

The Pangkor Treaty thus pioneered the formula by which the British would achieve authority in the peninsular states. Constitutionally, the states would be "protected" sovereign states, retaining their rulers. Practically, the Resident (or, in some cases, "Adviser") could extend his control as far as the British wished. By the 1880s, not only Perak but Selangor, Negeri Sembilan and Pahang were under such a system. In 1896 these states became the Federated Malay States (FMS) with their federal administrative centre at Kuala Lumpur, a young city growing out of a tin-mining camp.

In 1909, Thailand relinquished its imperial claims to the northern Malay states of Kedah, Perlis, Kelantan and Trengganu, and Britain moved to instal Advisers in these states. In 1914, Johor was also obliged to accept an Adviser, despite its long record of satisfactory administration. Johor and the northern states were not brought under federal administration and became the Unfederated Malay States (UMS). Even so, by the second decade of the 20th century the British had begun to talk about "Malaya" – that term disguising a constitutional hotchpotch of Crown colony (the Straits Settlements) and nine protected sovereign states, four of which were federated and five not.

In northern Borneo, meanwhile, two unique – indeed, eccentric – expressions of British colonialism had emerged at the expense of the sultanate of Brunei. Brunei was impoverished in the 19th century and further weakened by bitter factionalism within its ruling class. In 1840, a British adventurer, James Brooke, was recruited to quell a revolt in the Sarawak river region, at the sultanate's western extremity. Between 1841 and 1843 Brooke acquired full possession of the region and made the town of Kuching his base. From there, he, and his nephew and successor as "White Raja", Charles Brooke (ruler 1868-1917), expanded their territory eastward, establishing Sarawak's final borders shortly after the turn of the century. Brunei would be left as two small enclaves within Sarawak.

Several factors propelled the Brookes' expansionism, the most important being Brunei's poverty and the dispersal of power in the sultanate, which made the piecemeal acquisition of territory for small sums relatively easy. In addition, in the 1840s the British navy saw James Brooke as an ally in its efforts to stamp out piracy in South-East Asian waters. Brooke was backed on several occasions by intimidating displays of British naval power when dealing with Brunei. From the 1850s, British support was withheld from the Brookes, for fear that such private imperial ventures might embarrass Britain, but this made no difference. The Brookes had their own source of intimidating power – large contingents of Dayak warriors. They also had an idealistic rationale for their advance, believing that they were developing a unique experiment in efficient and benevolent government for native peoples.

Competition would add further urgency to Charles Brooke's expansionism from the 1870s. In 1877–1878, a British business consortium acquired the rights to most of the territory of Sabah, to Brunei's east, from Brunei and from the sultanate of Sulu in what is now the southern Philippines. (Here was the origin of a dormant but still unresolved dispute over Sabah between the Philippines and Malaysia. The Philippines, as successor state to Sulu, claims that Sulu merely "leased" rather than "ceded" its rights in Sabah.) By 1881, the business consortium had persuaded the British government to charter a company, financed by shares, to administer the Sabahan territories, hopefully at a profit. Thus Sabah became British North Borneo, and was governed by the British North Borneo Chartered Company.

Charles Brooke was outraged. During the 1880s and 1890s there was fierce competition between him and the Chartered Company over the Brunei territories that remained unceded. In 1888, Britain moved to guarantee that at least the core lands of the sultanate should survive, making Brunei a British protectorate. In 1906, Brunei received a British Adviser, with powers similar to those of Residents in the Peninsular states. By then Brunei had new-found economic significance; large oil deposits had been located in Brunei Bay.

THE COLONIAL ERA

On the peninsula, the extension of British control met with some opposition but it was soon quelled. The British now set about creating an environment for economic expansion. The tin industry which had boomed in the 1840s continued to grow, moving from Chinese to Western control with the arrival of capital-intensive mechanisation in the 20th century. In the first decade of the 20th century, rubber cultivation boomed. By 1930, two-thirds of the cultivated land on the peninsula would be under rubber.

Malayan tin and Malayan rubber would dominate their respective world markets, and despite their price instability, would make the peninsula one of Britain's most valued imperial possessions. The success of these commodities meant that economic diversification was limited. Crops such as pepper, sugar and coffee were largely swept aside by rubber after 1900. Some limited progress was made with palm oil, pineapples and timber in the more cautious 1920s and 1930s. No significant industrialisation occurred. However, the road and rail networks which the British established formed the basis for a good communications infrastructure. Chinese activity in such areas as finance, transportation, construction, petty industry and retail trading was also establishing a strong base for the area's economic future.

Chinese immigration swelled in the colonial era, pulled by the economic opportunities opening up and pushed by the dire conditions in China. The British left Chinese immigration uncontrolled until 1930, when the Great Depression ended any demand for additional labour. Meanwhile, the British had also recruited Indian labour. The Chinese and Indians had always been regarded as transients, but by the 1930s significant numbers had either decided to settle or lacked the ability to return to their homelands. The 1931 census revealed that Malays no longer formed the majority in the total population of the Malay States and Straits Settlements. This was despite another aspect of immigration to the Peninsula in this era – the arrival in substantial numbers of Malay-Muslim people from various parts of the archipelago.

Divisions between Malays, Chinese and Indians, already culturally profound, were deepened by British perceptions and policies. Racial stereotyping meant that the Malays were effectively excluded from the modernising economy. Their upper class was encouraged to think about an English public school-style education and a career within the branch of government which administered the Malays. Ordinary Malays were envisaged as rice farmers and fisherfolk, and their vernacular education was tailored to such humble goals. The growing towns and cities of colonial Malaya, predominantly populated by Chinese, became alien places to most Malays. Meanwhile, the Chinese were subject to a separate branch of government and managed their own education systems, in Chinese languages or English. Most Indians were effectively subjects of the rubber estates on which they laboured; their children received Indian-language education.

Such separation of the communities made the emergence of nationalism, in the sense of a pan-ethnic movement, unlikely. Prior to World War II, the British in Malaya were virtually unbothered by the sort of anti-colonial sentiment disturbing other Western colonies in Asia. Divisions within Malaya's communities furthered this state of affairs. Most Malays still tended to be loyal to their particular state and sultan. The Chinese were divided by differences of clan and dialect, and by the battle between the Kuomintang and the Chinese Communist Party in China.

However, education in various forms was beginning to produce people within each of the ethnic communities who were not content to leave the future entirely to the British. Amongst Malays, pan-Malay and pan-Muslim attitudes were stirring in the 1930s, heralding strong Malay political organisation later. A few Malay radicals believed that the peninsula should become part of the Indonesia envisaged by the nationalists of the Netherlands East Indies. The Communist Party of Malaya, founded in 1930, was mainly Chinese in membership and in the 1930s mainly interested in events in China, but it had begun to analyse the potential for revolution in Malaya. Many Indians were gaining political confidence from news about the struggle against the British on the subcontinent. Soon, war would accelerate dramatically the significance of these political awakenings.

Meanwhile, Sarawak and British North Borneo were quiet back-waters of the colonial world. Both had experienced major rebellions against the imposition of white authority, but resistance had been largely put down by 1900. Thereafter, change was slow. Neither territory attracted more than minor economic development, and the Brooke government (from 1917 under the third raja, Vyner Brooke) and the Chartered Company always survived on tight budgets. The Brookes made a virtue of that fact by arguing that they were deliberately protecting their subjects from the evils of modernisation. The provision of education was extremely limited in both territories, much of it being left to Christian missions.

In one regard – that of racial stereotyping – the theory of administration in Sarawak conformed closely to British theory in the peninsular states. In Brooke's eyes, Sarawak's Malay-Muslims would provide native administrators, the immigrant Chinese (over 30 per cent of the population by the early 20th century) would drive the commercial economy, while the Dayaks (Ibans) would remain within their traditional culture, except in the matter of head-hunting, for which the administration substituted police and military work. The Chartered Company, by contrast, was relatively relaxed in its dealings with its ethnically diverse population. It welcomed administrative and commercial talent from any group, and allowed complex inter-communal relationships to flourish. The communal rigidities of Sarawak and the peninsular states did not, therefore, develop to the same degree in Sabah.

JAPANESE OCCUPATION

Japanese forces attacked British Malaya on 8 December, 1941. Singapore, the supreme symbol of British power in South-East Asia, fell on 15 February, 1942. Sarawak and British North Borneo were occupied without a shot being fired. Over three and a half years of Japanese occupation would follow, until British military administrators returned in August/September 1945. The principal results of these years were devastation of the pre-war economy, a much more politicised populace, and a much more divided populace.

The Japanese presented themselves to Malay-Muslims as their patron, respectful of Islam and of Malay culture. They fostered pan-Malay consciousness and gave Malays new opportunities in administration. They also encouraged those young Malay radicals hoping for links with the Indonesian nationalists, though few Peninsular Malays supported them and the idea would not get far. Japanese regard for the Malays was thrown into question in 1943 when they handed over the four northern Malay states to Thailand. However, these states would return to British control in 1945.

The Chinese were treated by the Japanese as war enemies, often with appalling brutality. Not surprisingly, Chinese formed the majority of the underground resistance forces which developed in the peninsula and in the Borneo territories. The peninsular forces were known as the MPAJA (Malayan People's Anti-Japanese Army), and were to a large degree controlled by members of the CPM (Communist Party of Malaya).

The Indians of Malaya, by contrast, were encouraged by the Japanese to focus their political thoughts on India. Many young Malayan Indians were recruited for service in the Japanese-sponsored but ill-fated INA (Indian National Army).

THE POST-WAR PERIOD

When the British returned in 1945, they quickly subdued the open inter-communal hostilities which had flared at the war's end. They were aware, however, that there could be no going back to the complacency of pre-war days. Alongside the massive reconstruction of the economy, they also set about fundamental administrative reform. In 1946, Sarawak and British North Borneo – the latter particularly badly damaged by war – were acquired from their former owners and finally became the full responsibility of Britain. On the peninsula, the British introduced a plan for 'Malayan Union', uniting administratively the Malay States, Penang and Melaka (though not Singapore) and giving all residents equal rights of citizenship.

Malays from all states were galvanised by the blithe disregard for states' rights and Malay pre-eminence over the immigrant peoples. UMNO (United Malays National Organisation) was swiftly formed in protest, and the British were forced to abandon the idea of union. However, in subsequent talks, UMNO agreed to a federal administrative structure, and to citizenship for non-Malays who filled certain strict criteria. The Federation of Malaya was launched in 1948.

In the same year, the CPM attempted revolution, using guerilla warfare tactics and drawing on the experience and organisation gained during the war in the MPAJA. The British declared a state of emergency (the event became known as "the Emergency") and developed counter-insurgency policies which, crucially, won the support of the majority of the population. By the early 1950s, CPM terrorism had been reduced to a minor problem, though Emergency regulations were not lifted until 1960. One permanent result of the Emergency was a highly centralised federation, the states having relinquished most of their sovereign powers so that the crisis could be handled efficiently.

ALLIANCE GOVERNMENT AND INDEPENDENCE

During the Emergency, the British promised self-government for Malaya, though at the time it was not clear how this could be achieved in a way acceptable to all communities. Attempts to establish multiracial political parties met with little success. The largest and best-organised party in Malaya, UMNO, was exclusively for Malays. The peril of politicised ethnic rivalry loomed large.

Beginning in 1952, however, a formula for potentially stable self-government was worked out. This was the Alliance, a coalition of three communal-based parties. UMNO represented the Malays. The Chinese were represented by the new and politically conservative MCA (Malayan – later Malaysian – Chinese Association). The Malayan – later Malaysian – Indian Congress (MIC) represented the Indian community. The Alliance testified to the pragmatic good sense, diplomatic skills and political generosity of its founders, supremely Tunku Abdul Rahman, UMNO leader and first Prime Minister until 1970. Hugely successful at national elections in 1955, the Alliance achieved *merdeka* (independence) for the Federation of

Malaya in 1957. The new nation's democratic parliamentary system and its legal system were broadly derived from British models.

The Alliance was not without its flaws, leaving unresolved many issues which Malaysia is still working out. It was a pact, or bargain, between three communal élites which gave the economically weak Malays access to political and administrative power while assuring the other communities of respect for their interests. The Malays were offered a degree of "positive discrimination" but Alliance government basically left the socio-economic imbalances between communities to be worked out by laissez faire forces. In addition, questions of national cultural integration were left largely unresolved. Malay pre-eminence was acknowledged in the adoption of Islam as the national religion, in the form of monarchy devised (the nine hereditary state rulers would elect a king from their number every five years), and in making Malay the national language, but the application of the national religion and language to the daily lives of non-Malays was extremely circumscribed. It was believed that inter-ethnic suspicions were running too high for such issues to be determined at once.

THE CREATION OF MALAYSIA
Ethnic issues dominated the formation of the Federation of Malaysia. First mooted in 1961, Malaysia was envisaged as a merger of Malaya with Singapore, Sarawak, Sabah (then still British North Borneo) and, perhaps, the sultanate of Brunei. In the event Brunei remained apart but, after cautious negotiation, the other territories established Malaysia on 16 September, 1963.

The new nation was a delicate exercise in ethnic arithmetic. The non-Chinese majorities of the Borneo states helped balance the inclusion of the predominantly Chinese Singapore, but Singapore entered Malaysia with many constitutional, political and administrative issues left unresolved. Tensions escalated and, in August 1965, Tunku Abdul Rahman and Lee Kuan Yew signed a separation agreement.

THE 1969 CRISIS
The 1960s saw Malaysian democracy at its most open, and a number of parties engaging in vigorous criticism of the Alliance. The most notable opposition parties were Pas (Parti Islam Se-Malaysia, originally PMIP, Pan-Malayan Islamic Party), and DAP (Democratic Action Party). Pas was dedicated to building an Islamic state in Malaysia and appealed to Malay voters who saw UMNO as being

compromised by Western and non-Islamic influences and too ready to bargain with the non-Malays. The DAP picked up support mainly from Chinese voters unhappy with the conservative and Malay-dominated Alliance.

Political passions ran high during the general election campaign of May 1969. The results appeared to diminish the absolute control over government which the Alliance had previously enjoyed. Violent clashes erupted in Kuala Lumpur between perturbed Malays and celebratory Chinese. The riots lasted four days and caused several hundred deaths and heavy destruction of property. A state of emergency was declared, with government placed effectively in the hands of a body coordinating military and police action, the National Operations Council (NOC). Some observers feared that Malaysian democracy was dead. This did not prove to be the case, the rage and trauma did lead to substantial political changes.

UMNO AND BARISAN NASIONAL GOVERNMENT

Government by NOC ended in 1971 and government by federal cabinet, based on parliamentary voting strength, was restored. But the level of political freedom allowed to critics of government policy in the 1960s did not return. Conciliation and consensus-building were to remain a key feature of the Malaysian political scene, but now non-Malays were left in no doubt that their bargaining position was weaker than it may have seemed before May 1969. The Malaysian Government now adopted much more frankly the character of a primarily Malay government of a primarily Malay nation. Malay interests became paramount in the formulation of government goals and policies. UMNO became, unapologetically, the dominant political party in Malaysia, and was to increase its power further over the next two decades.

Under Tun Abdul Razak, prime minister until his death in 1976, the Alliance was superseded by a broader coalition of parties, Barisan Nasional (or, popularly 'Barisan'). MCA and MIC remained within this coalition but with their influence diluted. The leading pre-1969 opposition parties, however, refused to be subsumed within the UMNO-dominated coalition. The DAP has always remained outside Barisan. Pas joined briefly but soon departed. At the present time Pas controls the state governments of Kelantan and Kedah, but has never been able to win many federal seats.

Barisan was to prove a device for strong UMNO-led government. The composition of the coalition fluctuated during the 1970s and 1980s, as did the extent of its winning margins at elections, but following the 1990 general election, Barisan, comprised of nine parties, held 127 of the 180 seats in the federal lower house. Of the 127 Barisan seats, UMNO held 71; no other component party held more than 18. DAP, with 20 seats, led the five opposition parties.

THE NEP AND ECONOMIC GROWTH

Even more important for the direction of Malaysian politics was the establishment in 1971 of the New Economic Policy (NEP). Tun Razak and the "second generation" of Malay politicians saw the need to tackle vigorously the economic and social disparities which fuelled racial antagonism. The NEP set two basic goals with a 1990 target date – to reduce and eventually eradicate poverty, and to reduce and eventually eradicate identification of economic function with race. These goals were to be achieved in the context of high economic growth rates over the next two decades. While NEP would be socially redistributive, there would be no absolute "losers".

To meet NEP goals, however, NEP would inevitably mean government favour for the Malays, by far the largest component of Malaysia's Bumiputera peoples. In the early 1970s, Bumiputeras were still predominantly rural-based and involved in agriculture. Around half of Bumiputera households existed below the poverty line. Bumiputeras owned a mere 1.5 per cent of the share capital of companies operating in Malaysia, and accounted for only 4.9 per cent of the country's registered professionals.

The NEP necessitated a dramatic increase in governmental intervention in Malaysian business and in Malaysian society in general. The NEP's "big government" strategies vastly increased UMNO's power and influence. Under the NEP the volumes of public investment and public consumption expenditure increased substantially. In order to increase the Bumiputera stake in the economy, major public enterprises were established to take up share capital "in trust" for Bumiputeras until they were in a position to purchase share capital privately. Some of these enterprises developed elaborate conglomerate business interests.

The government promoted the education and training of Bumiputeras, and access for them at all levels of the public and private sectors. It also promoted the modernisation of the rural economy, with its predominantly Bumiputera workforce, and of rural life in general, while also supervising the balanced expansion of urban areas. In general, NEP saw the creation of significant Bumiputera commercial, industrial and professional communities. By 1987, the percentage of Bumiputera households in peninsular Malaysia deemed to be in poverty dropped to 17.3 per cent in rural areas and about eight per cent in urban areas.

Simultaneously with the implementation of the NEP, the Malaysian economy experienced dramatic growth. In the years 1971-90, the country's annual average growth in GNP was 6.8 per cent. Per-capita GDP moved from $380 to $2,200 (in current US dollar terms). Once the purveyor of just two important commodities, rubber and tin, Malaysia became a major exporter of oil/LNG, palm oil, timber and manufactures. Growth in manufacturing was particularly spectacular. By the late 1980s, manufactures dominated Malaysia's exports. Major manufactures included electrical and electronic products, chemicals, processed foods, textiles and processed timber and rubber products. Steel and automobile industries had also been established.

The opening of new economic opportunities and the solid rise in prosperity helped mollify those non-Bumiputeras who had feared the NEP and who still disliked many of its features, notably the level of government control over business and the favouritism shown towards Malays in areas such as education and employment. Critics of the NEP also argued that its implementation had paid insufficient attention to the non-Malay Bumiputera communities of Sarawak and Sabah, which were now the states with the worst figures on poverty in Malaysia. In 1987, the percentage of Bumiputera households deemed to be in poverty in Sarawak was 33 per cent; the percentage for Sabah was almost 42 per cent. The critics also argued that the Chinese and Indian poor had been ignored and that, even within the Malay community, NEP benefits had tended to be spread to UMNO's political advantage rather than on the basis of equity.

Eventually economic pressures compelled modification of the NEP's 'big government' strategies. In the mid 1980s a drastic fall in commodity prices, virtually across the board, threatened a serious balance-of-payments crisis. Dr Mahathir pegged back government spending and instituted a policy of privatisation of public enterprises. Mahathir, a strident champion of Malay advancement, was also motivated to modify the NEP strategies by his fear that Malay "feather bedding" would prove self-defeating. The NEP has now been replaced by the NDP (New Development Policy) which, though retaining NEP's broad goals, aims in Dr Mahathir's words to "strike an optimum balance between the goals of economic growth and equity". It is claimed that the NDP strategies will concentrate on the more glaring pockets of poverty and disadvantaged still existing in a now relatively prosperous Malaysia.

MAHATHIR AND THE CENTRALISATION OF POWER

Malaysia's fourth prime minister, Datuk Seri (now Tun) Dr Mahathir Mohamad was a controversial figure. Before achieving the prime ministership in 1981 he was often viewed as a Malay radical who might exacerbate Malaysia's ethnic tensions. In power, however, he proved a more complex political personality.

Mahathir championed the Malays yet he lambasted the dependent attitudes which he considered the NEP fostered. He promoted Islam in Malaysia, yet reined in its more doctrinaire elements and sharply rebuked Islamic "fanaticism". He insisted on the political overlordship of UMNO more forcefully than any previous administration, yet made it clear that non-Malays could work within the Barisan system securely and profitably. Mahathir went to the brink in pursuit of his political goals, yet never actually plunged Malaysia into any of the impasses, ethnic or cultural, of which it could have been capable, and even his controversial methods of dealing with the regional economic crisis of 1997, described below, appear not to have harmed the country's long-term prospects.

Even so, there was a clear theme to Mahathir's prime ministership – the centralisation of all significant power in the hands of the person who jointly headed UMNO and, as prime minister, the national government. Mahathir argued that such concentration of power was necessary for social stability and economic development. Critics argued that he unnecessarily diminished the democratic freedoms which Malaysia – unusually in its region – enjoyed. They also claimed that the growth of government power led to the abuse of power. Barisan government is continually dogged with rumours of corruption and crony capitalism, though the rumours remain unproven and Malaysia has not experienced the levels of corruption of some neighbouring nations.

Ironically, Mahathir's major battles for control concerned divisions within the Malay community, not inter-communal divisions. The opposition party, DAP, has commanded a majority of Chinese votes but is politically impotent except as a persistent if cautious critic of government. Mahathir's biggest political challenge occurred in 1986/7 when elements of his own party rebelled against his leadership. Partly this was a matter of personalities and of discontent with Mahathir's dominating style, but the revolt also signalled Malay alarm at the administration's retreat from the NEP's "big government" strategies. Mahathir retained the UMNO presidency by a mere 43-vote margin over his rival Tunku Razaleigh Hamzah (the voting was 761 to 718). After his victory, Mahathir purged his cabinet.

Political tension persisted and, in October 1987, Mahathir clamped down, detaining 106 people including leading opposition personalities. Three newspapers were closed, including *The Star*, which carried a column by the late former prime minister, Tunku Abdul Rahman, which was often critical of Mahathir's government. Most of the detainees were released within weeks, Mahathir's drastic action having subdued much of the political agitation.

Elements of the judiciary questioned the legal extent of the government's powers of detention without trial. The detentions had been ordered under the Internal Security Act (ISA), a measure originating in Emergency days and originally intended for use against communists. More recently, the threat of invoking the ISA has been a useful tool to intern Islamic fundamentalists suspected of being associated with extremist organisations in the wake of the 11 September, 2001 terrorist attacks in the United States. This also explains the lessening of criticism by Western governments, especially the US, who had at times been critical of the ISA but during the Bush Presidency supported its invocation to intern suspects indefinitely without trial. In 2002, Malaysia and the US announced plans for the establishment of a joint anti-terrorism training centre in Malaysia to serve the ASEAN countries.

Other areas in which Mahathir insisted on imposing his power included the promotion of Islam in Malaysia, the powers of Malaysian royalty and centre-state relationships.

From the 1960s, Malaysian government has had to deal with increased levels of Muslim political assertiveness. The traditionally quiet religious culture of the Malays has been shaken by the *dakwah* (mission) movement and by the claims of party, Pas, that UMNO is insufficiently concerned with religious matters. The dual thrust of the *dakwah* movement has been to foster personal devoutness and to pressure Malaysian government to support a more Islamic society. The movement has been particularly identified with young, educated and politically aware Malays.

In response, Barisan government has demonstrated strong support for Islam in a range of ways. With government patronage, Malaysia today is a much more insistently Islamic society than it was. But government activity in this area has also had a restraining dimension, aiming to bring Islamic enthusiasms under government oversight and regulation. Since the 1980s, successive legislative measures have tightened government powers over religious organisations and their teaching. On occasion, the government has resorted to its tough detention and censorship powers to silence persons considered a threat to social order on religious grounds. As well, government has used all its political skills and media control to diminish the credibility of Pas in Malay eyes. In 2002, Pas suffered a setback when Trengganu's assembly was forced by the federal government to reverse a decision to ban the wearing of bikinis and force all future resorts to have separate swimming pools for men and women. Aside from concern at the drop-off in tourism which would have resulted, Mahathir was acting to ensure there would be no threat to his positioning of Malaysia overseas as an advanced, moderate, Islamic nation deftly able to reconcile Western economic modernity with custom and tradition.

The prime minister's determination to curtail the influence of Pas among Malaysia's youth was again in evidence following controversial plans announced in late 2002 to overhaul the education system following a major government review inspired by Mahathir himself. The changes effectively ended all government subsidies to Islamic schools in an effort to absorb the approximately 126,000 students enrolled within them back into the government education system. There have even been suggestions that these schools – which Mahathir baldly stated were engaged in "brainwashing" – may eventually be banned entirely in an effort to address concerns that young Muslim children were being radicalised and led astray by the promotion of political Islam which, the government fears, will serve only to drive the youths into the embrace of Pas and other even more extreme groups. The guidelines also served to remove all religious instruction from the state school curriculum, with students instead receiving it during special after-school classes from which all political content had been removed. By so doing, the government can carefully regulate and monitor the administration of religious learning.

Besides this, the government has become alarmed at the fact that, by 2002, only one in 20 ethnic Chinese students attended government schools, down from 98 per cent in 1964, and has floated the possibility of compulsory national service for all 18-year-old boys, regardless of social class, religion or race, in an effort to force them to mix with other Malaysian youths and counteract the effects of a growing ethnic polarisation evident in the county's schools. In addition, in 2003 it was announced that, as a result of falling English-language standards affecting Malaysia's ability to compete in world markets, all schools would soon be forced to conduct mathematics and science classes in English. Mahathir, who as education minister in the 1970s had spearheaded the push to replace English with Malay, was behind this U-turn stating, "We have to accept English whether we like it or not".

Mahathir removed the powers of the Malaysian king to veto legislation, and minimised royal power to delay legislation. He also cut the powers and privileges of the country's nine royal state rulers, following an orchestrated media campaign in the mid 1990s which alleged the contempt of some rulers for the law, their questionable business dealings and extravagant lifestyles. Once held up as the symbols of historic Malay culture, the rulers were instead satorised as "feudal relics", at odds with the contemporary business and technology-oriented Malay. The Malaysian Bar Council's view was that the executive's reduction of the rulers' powers was a further attack on constitutional democracy in Malaysia.

A traumatic external shock occurred in August 1997, when currency woes brought on by the devaluation of the Thai baht spread to Malaysia's financial markets and, within six months, precipitated a halving of the value of the ringgit and a three-quarter slide in the value of the share market. Western economists blamed a combination of structural problems for this fall, including an unsustainably large current account deficit, a diversion of private domestic capital into economically unproductive sectors such as land and stock-market speculation, and massive government and private-sector spending on unnecessary prestige infrastructure projects. In addition, a culture of cronyism and nepotism enabled individuals and companies connected to UMNO to obtain government contracts for projects of dubious economic merit. While this worked fine during the good times, when the economy turned sour the effects were amplified by this lack of transparency, leading to a crisis of investor confidence.

Mahathir, characteristically had his own explanation for this. Malaysia was, he said, the victim of conspiracy of international financiers, whose aim was to destroy the prospects of an industrialising country and, moreover, to profit from its misfortune. He particularly targeted the currency hedge funds based in New York and Western Europe which sought to exploit instability in emerging markets by "taking a position" in the currency, precipitating instability and then causing a crisis of confidence.

Mahathir's strident calls for reform of the international financial sector, especially as regards leveraging, found many sympathetic ears both at home and abroad. In a radical experiment, in 1998 Kuala Lumpur imposed strict controls on the ringgit and the domestic equity market in order to try to insulate them from foreign manipulation and thereby prop up their value, at least in the short to medium term. His unorthodox response not only stabilised the economy but positioned Malaysia for a resumption of sustained growth in the new century. (It is also true that two countries in the region that also suffered severe downturns, Thailand and South Korea, have recovered and grown as well, and they both followed orthodox policies laid down by the International Monetary Fund.)

A further issue confronting Malaysia in the new millennium is the extent to which the entrenched rights afforded Malays will be lessened, thereby pushing Malaysia towards a meritocracy with greater inclusion for the ethnic Chinese and Indians. The momentum against affirmative action was driven by Mahathir, who repeatedly accused Malays of becoming soft and squandering their government-prescribed privileges. In 2002, an editorial in a leading newspaper thought to have been inspired by the prime minister created a storm when it stated that affirmative action had fostered a subsidy mentality that was counter-productive to economic growth. Shortly afterwards, deputy prime minister Badawi (who replaced Mahathir as prime minister in 2003) stated, "the Malays must think positively of their own ability, for it is one's own negative perception that makes one weak. The time has come for us to give up the crutches and start walking independently." In practice, any such moves may see an end to, or reduction in, minimum quotas for Malays entering the civil service, higher education and bidding for government contracts. Such comments increased UMNO's palatability among Malaysia's non-Malays.

The question of succession, never far from the surface during the close of the 20th century, came to the fore explosively in 1998 with the arrest of the deputy prime minister, finance minister and anointed heir, Anwar Ibrahim. During a mid-year UMNO conference, Anwar was the victim of a whispering campaign, apparently undertaken with the approval of the prime minister, in which his ability to continue in his ministerial role was undermined with the circulation of a highly personal pamphlet attacking his right to succeed Mahathir. This was the first tangible evidence pointing to a rumoured falling out between the two men. In September, Mahathir claimed Anwar had acted incompetently in the face of the financial crisis and promptly sacked him. Soon afterwards, the police formally charged him with perform-ing homosexual acts and corruption. Taken into custody, he was subsequently assaulted by the police commissioner, who was later forced to resign after admitting his role. In 1999, he was sentenced to a minimum of five years in prison, with a further nine years added for additional offences the following year. He was freed in 2004 when the federal court overturned his conviction for sodomy and, since he had already served his sentence for corruption, ordered his release from prison. He returned triumphantly to parliament after winning a landslide by-election victory in the seat of Penang in August 2008. This was in spite of UMNO vigorously campaigning against him and attempting to discredit his political party, the People's Justice Party. Anwar described his victory as "an endorsement of our policies and a rejection of the obsolete and corrupt policies of the government." Although only a single seat was at stake, the event transfixed Malaysians. While the result did not change the balance of power, it will strengthen Anwar's hand in his campaign to one day become prime minister.

Mahathir took Malaysia—and indeed, the world—by surprise when he abruptly announced his resignation in front of delegates and on live television at an UMNO party conference on 22 June, 2002. Although he withdrew it an hour later, he nonetheless said he would hand over power to his deputy, Abdullah Ahmad Badawi, in a phased transition. He resigned on 31 October, 2003 and Badawi was sworn in the following day. Preparations immediately commenced for the March 2004 general election, in which Badawi's ruling Barisan Nasional Party alliance gained 90 per cent of the seats in the House of Representatives.

This result was viewed as a ringing endorsement of the new prime minister. His popular mandate was assisted by his promises to reduce poverty and combat corruption, and via the support of many middle-class voters disenchanted with his predecessor's treatment of Anwar Ibrahim. Badawi was initially viewed as a consensus builder with impeccable Islamic credentials. But within a couple of years he came to be viewed as weak and indecisive by the electorate, from within his own party and even from Mahathir himself, who said publicly he regretted anointing Badawi his heir. Badawi's many critics also accused him of squandering the strong mandate for change handed to him in 2004; this seemed to be born out by the results of the 2008 general election in which he led UMNO to victory, but with a much reduced majority. Support for the opposition swelled to unprecedented levels and, as mentioned above, Anwar Ibrahim re-entered parliament late in 2008 as a powerful voice against the Government. Badawi accepted responsibility for the ruling coalition's poor performance and in mid-2008 agreed to step aside in March 2009 in favour of his deputy Najib Razak. Razak is the son of Malaysia's second prime minister and has been in parliament since his early 20s.

Mahathir left behind a legacy in which multiracial Malaysia was provided with the stability and guidance necessary to develop rapidly into a sophisticated modern economy, with a largely educated workforce who have greatly benefited from the changes Mahathir oversaw. But his critics accused him of maintaining an autocratic leadership style, muzzling the press and compromising the independence of the judiciary. The extent to which popular aspirations for greater political openness to match the increasing material prosperity will be accommodated by his successors still remains to be seen.

7 MYANMAR

1044

End 13th century

Mid 16th century

Mid 18th century

1824–26 & 1850s

1886

1948

1948–62

1962

Period of
democratic
governments

Independence
granted and the
Union of Burma
formed

New
kingdom
emerges
at Ava (near
Mandalay)

New kingdom
emerges at Pegu
(near Yangon)

Britain annexes the
remainder of
Myanmar

Mongols from
China attack
Pagan; empire
is destroyed

First and Second
Anglo-Burmese
Wars result in the
loss of territory to
the British East
India Company

Military coup
led by General
Ne Win ushers
in "Burmese
Way to
Socialism"

Pagan empire founded

Temples in Myanmar

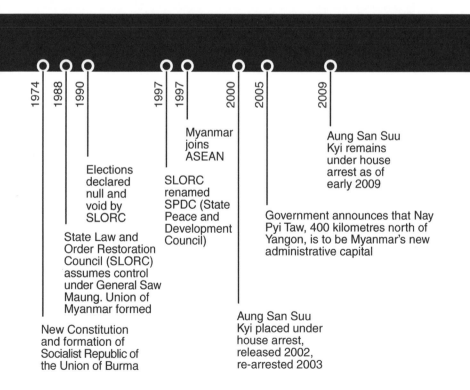

1974

1988

1990

1997

1997

2000

2005

2009

Myanmar
joins
ASEAN

Aung San Suu
Kyi remains
under house
arrest as of
early 2009

Elections
declared
null and
void by
SLORC

SLORC
renamed
SPDC (State
Peace and
Development
Council)

Government announces that Nay
Pyi Taw, 400 kilometres north of
Yangon, is to be Myanmar's new
administrative capital

State Law and
Order Restoration
Council (SLORC)
assumes control
under General Saw
Maung. Union of
Myanmar formed

New Constitution
and formation of
Socialist Republic of
the Union of Burma

Aung San Suu
Kyi placed under
house arrest,
released 2002,
re-arrested 2003

7 MYANMAR

Myanmar, formerly known as Burma, is a unique country in South-East Asia. For most of the six decades since achieving independence in the aftermath of World War II, Myanmar has isolated itself from the outside world. From its pre-war position as a relatively rich agricultural colony and a major exporter of rice, it has slumped to being the poorest nation in South-East Asia. Mineral rich, in the new century it is dependent on oil imports to keep its shaky economy running. Ruled by a military regime since 1962, for 40 years it deliberately isolated itself from the political, social and economic forces that have swept over the rest of South East Asia. Whilst in the early 1990s there were signs that economic imperatives and political pressure from both inside and outside the country were at least leading to more outward-looking economic policies, by the first years of the new century the Asian economic crisis, continuing un-resolved domestic political disputes and international condemnation by Western governments, has led to a stagnant economy.

Myanmar is the most ethnically diverse state in mainland South-East Asia. The Burmese comprise around 68 per cent of the population of 49 million, but there are more than 100 ethnic groups in the country. The Burmese dominate the alluvial plains and the major towns and cities. The hills bordering neighbouring countries of India, Bangladesh, China, Laos and Thailand are populated by ethnic minorities. These peoples have long resisted Burmese domination.

The largest of the ethnic minorities are the Shans, the Karens and the Arakanese (on the Bangladesh border). The multi-ethnic nature of Myanmar and the antipathy between Burmese and ethnic minorities is one important theme in Myanmar's history.

There is a strong coincidence between religious adherence and ethnic divisions. The Burmese are predominantly Buddhist, whereas the Karen and the Shan are predominantly Christian and the Arakanese are split between Buddhists and Muslims. Buddhism entered Myanmar from India from the seventh century and along with it came Hindu-Buddhist cosmological ideas. The ethnic Burmese began their migration from southern China in the ninth century and over the succeeding thousand years steadily spread through the lowland plains of present-day Myanmar. The Burmese embraced Buddhism. Christianity was introduced during British rule. British missionaries evangelised among the animistic hill peoples, converting the Shan, Karen and other ethnic minorities to the Christian faith. The coincidence of ethnicity and religion has deepened the divisions between ethnic groups in Myanmar.

A second major theme in Myanmar's history is a deep concern about its neighbours. The Burmese and the Thais have competed for territory, power and wealth over hundreds of years, resorting to war where necessary and thoroughly distrusting each other in periods of peace. The Burmese have also ingrained fears of their huge northern neighbor, China (remembering the Mongol conquest at the end of the 13th century), and still fresh memories of the colonial period, when Indian migrants dominated the modern sector of the economy. Ruled by an inward-looking elite, who are wary of their neighbours, fearful of foreign influences and steeped in distrust of ethnic minorities, Myanmar is very different from any other country in South-East Asia.

PRE-COLONIAL HISTORY

The territorial boundaries of Myanmar are the creation of British colonialism. Prior to British conquest no indigenous kingdom controlled the territory that now comprises Myanmar. The division between the alluvial plains (the lowlands) and the mountainous regions (the highlands) is central not just to the history of Myanmar but to the history of all mainland South-East Asian states. Lowland Myanmar is dominated by the Irrawaddy River and the rich alluvial plain created and recreated by thousands of years of annual monsoonal flooding.

The first known kingdoms emerged in the lower Irrawaddy valley from the fifth century. They were non-Burmese kingdoms but strongly influenced by Hindu-Buddhism ideas. The first major kingdom was founded around 1044, on the banks of the Irrawaddy

River at Pagan, north of the present day capital of Yangon (formerly known as Rangoon). For over 200 years, until the end of the 13th century, the Pagan empire flourished, at its peak controlling much of the territory of present-day Myanmar. It was a Buddhist kingdom whose temple remains at Pagan attest not only to its great agricultural wealth but also to its people's knowledge of mathematics, geometry and engineering. The temples of Pagan stretch along a 40-square kilometre zone. Some are as large as medieval European cathedrals, though built a century or more earlier. Pagan remains a golden era in the Burmese mind, when a strong, prosperous Burmese kingdom created beautiful temples and religiously inspired works of arts, and was a renowned centre for Buddhist scholarship.

The first major Burmese kingdom was destroyed by a northern invader. Pagan was attacked by the Mongols from China at the end of the 13th century. The city of Pagan itself was sacked and subsequently abandoned. Only the temples remained, under the control of Buddhist monasteries. In its place for the next 300 years were a series of small competing rulers all of whom failed to recreate the glories of Pagan. In the middle of the 16th century, a new Burmese kingdom emerged at Pegu, near Yangon, and tried to reunite the Burmese. It quickly exerted control over much of lower Myanmar and north to the Shan states. But it was a short-lived state, collapsing after only 50 years. Once again the Burmese were divided by a number of small, competing kingdoms.

In the middle of the 18th century, a new Burmese kingdom emerged at Ava (near Mandalay). It gradually extended its control over much of what is now Myanmar, including conquering the hill states of the Shan people. It became a major regional power, competing with the Thai kingdom of Ayudhya for territory and people. The Thai/ Burmese rivalry was strong and often bitter. In 1767, Ava was strong enough to despatch an army to Ayudhya. The capital was sacked, treasures were looted (with many finding a home today in Myanmar's museums), and tens of thousands of Thais were captured and transported back to Myanmar as slaves. The Thai kingdom collapsed, to be replaced a few years later by a new kingdom, the Chakri dynasty, which continues today in Thailand and whose capital was built further south at Bangkok away from the threat of Burmese attack.

At the end of the 18th century Myanmar was the strongest state in mainland South-East Asia. The Chakri dynasty in Thailand was in its infancy, recovering from the Burmese destruction of Ayudhya, and the Vietnamese kingdom was torn by rebellion. The balance changed in the early 19th century: the Thai and Vietnamese kingdoms flourished while the Burmese kingdom declined. The Burmese ruling elite was noticeably more inward-looking than its Thai and Vietnamese counterparts and less involved in commercial relations with the outside world. As Britain increased its presence in South-East Asia in the 19th century, the Burmese elite proved less able than the Thais to appreciate the threat posed to them and therefore less able to adopt strategies to cope with them.

THE COLONIAL PERIOD

The English East India Company (EIC) steadily extended its territory in India from early in the 17th century. Bengal, on the east coast of India adjacent to the Burmese kingdom of Ava, was the British stepping-stone into India. Calcutta was the capital from which emanated EIC influence, territorial expansion and commercial dealings. Myanmar was primarily seen by the EIC as a buffer zone. It had potential commercial importance but its greater importance was strategic. No other European power could be allowed to gain influence there and the Burmese rulers were expected to acknowledge the superiority of British India and create stable conditions for successful trade. The Burmese king and elite had a very different view of the world and the Burmese place in it. Fresh from the defeat of Ayudhya, in the 1820s the Burmese kingdom extended its control over Arakan, bordering Bengal. Refugees fled across the border, from where they organised resistance to the Burmese. The Burmese king finally demanded the British return them. For their part, the British became increasingly concerned about political instability on their colonial frontier.

The Burmese court greatly underestimated the strength of the EIC. In 1822, Burmese forces invaded Bengal and threatened to march on Chittagong in a dispute over the return of political refugees from Ava. The result was a British expedition to Myanmar. The Burmese were no easy opponents. The first Anglo-Burmese war lasted two years, from 1824 until 1826. Eventually, superior British weaponry and tactics, backed by a strong rear base in Bengal, ensured a British victory. The Burmese were forced to cede a large amount of territory on the coast of the Bay of Bengal, enabling the EIC to control the Bay from both sides. Over the next two decades, the EIC exploited the agricultural potential of its new territory, increasing rice production four-fold and developing a strong export trade in rice, timber and shipbuilding.

Despite this defeat and loss of territory, the Burmese elite contin-ued to underestimate British power in Bengal, demanding respect as equals and taking whatever opportunities they could to remind British envoys, traders and visitors of their equal status. In the 1850s, a second Anglo-Burmese war broke out, the immediate cause of which was a conflict between British traders and the Burmese governor of Yangon.

The result was that Bengal acquired more territory in lower Myanmar. The final act in the British acquisition of Myanmar occurred in 1885 when Mandalay was captured and the King and his family exiled to Calcutta. Myanmar was formally annexed by Britain on 1 January, 1886.

The British impact on Myanmar was profound. At the political level, the monarchy was abolished and the Burmese aristocracy was stripped of their power. Myanmar was ruled from Calcutta, as a minor part of the British Indian empire. Indian models of administration were imposed by Englishmen, who by and large, had no under-standing of or respect for local social structures. Lower Myanmar, that is the alluvial plains which were ethnically Burmese and the heart of the Burmese empires, was ruled directly by the colonial govern-ment, with the powers of traditional regional and local elites de-stroyed. It was here that the full force of British political and economic policies were felt. In Upland Myanmar, in areas populated by ethnic groups such as the Shan and Karen, a policy of indirect rule was introduced. Social structures and local elites were more or less left intact, with administrations separate from that of the Burmese heart-land. A major consequence of this was a strengthening of the division between the Burmese and ethnic minorities, with the latter developing a stronger sense of identity under British rule.

It has been argued that one of the most important consequences of British conquest was that the two most vital institutions of Burmese society, which together defined what it meant to be Burmese, were destroyed or seriously weakened. The exile of the King and his family meant that the ritual and symbolism of the court was abruptly ended. The Burmese state no longer had a centre; indeed, the throne itself was transported to a museum in Calcutta. The king was also the patron and, in many senses, the head of the Buddhist hierarchy. His demise reduced the authority of the religious hierarchy, leaving Buddhist religious institutions with a much weakened central leadership. As a consequence, Burma became fragmented. These two binding forces in Burmese society were eliminated, with no indigenous replacements.

British colonial rule introduced a strong bureaucracy supported in its maintenance of social control by an efficient police and army. The British distrusted the Burmese. The police and the army were largely composed of ethnic minorities who would have few qualms about quashing Burmese dissent. The bureaucracy was supervised by the British but staffed largely by Anglo-Burmese and Indians. The new bureaucratic elite created by Britain was dominated by Anglo-Burmese, whose cultural models were influenced more by Britain than by Myanmar. This was to pose considerable problems after independence.

British rule increased the ethnic diversity of Myanmar. The administrative link with India meant that Indians were free to migrate. By 1931, about seven per cent of the population of Myanmar was Indian, predominantly from Bengal and Madras. Yangon was an immigrant city. Two-thirds of its population in 1931 were immigrants, including 53 per cent Indians. Much of the capital for the agricultural expansion in the Myanmar Delta came from Indian moneylenders. Chinese immigrants were recruited from British Malaya and Singapore. In 1931, they comprised about two per cent of the total population of Myanmar. They worked in the mines in the Shan states, provided much of the urban labour force, operated small businesses and built rice mills in central Myanmar. On the eve of British conquest, the Myanmar lowlands were populated predominantly by ethnic Burmese. By 1941, this ethnic homogeneity had given way to a multi-ethnic and multi-religious society.

The British transformed Myanmar's economy. They encouraged the settlement of the Myanmar Delta, which, in the 1850s, was largely malarial infested jungle and swamps in the 1850s. Roads and bridges were built, land was opened up at cheap prices with significant tax concessions and the infrastructure of ports and communications was greatly improved to enable crops to be exported to world markets. The result was a dramatic southward migration of Burmese from the dry northern zone to the fertile delta. The Myanmar Delta became a major producer of rice and little else, commercialised and dependent on the vagaries of international markets. The extent of the transformation can be gauged by the raw economic statistics. In 1855, lower Myanmar exported 162,000 tons of rice: in 1905–6, it exported two million tons, with the price of rice increasing threefold in that time. The area under rice cultivation expanded from around 800,000 acres to around six million acres and the population grew from one million in 1852 to four million in 1901.

Land was plentiful until the 1920s, when the limits of cultivation were reached. Until then, the Myanmar Delta was generally prosperous, for those who tilled the land as well as for those who financed the development and traded rice and teak on world markets. From the 1920s population pressure on the land became a major problem, as did farmers' indebtedness. Tensions between Burmese and immigrant Chinese and Indians then became more open and, at times, more violent.

Britain transformed the economy but was content for Myanmar to be a rice, teak and mineral exporter. There was no attempt to industrialise the country. In 1941, Myanmar was still a relatively prosperous agrarian society, though serious indebtedness and population pressure had expressed themselves in peasant protests and violence in the 1930s. What capitalism existed was in foreign hands: European companies controlled the export trade; the petty traders and small-scale capitalists were Chinese; and the financiers and rural moneylenders were Indians. Myanmar was a pluralistic society in which economic position was coterminous with ethnicity.

Economic development under colonial rule was accompanied by the spread of Western education. A new Western-educated, urban elite emerged in the 20th century, out of which a nationalist movement was to emerge. As part of the Indian empire, until its separation into an independent colony in 1937, Myanmar's political development closely parallelled that of India. The political reforms introduced in India from the beginning of the 20th century were extended to Myanmar. In 1935, a new Constitution was introduced into Myanmar under which limited self-government was permitted. The first elections for a Burmese Parliament were held in 1936 and a Westminster-style parliamentary government operated until the Japanese occupation in 1942.

The nationalist movement in Myanmar had a number of distinctive characteristics. First, it was dominated by the ethnic Burmese. Their promotion of Burmese language, literature and cultural symbols as "national", led to an ambiguous relationship with the ethnic minorities. Ethnic minorities were suspicious of the nationalist movement. They feared Burmese domination of an independent Myanmar and their assimilation into Burmese majority culture. Second, the nationalist movement was strongly anti-Chinese and anti-Indian, in reaction to the domination of the Myanmar economy by these groups. Third, the domination of the Myanmar economy by foreign capital stimulated the development of socialist ideology among all strands of Burmese nationalism. Fourth, the stress on Buddhism as being at the core of cultural, religious and personal identity further alienated the non-Burmese minorities, especially those who were Christians.

On the eve of World War II, there was a strong urban-based, Western-educated, nationalist elite which had developed no single or widely accepted view of what independent Myanmar would look like, apart from an emphasis on the unity of Myanmar, the "Burmeseness" of Myanmar and the need to take control of the economy out of the hands of foreigners. Two of the most prominent nationalists in the 1930s were U (meaning "Mr") Aung San and U Nu, the latter of whom was to be the first prime minister. Another was U Ne Win who, in 1962 led the coup that placed the military in power, where they remain today. Japan became a magnet for many nationalists in the 1930s. They were impressed by its propaganda support of anti-colonial movements in South-East Asia. When World War II broke out, Aung San was one of a group known as the Thirty Comrades who accepted Japanese-sponsored military training in Hainan. The Thirty Comrades returned to Myanmar in 1942 along with the invading Japanese army as leaders of the Myanmar Independence Army. From the Thirty Comrades came many of the political and military leaders of post-independence Myanmar.

JAPANESE OCCUPATION

The Japanese occupation was welcomed by many Burmese, including, of course, the Thirty Comrades. The attraction of Japan in the 1930s was shared by most South-East Asian nationalists. Not only did the Japanese decisively end European colonialism but their slogans of "Asia for the Asians" and building a "Co-Prosperity Sphere" were seductive. The destruction of white rule was itself a major fillip to South-East Asian nationalists. The introduction of military training, the promotion of locals to administrative positions far higher than they could achieve under colonial rule and the promotion of indigenous languages all contributed to a growing self- confidence among nationalists throughout the region.

The realities of the Japanese exercise of power were far different from the promises held out by the propaganda, however. South-East Asians quickly found Japanese rule to be no less exploitative and far more brutal than that of their former European colonial masters. In 1944, Aung San and fellow members of the Thirty Comrades group established the Anti-Fascist People's Freedom League, which opposed the Japanese and worked to develop a vision of an independent Myanmar.

INDEPENDENCE

The activities of the Anti-Fascist People's Freedom League against the Japanese made its leader, Aung San, a Burmese hero and ensured that at the end of the war Britain would have to negotiate with the League. In May 1945, just two weeks after Yangon had been recaptured, Britain announced its plans for post-war Myanmar. Its stated intention was to move Myanmar towards full self-government within the British Commonwealth but, in the meantime, to suspend the political reforms of the 1930s and rule directly in order to reconstruct the economy. The plan had no timetable for independence.

Britain's position was unrealistic. It took no account of the political and psychological impact of the Japanese occupation of South-East Asia, whose people were no longer prepared to acquiesce in colonial rule. In Myanmar, the Anti-Fascist People's Freedom League, the Burmese Communist Party and parties based on ethnic minorities campaigned for independence and struggled with each other for dominance. In January 1947 Aung San led an Anti-Fascist People's Freedom League delegation to London and negotiated the election of a constituent assembly to prepare a constitution for an independent Myanmar. In April 1947, the Anti-Fascist People's Freedom League won the election handsomely but, in July, Aung San and six of his Cabinet were assassinated by political rivals. The assassinations created a national martyr but made it even more difficult for Myanmar to create a consensus on the structure of the independent state.

Aung San was replaced by his deputy, U Nu, and the League led Myanmar into independence on 4 January, 1948. The Union of Burma was constituted as a federal state composed of the large Burmese area and four upland states, home to the ethnic minorities. Though these states were promised a great deal of autonomy, power was quickly concentrated in the central government. The failure of the federal system and the concentration of power in Yangon have been a major cause of the instability Myanmar has suffered since 1948. Shortly after independence was declared, the Burmese Communist Party and the Karen nationalist movement launched insurrections which continue through today—though in recent years there have been some conciliatory moves by Yangon to accommodate the rebels and the scale of the fighting has, temporarily at least, been reduced. The cause of the insurrections remains. Many of the minorities see independent Myanmar as a Burmese state. The army, the police and the apparatus of government are controlled by Burmese. The substantial ethnic minorities fear absorption and the consequent disappearance of their separate and distinct cultural identities.

Myanmar was a democratic state between 1948 and 1962. Governments were elected, accepted the need to operate within the limits of the Constitution, held national elections and abided by the results and accepted decisions of the Supreme Court when it ruled against the government. Power was in the hands of the Anti-Fascist People's Freedom League, which drew on the name of Aung San to bolster its support. There was a 16-month period of military rule between 1958 and 1960, but General Ne Win abided by the Constitution and fulfilled an undertaking to hold elections in 1960. Though the political party favoured by the military did not win the elections, the military accepted the decision and returned to barracks.

The failings of the democratic period were critical. The declining economy and the emphasis on the "Burmeseness" of Myanmar were the prime causes of regional insurrections and social unrest in both urban and rural areas. All efforts to create a social consensus on the kind of society that should be created failed. Corruption became rampant as inflation ate away remorselessly at civil servants' salaries, forcing them to resort to illegal impositions in order to survive.

In March 1962, a military coup led by General Ne Win over-threw the elected government of U Nu, ushering in a period of military rule that has lasted more than 40 years. The ostensible reason for the coup was the military's fear that U Nu's government would allow the Shan and other ethnic minorities to secede from Myanmar. Many Burmese cautiously welcomed the coup because it promised to put an end to the corruption, instability, inflation and social unrest of the previous decade and a half.

The coup leaders arrested political and ethnic minority leaders, closed down the parliament and demolished the federal structure. Opposition from Yangon students and from Burmese monks was ruthlessly suppressed. The country was ruled by a Revolutionary Council composed entirely of military officials loyal to General Ne Win. The military created its own political party, the Burma Socialist Program Party, as the only legal party in the country and described its ideology as the "Burmese Way to Socialism". In 1974, a new Constitution was put into effect, creating the Socialist Republic of the Union of Burma. An elected parliament was formed, but only one candidate was allowed to stand for each constituency and that candidate had to be approved by the Burma Socialist Program Party.

The leaders of the coup argued that the army was the only cohesive and disciplined organisation capable of providing the strong leadership needed to overcome the social chaos that prevailed. They were fiercely anti-foreign and determined to rid Myanmar of all vestiges of colonial-ism by refocussing on Burmese culture, language, tradition and religion. Like the royal elite that had ruled Myanmar in the 1800s, they were, and to a certain extent remain, an inward-looking elite, suspicious of its immediate neighbours and determined to keep outside political, cultural and economic influences to a minimum. The new regime moved quickly to eliminate the predominantly Indian and Chinese business class, seeing state socialism as the only way to deliver economic independence to the country. The Westernised, often Anglo-Burmese, elite that had run the country under colonial rule and through the 1950s fled the country, along with the Indian and Chinese communities. In the 1990s, they were followed by the Muslim minority on the western border with Bangladesh who, too, became a target for a government intent on removing all non-Burmese elements from society.

Ne Win's military government was even less successful in devel-oping the economy than the democratically elected governments before it. Indeed, the economy worsened acutely under military rule, with the expulsion of Indians and Pakistanis, the prohibition on foreign investment and the efforts of the one-party State to impose a command economy. In 1987, the United Nations gave Myanmar "Least Developed Nation" status, recognising it as one of the world's ten poorest countries. Estimates of per-capita income vary and even official statistics are difficult to obtain, as the government has released few figures pertaining to the country's financial and social conditions since 1999. There are, however, two economies: the legal, largely state-controlled economy and the black-market economy. It is estimated that illegal trade in Myanmar is three times the official trade, and that the total, non-drug, illegal trade makes up about 40 per cent of GNP.

The illegal trade filters through Myanmar's porous borders with China, Thailand, Bangladesh and India. The illegal drug trade would add considerably to the black market figures as the Golden Triangle, centred on Myanmar, is the world's major opium producer. The military elite, which on assuming power in 1962 spoke much of the need to combat corruption, is one of the main beneficiaries of the black market. It is directly involved as broker and rentier, raking off a percentage of the money made from the trade. In 2006 the global organisation which monitors corruption, Transparency International, listed Myanmar as the world's second most corrupt country after Haiti. The black market is crucial to Myanmar's economic survival. Without it the country would fall even further into abject poverty and the people's lot would be truly appalling. The military regime's continued hold on power is to a large extent dependent on the ability of the black market to keep consumer goods and essential supplies trickling into Myanmar.

There were sporadic student protests and riots in the 1970s, but these were ruthlessly quelled by the military. A new series of protests began early in 1988, led by students and Buddhist monks. The usual violent reaction from the military this time failed to stop the riots growing in intensity. In August and September 1988, they culminated in widespread strikes and massive demonstrations in the urban areas, coalescing into a demand for an end to military rule. The army reacted, killing thousands of protesters. The horrors of these acts were relayed daily to the television screens of the Western world, eliciting widespread protests from Western governments. A new organisation, the State Law and Order Restoration Council (SLORC), took over government under the control of the army chief of staff, General Saw Maung. However, Ne Win, who had resigned as chairman of the Burmese Socialist Program Party in August 1988, retained an important behind-the-scene role during the 1990s. By the turn of the century, though, his star has waned. In a dramatic move in March 2002, Ne Win's son-in-law and three grandsons were charged with plotting a coup to restore him to power and sentenced to death in August, though this was later commuted to life imprisonment. Ne Win himself died under house arrest in December 2002 and was buried in a private ceremony ignored by the country's military rulers.

SLORC decided to hold elections in 1990, presumably because it was concerned at the strong international reaction to the repression of August and September 1988. It also thought that it could control the results of the election through its powerful intelligence service. The election campaign did not go as planned. Daw (meaning "Mrs") Aung San Suu Kyi, daughter of Myanmar's first prime minister and revered national martyr Aung San, returned from London and quickly became the major spokesman for the National League for Democracy (NLD). The NLD campaigned vigorously in 1989, drawing large crowds to its meetings despite the restrictions placed by the military and the fear campaign waged by the intelligence service. Aung San Suu Kyi was a powerful orator and magnetic public figure, and was able to draw on the aura surrounding her father's name. In July 1989, she was placed under house arrest and thousands of NLD supporters, students and other political activists were arrested.

Despite the tough military line, the NLD won over three-quarters of the seats when the elections were eventually held in May 1990. The renamed Myanmar Socialist Program Party—now the National Union Party—won only ten seats. SLORC responded by arresting NLD leaders and declaring the election null and void. The military subsequently stated that they would retain power. Although Aung San Suu Kyi was released from house arrest in 1995, between September 2000 and May 2002 she was again subject to house arrest and imprisoned in May 2003. She is currently under house arrest once again. The military government (which changed its name from SLORC to the State Peace and Development Council, or SPDC, in 1997) has shown no sign that it is prepared to relinquish political power or lessen its repression of the NLD and popular dissent generally. In 1999, Suu Kyi's British husband, Michael Aris, died of cancer in London. The Myanmar authorities refused him permission for a last visit to see his wife in Yangon. She in turn refused to leave the country, fearing the Myanmar government would deny her a re-entry permit when it came time to return home.

International pressure for reform has come mostly from the European Union and the US, both of which have imposed economic sanctions and placed travel restrictions on government officials. In contrast, neighbouring countries have mostly refused to condemn the SPDC, stating that this would amount to an unacceptable interference in the country's internal affairs. In 1997, Myanmar entered ASEAN and the other members have relied on a policy of "constructive engagement" in an effort to quietly persuade the SPDC to be more accommodating of the aspirations of its citizens and to seek a political compromise with Aung San Suu Kyi. But following the 1997 Asian financial crisis ASEAN has had other issues to deal with and international controversy regarding its support for the SPDC have become a liability. Thus, during a visit in January 2001, one of ASEAN's most influential leaders, Malaysia's prime minister Mahathir, stated quite baldly that his hosts had become an "embarrassment to ASEAN" because of their failure to enact reforms to address the pariah status accorded their country by Western nations. This, he said, was tarnishing not only Myanmar's reputation, but those of other ASEAN member-states too. In 2005 a group of South-East Asian parliamentarians demanded that Myanmar be expelled from ASEAN unless the regime improved its human rights record. While their calls went unheeded, ASEAN members did become concerned that the Association's image would suffer irredeemably if Myanmar insisted on taking its turn as ASEAN's rotating chair in 2006. Subtle pressure was applied behind the scenes and in July 2005, the government announced it would forego its right to chair ASEAN, citing the need to concentrate on domestic considerations.

Aung San Suu Kyi, meanwhile, continues to call for a continuation of foreign boycotts on trade, aid and tourism. Indeed, foreign donor countries have largely cut off development aid since 1998. To add to Myanmar's woes, in 2002 the United Nations announced that the country was facing an AIDS epidemic, with one in 50 adults estimated to be HIV positive, one of the highest rates in the world. In the same year, the US State Department reported that "poverty is widespread and the economy has continued to show the effects of a growing government deficit, rising inflation, shortfalls in energy supplies and continuing foreign exchange shortages". In September 2007 major riots, triggered by fuel price rises, broke out in the capital. Thousands of Buddhist monks and nuns joined the protests, which were ruthlessly suppressed by the authorities, sparking sharp international condemnation.

Also attracting international criticism was the government's response to Cyclone Nargis, which wrought havoc in the Irrawaddy delta (the source of 65 per cent of the rice grown in Myanmar) on 2–3 May 2008. The cyclone is said to have killed an estimated 134,000 people, affected 2.4 million farmers and swamped 200,000 hectares of delta rice paddies (16 per cent of the total) with seawater, rendering it unusable for several harvests. The tragedy was compounded by the government's refusal to avail itself of offers of assistance which flooded in from the United Nations, foreign aid groups and other governments. These offers were either delayed or rejected outright, which needlessly led to the deaths of many thousands of cyclone victims. This was further evidence of the extent to which the regime remains insular and suspicious of outside interference, even during a humanitarian catastrophe such as Nargis.

In January 2004, the government and the Karen National Union (the most significant ethnic group fighting the government) agreed to a ceasefire. Since then, however, sporadic clashes between Myanmar's army and the insurgents have occurred. In October 2004, Khin Nyunt was dismissed as prime minister ostensibly for corruption, but more likely the victim of a power struggle. In July 2005 he received a suspended sentence of 44 years from a special tribunal and remains under house arrest, along with his two sons who were found guilty of similar charges. Khin Nyunt was replaced by General Soe Win, the former first secretary of the SPDC, who had a reputation as a hardliner in dealings with the NLD. Soe Win stepped aside due to ill-health in May 2007 (and died in October that year), and was, in turn, replaced as Prime Minister by SPDC first secretary Lt-Gen Thein Sein. However, the real power in Myanmar still lies with Senior General Than Shwe, who is chairman of the SPDC, commander-in-chief of the defence force, minister of defence and also taken on the functions of state president.

In an announcement that took most Yangon-based diplomats by surprise (including, it was reported, those representing other ASEAN countries), the Ministry of Foreign Affairs announced in November 2005 that government ministries and military headquarters were to be transferred to Nay Pyi Taw, approximately 400 kilometres north of Yangon. The government also promised a ten-fold increase in salaries paid to civil servants required to relocate to the new site. The official reason given for the creation of a new administrative capital was that Nay Pyi Taw is centrally located and therefore more accessible from all parts of the country. However observers have speculated that an enhanced capacity to quarantine key government and security installations from potentially debilitating unrest in Yangon (such as that which swept the capital in 1988), to be a more plausible explanation. In March 2006 Armed Forces Day festivities were held at the new site to inaugurate it officially.

Myanmar's history continues to haunt it and a stable and prosperous future will, to a large extent, depend upon establishing a political system which skilfully handles the aspirations of the various ethnic groups.

8 PHILIPPINES

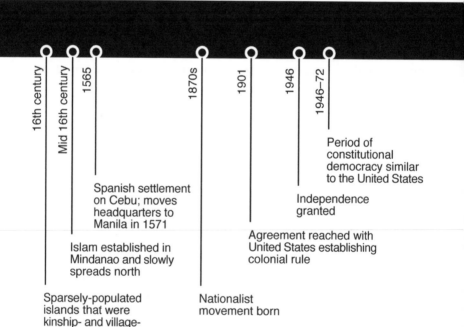

16th century

Mid 16th century

1565

1870s

1901

1946

1946–72

Period of
constitutional
democracy similar
to the United States

Independence
granted

Spanish settlement
on Cebu; moves
headquarters to
Manila in 1571

Agreement reached with
United States establishing
colonial rule

Islam established in
Mindanao and slowly
spreads north

Sparsely-populated
islands that were
kinship- and village-
based

Nationalist
movement born

Fort Santiago in Manila

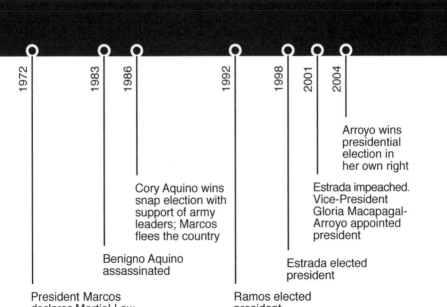

1972

1983

1986

1992

1998

2001

2004

Arroyo wins
presidential
election in
her own right

Cory Aquino wins
snap election with
support of army
leaders; Marcos
flees the country

Estrada impeached.
Vice-President
Gloria Macapagal-
Arroyo appointed
president

Benigno Aquino
assassinated

Estrada elected
president

President Marcos
declares Martial Law

Ramos elected
president

8 PHILIPPINES

In 1967, the Philippines joined Indonesia, Malaysia, Thailand and Singapore to form ASEAN. The country was seen by many as a model of what its partners might become. It had a strong economy, a well-educated English-speaking workforce, strong technical and managerial classes and an apparently thriving industrial sector. Within the South-East Asian region it was favoured by foreign investors. Moreover, it was a parliamentary democracy with a vigorous press and a strong civil society, again pointing to what the rest of ASEAN might become. In 2002, after more than a decade of regression, the Philippines economy had only slowly restarted. Although stability has now returned for many years following the downfall of President Marcos, the Philippines experienced enormous social and political instability, including a civil war in the south and private armies in many other areas. If one characteristic of many contemporary ASEAN countries is the presence of a strong state and a weak civil society then the Philippines has been the major exception. It had a weak state and a fragmented society. That seems to be changing through the successive leadership of presidents Aquino, Ramos, Estrada and Arroyo, and their compliance with the Constitution.

The Philippines is different from the rest of South-East Asia in a number of ways. It shares with Indonesia and Malaysia, a Malay ethnic base (its underlying animistic beliefs have much in common with other countries in the region) and it has, for many centuries, been part of regional trading networks, albeit in a minor way. Yet unique among South-East Asian countries, it was unaffected by Hinduism or Buddhism. The great majority of the Philippines' 88 million people are Roman Catholic. The Spanish colonisers probably prevented the conversion of the islands to Islam and only the southern islands of Mindanao and the Sulu archipelago are Islamic. It is also unique in another way. The absence of Hindu/Buddhist influences meant that sophisticated concepts of the state and cosmologies which linked the temporal and the spiritual realms were lacking in the pre-colonial Philippines. There were no pre-colonial state structures, socially integrating ideologies or "great traditions".

One important consequence is that contemporary Filipinos lack a concrete pre-colonial history from which they can draw inspiration and create national myths. There is nothing in the Philippines' past remotely comparable to the "golden eras" of Angkor in Cambodia, Pagan in Burma or Majapahit in Indonesia. There is only a pattern of regionalism under the control of local trading families and kinship networks.

EARLY HISTORY

We know little about the political, social or economic structures of the islands now known as the Philippines before the arrival of the Spanish in the mid 16th century. The islands were sparsely populated with largely kinship- and village-based political organisation. There were well-established trading networks between the islands and links into wider regional trading networks in South-East Asia and beyond to China and India. There were also some relatively large entrepots exchanging local products, ranging from exotic foods to gold, for Chinese pottery, silk and other wares.

Islam was the first of the world religions to have an impact upon the folk-religious base of the peoples of the Philippines. It is impossible to date precisely the arrival of Islam in the southern islands of the Philippines, but we do know that Aceh on the northern tip of Sumatra converted to Islam in the middle of the 14th century and that when Melaka was closed to Muslim traders as a consequence of the Portuguese conquest in 1511 the process of Islamisation in the Indonesian archipelago quickened. The ruler of the northern Borneo state of Brunei converted to Islam soon after the fall of Melaka. Brunei then became the base for the spread of Islam into the southern islands of the Philippines. By the middle of the 16th century, the ruler of Sulu had converted to Islam, as had the court in Mindanao island. The influence of Islam slowly moved north to the island of Luzon. By the middle of the 16th century, the Manila region was under the control of an Islamic ruler.

SPANISH RULE

In 1494, the Pope endeavoured to settle the commercial and political rivalries of Europe's major powers, Portugal and Spain, by determining that Spanish expeditions should sail westwards and Portuguese expeditions eastwards of an imaginary north/south line in the middle of the Atlantic ocean. Hence, Portugal established colonies in Africa, India, Malaya, the Indonesian archipelago and on the China coast, while Spain moved into the New World, establishing a base in New Spain (present-day Mexico) and from there moving to conquer much of Central and South America. In the 16th and 17th centuries, Mexico was a valuable source of silver and gold, carried across the Atlantic to Spain in great galleon fleets.

The Portuguese-born explorer Ferdinand Magellan led an expedition that became the first to circumnavigate the globe in 1522. Magellan did not survive the trip. He was killed in a skirmish with natives in the Philippines. A few years later, another expedition arrived in the Philippines in search of the fabled spice islands, which were known as the Malukas in the Indonesian archipelago. They had long been the source of expensive spices traded in Europe. Spanish, Portuguese and later Dutch merchants dreamed of acquiring control of the islands in order to monopolise the supply of spices to Europe. The dreams of the Spanish expedition were shattered when they discovered that Portugal had beaten them to it in 1512. The world proved to be spherical rather than flat, as believed at the time. Sailing east, the Portuguese arrived in the Indonesian archipelago, a decade before the Spanish.

Other expeditions were sent to the western Pacific by the Spanish governors of New Mexico, but it was not until 1564 that the New Mexican governor decided to occupy the islands of the Philippines. Two motives drove the Spanish to the Philippines: first, a determination to spread the Faith; second, the possibility of opening new trading posts and expanding trade to Asia. The first Spanish settlement was established on the island of Cebu, in the southern Philippines, in 1565. In 1571, Spanish headquarters were moved to Manila, then a thriving entrepot dominated by Chinese merchants. Thus began more than 300 years of Spanish influence on the Philippines. The islands were named after the Spanish Crown Prince Felipe, quickly becoming known as the Philippines.

In the 17th century, Spain tried to create an Asian trading empire, based on Manila as both an entrepot and a naval base from which it could challenge the Dutch in the Malukas. The attempt failed. Spanish economic and political power steadily declined and Spain was no match for the resurgent northern European Protestant nations of Britain and the Netherlands, both of which aggressively sought Asian empires. The economic base of Spanish occupation of the Philippines in the 17th and 18th centuries was the galleon trade between the Portuguese port of Macau on the south China coast, Manila and Acapulco in New Mexico. It underpinned the Philippines until the Mexican Revolution in 1820 brought it to an end. The first Spanish governor of the Philippines, Miguel Legaspi, admired the fine Chinese silks traded at Manila by Chinese merchants and recognised a commercial opportunity for Spanish merchants to supply silk direct to the European market by exchanging silk for Mexican silver and gold. Great galleons left Acapulco for Manila, laden with silver. At Manila, the silver was exchanged for Chinese silk brought across from Macao. The silk was then transported to Acapulco and on to Europe, where it graced the lives of the European elite, in the process provided very profitable returns to the traders.

Manila was quickly transformed from a small but busy port town linked to regional trading networks into one of the major colonial port cities in South-East Asia. Its rival in the 17th and 18th centuries was Batavia (Jakarta). In the 19th century, Singapore outstripped both. Chinese merchants controlled Manila's trading lifeblood, although their numbers were only small. At the beginning of the 19th century, there were probably no more than 4,000 Chinese in the Philippines, mostly based in Manila. Many of the Chinese married locally and over time became a mestizo community. In many ways, 17th and 18th century Manila was a Chinese city or, at least, a city of Chinese and mestizos. They organised the entrepot trade and provided the internal trading and credit networks essential to that trade. There was never a large Spanish population in the Philippines and most who lived there resided in Manila. Most came via New Mexico and many were themselves creoles who married locally in the Philippines. The mestizo communities, one Spanish-derived and the other Chinese-derived, became the most powerful political and economic forces in the Philippines.

While Spanish rule in the 16th, 17th and 18th centuries had little economic impact on the peoples of the Philippines, its political and religious impact was considerable. In contrast to European invaders elsewhere in South-East Asia, the Spanish were not confronted by indigenous states supported by bureaucracies, aristocracies or religious organisations. Spanish rule defined the modern state of the Philippines and its social, religious and ideological underpinnings. Spanish power was centred in Manila, on the island of Luzon in the northern part of the island chain. However, Spanish control was only really assured in the lowlands of the northern and central islands. Despite constant efforts throughout the 18th and 19th centuries to conquer the southern islands, Spain was repeatedly rebuffed by the Islamic sultanate of Sulu. The Sulu archipelago and the island of Mindanao were not incorporated into the Philippines until the Americans took over the colony from Spain at the end of the 19th century. Even then it was only a partial incorporation. Independent Philippine governments from the 1940s to the 1990s have struggled to assert control over the Muslim south, tying up much of the Philippine armed forces in the effort to do so.

The key to Spanish control of the Philippines was the close relationship between state and church. Spain wanted to convert the peoples of the Philippines for the glory of God. Priests from Spanish orders, predominantly Jesuits, Dominicans and Columbians, were sent by the state to the countryside where they proselytised the faith, and at the same time, established the presence of the colonial state. Indeed, the friars were the state outside Manila, controlling large tracts of land, which they developed into plantations, and exercising considerable temporal powers alongside their spiritual powers. The people in the northern and central islands of the Philippines were gradually converted to Catholicism, albeit a Catholicism incorporating pre-Catholic animistic beliefs, symbols and ritual.

From the late 18th century and through to the early 20th century, social and economic structures in the Philippines were transformed. The Philippines, along with the rest of South-East Asia, was drawn into the world trading system. The catalyst was Britain's occupation of Manila in 1762. Spain had allied itself with France in the latter's war with Britain. Britain then occupied Manila in order to prevent a French threat to its China trade. Manila was sacked, galleons were captured and bullion confiscated. The British naval forces quickly departed, leaving behind a considerably poorer Spanish colony. In the context of a general decline in Spain's economic power in the 17th century, successive Spanish governors were forced to seek new sources of wealth and revenue.

One initiative was to create a state-controlled tobacco monopoly in northern Luzon. Local people were forced to provide labour on tobacco plantations, producing cheap tobacco for export to European markets and generating considerable profits for the treasuries of both the Philippines colony and the Spanish motherland. Another was the ending of the galleon merchants' trading monopoly. The Philippines was opened to private traders and investors. In addition to encouraging of private traders, in 1785 the Spanish Crown established The Royal Philippine Company, which became an investor in export crops in the Philippines, primarily sugar, coffee, indigo and pepper. In all of these crops, the Philippines was competing on world markets with the Netherlands East Indies.

The speed of social and economic change quickened after the end of the Napoleonic War. After the colony was opened to foreign traders and investors, the Philippines could be described as an Anglo-American colony flying the Spanish flag. In the 19th century, Anglo-American merchant houses dominated the burgeoning export economy. The Philippines became a major producer of cash crops for international markets. Between 1825 and 1875, the volume of international trade increased 15 times. Major exports were sugar, tobacco, coffee and abaca.

The incorporation of the Philippines into the world economy had two important consequences. First, it saw the emergence of Filipino nationalism and with it the emergence of a modern nation-state. Second, it created regional economic, social and political forces that served in the long term to weaken the nation-state. The growth of an export economy led to the creation of powerful regional elites who became the major political forces in the 20th century.

FILIPINO NATIONALISM

The Philippines nationalist movement was the earliest nationalist movement in South-East Asia. Many of its leaders saw their movement as a beacon for other South-East Asian colonies. In reality, it had little impact. Nationalism took a decidedly different course in the Philippines from elsewhere in South-East Asia. Philippine intellectual and political elites identified themselves more with Spain and, later, the United States than they did with anti-colonialists elsewhere in South-East Asia.

Philippine export crops were grown predominantly on land owned by the Chinese mestizo community. The haciendas developed by powerful regional families were worked by tenants. The landowners became rich and powerful while the tenants became increasingly impoverished, trapped in a grossly unequal relationship with the landowners. Here lie the origins of the major Philippine families who continue to control the rural Philippines today and who from this economic base continue to exert enormous political power. Their wealth continues to be based on large estates, even though many have diversified their investments in recent decades.

The landed elite which emerged in the 19th century, unique in South-East Asia for its social, economic and political power, educated their children in Spanish schools, seminaries and universities. Their Spanish-educated children, known as *ilustrados*, were influenced by the liberal reforms in Spain after 1868. From the 1870s, they began to demand the same rights as Spaniards, including representation in the Spanish parliament. Avowedly anti-clerical, they demanded the separation of state and church, the expulsion of the Spanish friars who dominated rural areas and the introduction of native clergy. Their demands were disregarded by both the colonial government and the Catholic Church. Disillusioned by Spain's refusal to treat them as equals and its dismissal of their proposals for social and economic reform, by the 1890s the *ilustrados* began to call themselves Filipinos. They were led by Jose Rizal, a wealthy fifth-generation Chinese mestizo. Hitherto, the Spanish had appropriated the term "Filipino" for Spaniards born in the Philippines, referring to natives as "Indios". The term "Filipino" now became a symbol of nationalism.

In contrast to their moderate nationalism of the *ilustrados*, a rebellion organised by a far more radical group known as the Katipunan and led by Andres Bonifacio, a relatively poorly educated Manila clerk broke out in Manila in 1896. The Spanish responded by arresting not only Katipunan leaders but also many *ilustrados* as well. Rizal was arrested, charged with treason and publicly executed. Philippine nationalism now had a martyr.

As well as being confronted by open rebellion in the Philippines, Spain was also fighting a major rebellion in its central American colony of Cuba. The drain on its limited resources was immense. United States intervention in Cuba resulted in the American-Spanish war. As a consequence, the US Pacific fleet sailed into Manila bay, destroyed the Spanish fleet and laid siege to Manila. Philippine nationalists took advantage of a weakened Spain by declaring independence on 12 June 1898 under the *ilustrado* leader, Apolinario Mabini. The Filipinos were the first people in Asia to defeat their colonial power and create a modern nation-state.

Unfortunately for the nascent Philippine Republic, the United States decided that occupation of the Philippines would provide it with a base in the western Pacific from which it could promote its political and economic interests in East Asia. Early in 1899, open hostilities broke out between the Philippine Republic and the United States, eventually involving more than 10,000 United States troops. Most hostilities ended in 1901 when the United States effectively bought off the *ilustrado* elite, promising to maintain their wealth and power in return for collaboration with American colonial rule. However, the Muslim south remained under American military jurisdiction until 1913. Even then sporadic violence continued against American authorities for some years.

The agreement of 1901 consolidated the power of the landed Chinese mestizo elite enabling them to dominate the political and economic structures of the Philippines in the 20th century. It also created a Filipino elite that looked to the United States not only for economic and political patronage but also as its intellectual and cultural model. The landed *ilustrado* elite in the Philippines had no parallel elsewhere in South-East Asia, their social and political power stemming from an economic base independent of the colonial state.

UNITED STATES COLONIALISM

It has been argued that if Spain occupied the Philippines for "the glory of God" then the United States occupied the Philippines for "the democratic mission". Certainly, Americans were uneasy about their status as an imperial nation. It ran counter to their perception of themselves as a people who had thrown off the colonial yoke to become the beacon for free, democratic and egalitarian values in the world. The Americans' own history of anti-colonialism ensured that there were significant differences in US rule in the Philippines from colonial rule elsewhere in South-East Asia. From the outset, the United States made clear that its goal was to lead the Philippines to independence. Nationalism was a legitimate force (to be moulded in its own image of course), not one to be distrusted and repressed. It followed from this that the role of the colonial state was to tutor Filipinos in the administration of a modern nation-state in order that they learn the skills necessary for independence as quickly as possible.

Given that the Americans saw themselves as being in the Philippines for the best of reasons—"the democratic mission"—it is not surprising that US colonial administrations emphasized the importance of developing education, health and democratic processes. Electoral systems were introduced at all levels of society and the national parliament was encouraged to monitor officials and influence colonial policies. By 1934, the United States Congress mandated Philippine independence within 12 years. As a first step towards this goal, in 1935 a Philippines Commonwealth was established and was given autonomy in domestic affairs. Manuel Quezon was its first president. Though political developments in the Philippines were unique in South-East Asia, in the long run the effect was to increase the wealth and power of the landed elite.

The United States government expended money on the Philippines rather than extracted money from it—another unique occurrence in colonial South-East Asia. Much of this money was spent on developing education and health systems far superior to anywhere else in the region. At home, the United States was committed to mass education at all levels, in contrast to Britain, France and Holland which restricted access to high schools and believed that a university education was only for a small elite. Education policies in the Philippines reflected American domestic educational philosophies, in the same way as education policies in British, French and Dutch colonies reflected their domestic policies. The contrast between the Philippines and Indonesia on the eve of World War II illustrates these differences. In 1938–39, there were 7,500 students at the University of the Philippines in Manila. For the same year in Indonesia there were a mere 128 students at Colleges of Law, Medicine and Engineering. In 1941, the literacy rate in the Philippines was five times that in Indonesia.

Nationalist movements in most of colonial South-East Asia flourished from the 1910s, demanding independence, by and large rejecting colonial cultural mores and vigorously debating the need for radical social and economic reform. They were generally led at the "national" level by the Western-educated sons of either the traditional aristocracy or the bureaucratic elite and at the local level by upwardly mobile clerks, schoolteachers and government officials. There was a wide spectrum of parties, ranging from conservative ones, who wanted independence and little social or economic change, to the communist parties which wanted thoroughgoing revolution. The Philippines was once again an exception. Its nationalist movement was dominated by the Nationalist Party under the leadership of Manuel Quezon. Leaders were from the landed elite, who were even more wealthy and powerful under American rule than they had been under Spain. While publicly demanding immediate independence, in fact their personal economic interests were well served by continued US rule. Enjoying self-government after 1935, and under a relatively benign colonialism, the Filipino nationalist elite remained pro-American. In many ways they were bi-cultural. The shape of Filipino nationalism—in ideology, myths and symbols—was very different from elsewhere in South-East Asia. With no need to foster a strong "national" consciousness and few "national" symbols, regionalism and regional loyalties based on regional landed elites remained strong. This had significant consequences after 1945. Filipino nationalists were barely conscious of the events going on elsewhere in South-East Asia and this left a legacy of separateness from the rest of the region which had only partially changed by the 1990s.

JAPANESE OCCUPATION

When General MacArthur was forced to flee the Philippines in 1942 he uttered the famous words "I shall return". When in 1944, he did return at the head of American troops charged with driving the Japanese back to Japan he was greeted as a hero. Fighting in the Philippines during the Pacific War was more intense than elsewhere in South-East Asia. It took six months of bloody warfare for the Japanese to oust the Americans in 1941–2 and another ten months for the Americans to expel the Japanese in 1944–5. There was a great cost in Filipino lives.

Japanese slogans such as "Asia for the Asians", "Japan the light of Asia" and "The Co-Prosperity Sphere" made much less sense to Filipinos than to other South-East Asians. The nature of American colonialism, the bi-culturalism of the Filipino elite, the experience of self-government and the realisation that they were due to get independence in 1946 anyway, placed Filipino nationalists in a different relationship to the Americans than nationalists elsewhere in South-East Asia to their colonial rulers. Though opinion was divided about the appropriate response to occupation, resistance to the Japanese in the Philippines was strong. The collaborationist government established by the Japanese lacked legitimacy in the eyes of many Filipinos.

Comparisons with other South-East Asian countries are striking. Elsewhere, the invading Japanese were seen as liberators. The iron grip of colonial rule was broken. Certainly, as time went by the mood changed to resentment and then hatred of Japanese brutality but Japanese occupation often opened the way for nationalists to seize power in August/September 1945 and to organise resistance to the re-invading Europeans. Filipino nationalists, by contrast, welcomed the returning American forces as liberators, restoring the country on the path to independence promised by 1946.

However, there were important long-term effects from the Japanese occupation of the Philippines. Its incorporation into Japan's South-East Asia empire broke the isolation of the Philippines from the rest of the region that had begun with the arrival of the Spanish and continued through United States rule. Filipinos became more aware than ever before of their place in Asia. The war also sharpened social, economic and political tensions in the Philippines. Throughout Japanese-occupied Asia people suffered badly. Filipinos were no exception. Corruption increased, the gap between the rich and the poor widened and social structures broke down. In 1946, the Communist Party of the Philippines took advantage of the deteriorating conditions in the countryside to arouse support for rebellion. The war also spawned an armed society. Filipinos put up strong resistance to the invading Japanese and the fighting between United States-Filipino and Japanese forces in 1944–45 was extensive. The violence of the war years led to a greater preparedness to use force to achieve political ends in the post-independence Philippines.

INDEPENDENCE AND THE DEMOCRATIC YEARS

Historians of the Philippines have stressed the importance of the family to an understanding of the political culture and the structures of the Philippines. They see independence in 1946 as having changed very little. A small number of wealthy families, generally based on extensive regionally land holdings, has controlled Philippines politics since the first elections in 1907. In the late 1960s, a prominent Philippines businessman summed up the failure of the Philippines political system with the statement: "We have no institutional loyalty, only personal loyalty." The political process in the 20th-century Philippines—both pre- and post-independence—has been based on extensive patron-client relations, linking at the base of the society exploited peasants and powerful landlords. Party politics has been free of ideology—with the exception of the Huks and the Communist Party of the Philippines. Party loyalty has been fickle and based on a complicated and extensive reward system linking party notables to politicians and local leaders.

Between the achievement of independence in 1946 and the Marcos coup in 1972, the Philippines was a constitutional democracy with all the trappings of an American-style political system. In practice, it was a system of intra-elite struggle based on powerful patron-client relations, at the apex of which were the landed families. The most serious opposition came from the Huk movement, based on support from impoverished tenant farmers and landless labourers in central Luzon. The Huks were in open rebellion against the Philippines state between 1946 and 1953. They were crushed by a combination of coordinated military activity and rural reforms introduced by President Magsaysay. However, rural discontent and unrest has remained a serious problem in the Philippines down to the present day. Local military and police forces are used by the local elites to contain rural resistance and, where they fail, extensive private armies owned by the landlords are brought into play.

In the 1950s and 1960s, the underlying rural problems were masked by the apparent success of the industrialisation policies of the Philippines government. The state promoted import-substitution manufacturing by imposing high tariffs and import controls and by managing the exchange rate. A new industrialist class emerged. Some were from the wealthy landed elite, diversifying their capital away from its rural origins. Others emerged from professionals and traders, who created joint ventures with foreign, predominantly American, companies or with wealthy local Chinese. By the 1960s, the Philippines was the most successful manufacturing country in South-East Asia and appeared to be the most prosperous. Urbanisation occurred apace. From the manufacturing companies built up behind tariff walls and state subsidies emerged a number of conglomerates with interests in agribusiness, real estate and banks as well as manufacturing. Some became multinationals.

THE MARCOS ERA

Ferdinand Marcos was elected president in 1965 and re-elected in 1969. He was a career politician. Neither he nor his wife, Imelda, came from the powerful landed oligarchy and thus he was dependent on powerful and wealthy patrons for financing his electoral machine. Marcos was openly unimpressed with the democratic system, arguing that it should be replaced by what he called "constitutional authoritarianism", a system he saw as being more in keeping with Filipino political culture.

In 1972, Marcos proclaimed martial law. Many explanations have been advanced for this decisive break with Philippines political history. First, Marcos was constitutionally barred from standing for a third term as president. In his determination to hold on to power, he was prepared to destroy the Constitution. Second, the halcyon days of the 1950s and 1960s had turned sour. The Philippines economy was stagnant, per-capita income was falling, foreign debt had grown to serious levels and there was growing middle-class discontent about political corruption and the inability of the political system to solve the country's social and economic problems. Third, the military leadership was willing to become more directly involved in running the country. Military leaders welcomed the suspension of democratic processes and the increased power that flowed to them as a consequence.

Many Filipinos initially welcomed Marcos' move. The New Society promoted by Marcos was attractive to many of the urban middle class and intellectuals. It promised law and order in a hitherto insecure society; it promised to provide the infrastructure and stability needed to attract the foreign investment essential if the economy was to revive; and it promised land reform and an end to the corruption that had bedevilled the Philippines since independence. Martial law was also welcomed by outsiders, including foreign investors, the United States government and other South-East Asian governments, most of which were themselves, in various degrees, military-dominated regimes.

Initially, the Marcos dictatorship did stimulate increased foreign investment and a return to economic growth. However, by the early 1980s new economic and political weaknesses had become obvious. Under the guise of creating a New Society, Marcos systematically undercut the political power of the landed elite at both national and local levels. Businesses belonging to his political opponents were confiscated, licenses were withdrawn and state enterprises became part of the president's personal fiefdom. He was able to do all of this because he had the support of the military leadership. The beneficiaries, apart from the Marcoses themselves and favoured military leaders, were a small group of friends and relatives who were provided with lucrative monopolies, government contracts and cheap finance. "Crony capitalism" was taken to spectacular heights by the late 1970s. Through all of this, Marcos and his family acquired enormous personal wealth, with the removal of the boundary between state finances and personal income. Corruption and nepotism were practiced on an unprecedented scale. While the landed oligarchy lost their political power, Marcos ensured that their economic interests were protected. Any notion of land reform and an end to rural poverty remained mere rhetoric.

Marcos centralised state power but did not create an institutionally strong state. The power of the state depended on personal loyalties, primarily from army commanders to Marcos. By the 1980s the Philippines was a society in danger of falling apart. The Moro Nationalist Liberation Front (MNLF) in the south had 50–60,000 guerrillas fighting for an independent Muslim state. More than half of the Philippines army was engaged in fighting it. The remainder was engaged against the New People's Army (NPA), the communist-controlled front organisation, which by the mid-1980s, had about 15,000 guerrillas and was able to launch commando-style raids in towns and cities, including Manila. Opposition to Marcos became more public and more strident. In August 1983, Benigno Aquino, Marcos' most prominent and popular political opponent, returned to the Philippines from his exile in the United States, but failed to set foot on Philippines soil. As he descended the aircraft steps at Manila airport, he was assassinated by one of the accompanying soldiers. The military leadership denied involvement, as did Marcos. The death of Aquino began a process of open resistance to Marcos, a resistance led by the Manila middle class.

Under pressure from the United States, and still supremely confident of his ability to fix elections, Marcos called a snap presidential election for early 1986. Despite the vote rigging he lost. In a few chaotic months in Manila, Cory Aquino, the widow of Benigno

Aquino, claimed victory and prepared for an inauguration organised by her supporters. Despite all the evidence to the contrary, Marcos continued to claim victory and moved towards his own inauguration. The imminent danger of serious bloodshed, if not outright civil war, was averted when a number of significant army leaders deserted Marcos and moved over to support Aquino. Marcos fled the Philippines. Cory Aquino became president. "People power" had won.

THE RESTORATION OF DEMOCRACY
With the end of martial law, the exile of Marcos and the inauguration of Cory Aquino, Philippines politics returned to its pre-1972 constitutional form. The landed gentry retained their wealth and restored their political power. Many of those who lost out under Marcos had their fortunes restored. The great families still dominate the Philippines. Despite all the promises of the post-Marcos era, land reform has been negligible and the interests of the landed elite have prevailed. Political loyalties remain personal rather than institutional. The state remains weak, especially compared to the counterparts in neighbouring ASEAN countries such as Singapore, Malaysia and Indonesia.

There have been major achievements since 1986. Not least of these were the peaceful and constitutionally correct elections in 1992 which brought Fidel Ramos to power as president. On the economic front, the first four or five years of the Aquino government saw an impressive economic turn-around from the negative growth of the last years of Marcos to a positive growth which peaked at 6.7 per cent in 1988. The growth fell away after 1990, in part because of the deteriorating world economy and the economic dislocation caused by the Gulf War of 1991, but also because of the failure of basic infrastructure, such as power, to keep up with demand. By the mid 1990s, the Philippines had been restored to economic growth levels approaching those achieved elsewhere in ASEAN.

President Ramos proved to be a popular leader, even though he took a number of tough economic decisions which won the praise of the finance sector and ensured the continuation of foreign investment, but understandably, alienated some sections of the community which suffered as a result of reductions in state subsidies of key commodities. However, these reforms did to a large extent cushion the economy from the full impact of the Asian economic crisis which swept the region in 1997 and 1998. Ramos also moved to force the police to act against a spate of kidnappings that targeted the wealthier business class. It emerged that the kidnapping gangs were aided by corrupt police and bank workers who passed on details of potential victims' worth. But law and order still remains a key concern for most Filipinos.

Since the Constitution expressly forbids an incumbent president from standing twice in 1998, Ramos stood aside—somewhat reluctantly it seems—and a former film star, Joseph Estrada, was elected on a populist platform in a landslide result. Initial fears by the finance sector that Estrada's playboy image, insupportable populist election promises and lack of experience in dealing with economic fundamentals—all in the midst of a regional financial crisis—would spell an end to the reform process initially proved unfounded. The new president proved willing to follow the advice of his experts and not engage in free-spending policies which might have unsettled investors and led to a flight of foreign capital. However, by the turn of the century, rumours were circulating that Estrada had taken bribes from illegal gambling syndicates. In late 2000, the House of Representatives began moves to impeach him amid claims of massive corruption. Estrada attempted to block the subsequent investigation, triggering large-scale protests that forced him to stand aside in January 2001. Vice-President Gloria Macapagal-Arroyo became president with strong support from the military, the business community and the Roman Catholic Church, although many poorer Filipinos refused to believe—and probably continue to do so—that their erstwhile hero was guilty of the corruption and mismanagement charges leveled against him.

Arroyo, a former economist, immediately set out to reassure foreign investors by focusing on the economy. In particular, she accelerated plans to deregulate the power industry, state mismanagement of which had led to the country being subject to repeated brown-outs in the 1990s. She also committed her government to enacting other liberalisation measures, such as simplifying the tax code, and pledged to re-invigorate stalled efforts on land reform and poverty-reduction programmes (though these promises have been made by Filipino leaders many times in the past). In June 2004, she was elected president, with 40 per cent of the vote. Her nearest rival received 37 per cent. Despite the narrow result, it was an important boost to her authority as she had been appointed, not elected, as leader in 2001 following Estrada's impeachment and could thus not hitherto claim a popular mandate. The next presidential context is scheduled for 2010 though in its present form, the constitution forbids Arroyo from seeking a second term.

While progress has been made by the government in accommodating the demands of various insurgent groups in the restive southern provinces, sporadic incidents still flare up. The MNLF have mostly abided by a peace agreement struck in 1996 under which they enjoy limited administrative autonomy on the island of Mindanao. The NPA's support declined sharply in the 1990s as a result of the restoration of democracy, more effective army operations and internal division. It re-emerged as a force in June 2003, when 200 insurgents raided an army camp, killing 17 soldiers. Arroyo initially ordered a military crackdown but agreed to peace talks in Norway in 2003, though these were cut short by the NPA after a few months because they claimed that their capacity to negotiate had been hamstrung by the NPA's listing on US and European prescribed terrorist lists. A low level insurgency continues.

The Moro Islamic Liberation Front (MILF), an Islamic separatist group which originally split from the MNLF, began negotiations with the government to end nearly four decades of fighting in 2001. In spite of a truce in 2003, intermittent fighting continued. Hopes were high that a comprehensive peace agreement brokered by Malaysia in 2008 would at last see an end to the fighting. The deal was designed to provide an expanded autonomous homeland for about four million Muslims in the southern Philippines. Indeed it did appear both sides would abide by the terms of the treaty, but at the 11th hour talks collapsed amid acrimony and counter-claim on both sides. The MILF had previously admitted allowing the Indonesia-based Jemaah Islamiah (JI) terrorist organisation to maintain training camps on territory it controls, though it vehemently denies doing so now—such denial being accepted by most observers. At present, MILF has little to gain by cooperating with international terrorist groups such as JI, though informal links may continue. Such links are unlikely to include JI operatives participating in MILF training camps (as in the past), though it is possible that JI members being pursued by Indonesia and Malaysia may be receiving sanctuary in the southern Philippines.

Another Islamic insurgency organisation, the Abu Sayyaf Group (ASG), has violently pressed its claims for the establishment of an Islamic state in the south by using kidnappings to extract large ransoms. In February 2004, the group masterminded the bombing of a new super-ferry resulting in 116 deaths. The MILF and ASG officially deny any links but informal contact is believed to occur.

Future progress in ending these insurgencies will depend on whether Muslims in the south can be persuaded to feel part of the Philippines, which in turn depends on central concessions to regional, cultural and religious differences as much as continued economic growth.

9 SINGAPORE

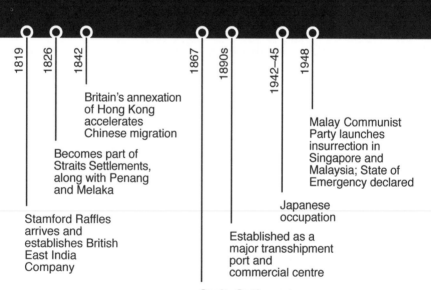

1819

1826

1842

1867

1890s

1942–45

1948

Britain's annexation
of Hong Kong
accelerates
Chinese migration

Becomes part of
Straits Settlements,
along with Penang
and Melaka

Malay Communist
Party launches
insurrection in
Singapore and
Malaysia; State of
Emergency declared

Stamford Raffles
arrives and
establishes British
East India
Company

Japanese
occupation

Established as a
major transshipment
port and
commercial centre

Straits Settlements
become a Crown
Colony

Statue of Sir Stamford Raffles

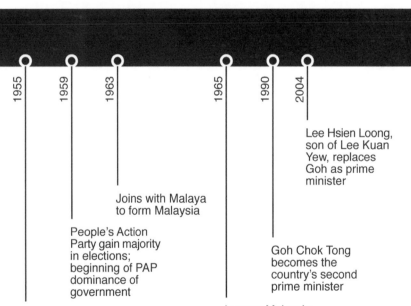

1955

1959

1963

1965

1990

2004

Lee Hsien Loong, son of Lee Kuan Yew, replaces Goh as prime minister

Joins with Malaya to form Malaysia

People's Action Party gain majority in elections; beginning of PAP dominance of government

Goh Chok Tong becomes the country's second prime minister

Limited self-government granted

Leaves Malaysia and becomes independent Republic, with Lee Kuan Yew as first prime minister

9 SINGAPORE

Singapore is an immigrant society. When acquired by Britain in 1819 it was populated by only a few hundred Malays living simple lives in fishing villages. It is now a thriving city-state, with a population of 4.6 million, and by far the highest per-capita income in Asia outside of Japan.

Geography is central to Singapore's history. Located at the foot of the Malay peninsula, separated from the mainland by a narrow stretch of shallow water, it is the pivotal island in the Straits of Melaka. Singapore's history has revolved around turning its strategic location to its commercial benefit while remaining on good terms with its larger neighbours.

Singapore is a Chinese city-state. There are minority Indian and Malay communities, but political, commercial and cultural power is in the hands of the ethnic Chinese. A major theme in Singapore's history since the end of World War II has been the continuous effort to create a national identity. What does it mean to be a Singaporean? How can the predominantly Chinese cultural heritage be transformed into a distinctly Singaporean culture? How best can a small, ethnically Chinese, island relate to its overwhelmingly more populous Malay-Muslim neighbours in Malaysia and Indonesia?

COLONIALISM

Stamford Raffles hoisted the British flag on the island of Singapore on 29 January, 1819. It was the second island in the region to be occupied by the English East India Company (EIC), following the acquisition of Penang in 1786. The EIC had a monopoly on the English trade between India and China, had acquired considerable territory in India and was eager to ensure control of the Straits of Melaka, the crucial passage of water through which most of its trading ships to China sailed. Penang gave it the ability to control the northern entrance of the Straits; Singapore gave it the ability to control the southern exit.

For nearly 200 years, the Netherlands United East India Company (VOC) had been the EIC's arch rival in the region. When Napoleon annexed the Netherlands in 1810, Britain occupied the major Dutch possessions in the Indonesian archipelago in order to prevent them from falling into the hands of the French. Melaka, Bencoolen on the west coast of Sumatra, and the island of Java were taken over by Britain. Stamford Raffles was appointed head of a civil government to run Java and Sumatra. The colony was added to the EIC Indian empire, reporting directly to Calcutta.

When the Napoleonic war ended in 1815, Britain wanted to bolster the Low Countries (the Netherlands and Belgium) as a bulwark against any future French revival. Dutch pressure, then, for the return of its colonies in the Indonesian archipelago fell on responsive ears. In 1818, Java was returned to Netherlands rule.

Raffles was extremely disappointed that wider European strategic considerations had forced him to return Java to the Dutch. He was an expansionist at heart, believing that Britain should acquire territory throughout the Indonesian archipelago and the Malay peninsula, should create European settler societies and should reap the benefits of what he saw as enormous commercial opportunities. On being forced to leave Java, he turned to a small island off the southern tip of the Malay peninsula, known locally first as Temasek (Sea Town) and later as Singapura (Lion City), persuading the Sultan of Johor to cede it to Britain. Sparsely occupied by Malay fishing communities and by local Malay pirates, in 1819, the island had no more than 1,000 inhabitants. In 1826, the East India Company amalgamated Singapore, Penang and Melaka into the Straits Settlements, administered from Singapore. The Straits Settlements remained in EIC control until 1867 when they became a Crown Colony under the control of a governor appointed by the Colonial Office.

The British commercial community gave strong support to the acquisition of Singapore, seeing it as a boost to trade in South-East Asia. In 1824, the Anglo-Dutch Treaty settled territorial disputes between the two countries, with the Netherlands recognising Britain's possession of Melaka and Singapore, and Britain handing Bencoolen back to the Netherlands. By the 1830s, Singapore had become the major trading port. It was challenged by Manila and Batavia but had three crucial advantages over the other colonial port cities and over the major indigenous ports. First, its geographic location: most ships trading between China, India and Europe had to pass Singapore. Second, its status as a free port: the Dutch in Batavia and the Spanish in Manila levied a range of tariffs and charges on imports, as did local rulers in the smaller ports. Third, its linkages into the British commercial and industrial empire: Britain was then the dominant colonial power.

Singapore was an integral part of Britain's empire in Asia, which had its centre in India. Singapore's prosperity stemmed from its geographic advantages and from its place in the colonial network. British traders were attracted in ever-increasing numbers and major trading houses, shipping lines and service companies quickly emerged. Equally importantly, Chinese traders long resident in South-East Asia were attracted to Singapore because of its free-port status, the certainty of the British legal system and the strategic position. Many came from Melaka and the Riau archipelago in the 1820s, relocating their trade to Singapore and thereby immediately linking Singapore into indigenous regional trading networks. Malay, Indian and Arab traders were also drawn to Singapore from other ports in the vicinity. Singapore quickly gained a dominant share of the inter-island regional trade as well as becoming the major victualling stop en-route to China. Chinese traders had worked in the region and had established a Chinese quarter in all of the major port cities well before the arrival of the Europeans. Their numbers increased greatly from the 17th century as, first, the Dutch and the Spanish and, later, the British and the French colonised the region. But it was not only colonised South-East Asia that attracted Chinese traders, entrepreneurs and labourers.

Thailand's kings encouraged the migration of Chinese in the 19th century, as did the sultans of the Malay states. Indeed, the tin-mining industry which developed in the Malay States from the 1830s was created by Chinese who worked under concessions granted to them by Malay rulers. The tin miners imported their needs through Singapore and used Singapore to export tin ore to the world. Tin mining in the Malay states and in southern Thailand was the source of wealth for a number of Chinese families who later went on to become major traders and financiers in the region.

The Chinese were the labour force on which British Singapore was built and Singapore was the conduit for the hundreds of thousands recruited to colonial Malaya and the Netherlands East Indies. Most Chinese came to Singapore as impoverished indentured labourers. The forced opening of the Treaty Ports in southern China and Britain's annexation of Hong Kong in 1842 accelerated the migration of Chinese from southern China to South-East Asia, Australia and the Pacific and the United States. The migration flow was organised and exploitative, with male Chinese signed on as indentured labourers. In the 19th century, the Chinese population of Singapore was predominantly male. Most came to Singapore hoping to make a fortune, send money back to families in their home villages in China and, one day, return home to marry, buy land and live as prosperous farmers. Some succeeded. Most lived and died in Singapore as coolie labourers, reliant on prostitution for female company and dependent on secret societies, opium dens and gambling parlours.

Singapore's economic history is interwoven with the economic history of the Malay states. The Singapore merchant community started to advocate British acquisition of the western Malay states from the 1840s. Chinese and Europeans in Singapore were significant investors in the tin-mining industry in the western Malay states and were increasingly frustrated at what they saw as the political instability there and the consequent lost commercial opportunities. Britain finally began to acquire control of the western Malay states in 1874, when the ambition's of the Singapore merchant and financial community were bolstered by imperial fears of French and German intentions in South-East Asia. Singapore was a major beneficiary of the addition of Malaya to the British empire. On the eve of World War II, over two-thirds of Malaya's imports and exports went through the port of Singapore.

By the late 19th century, Singapore was an important financial and commercial centre. It was a major transshipment port, where the products of South-East Asia were collected, packaged and re-exported and from where the products of industrial Britain and Europe were distributed. It had also become a major financial and commercial base for British companies in the region. Investment in tin mines in the Malay states was matched from the 1890s by investment in rubber plantations and on the transport infrastructure needed to get rubber to the ports for export. Investment finance came through Singapore, tin and rubber were exported through Singapore and Singapore was the warehousing and distribution centre for the imported goods needed by the growing European population.

The largest commercial firms were British-owned and managed. But there also emerged a growing number of Chinese-owned enterprises. Some were trading companies, some were financiers; and others were small-scale food processors and distributors. By 1942, when the Japanese invaded Singapore, there were a number of strong family companies in Singapore owned by second- or third-generation Chinese. While most Chinese immigrants who began life as rickshaw coolies or wharf labourers ended their lives much as they started, a few realised the immigrant's dream of making good. These Chinese enterprises were family companies linked into the commercial and financial network of the Chinese diaspora in Hong Kong and South-East Asia.

There was little manufacturing in Singapore before 1960. There was some food processing, primary processing of tin and rubber originating in Malaya and simple manufacturing, such as shoes and clothing. However, as late as 1960 between 70 and 75 per cent of Singapore's workforce was engaged in the service sector. In the early 1930s, a government-appointed commission investigated the possibility of Singapore developing an industrial base but concluded that it would only be feasible with high levels of protection and if the Singapore and Malayan economies were united. It concluded that the losses to Singapore from abandoning free-trade status would outweigh the gains from a protectionist industrial policy.

Singapore was an immigrant colony. However, the 1931 census revealed that 36 per cent of its residents had been born in the Straits Settlements. As a result of immigration restrictions introduced in the 1930s in response to the Depression, by 1947, 60 per cent of Singapore residents had been born in the Straits Settlements. However, with the exception of the elite, the mother tongue and language of day-to-day communication for the Chinese remained southern Chinese dialects.

By the early 20th century, there were nationalist movements demanding independence in most South-East Asian colonies, from Burma through to the Philippines. Singapore was an exception. There was no sense of being Singaporean: people identified themselves as Chinese or Nanyang Chinese. There was, therefore, no clearly articulated movement seeking the creation of an independent nation-state. Although the Malayan Communist Party (MCP) operated in Singapore in the 1920s and 1930s, as well as in British Malaya, and was involved in organising among Chinese and Indian workers, it made no attempt to develop a specifically Singapore identity or nationalism.

Political activity in Singapore in the 1920s and 1930s was focused on the struggle between the Chinese Communist Party (CCP) and the Kuomintang (KMT) for control of China. Both the CCP and the KMT gained ideological and financial support from the overseas Chinese. Singapore was a particular focus of propaganda and recruitment. Politically aware Chinese in Singapore were far more concerned about the great events convulsing China in the 1920s, 1930s and 1940s than events in Singapore. Whatever their ideology, they were united in opposition to Japan's invasion of China in the 1930s.

Chinese communities throughout South-East Asia were caught up in the events of their homeland and the battle for the hearts, minds and pockets was waged throughout the region. One important difference in Singapore was that because the dominant culture was Chinese, and to all intents and purposes there was no indigenous society, Chinese nationalism could focus on the ideological struggle in China unencumbered by an indigenous nationalist movement. Chinese communities elsewhere in South-East Asia were equally concerned about events in China but were forced by the existence of strong nationalist movements to ask fundamental questions about their individual and communal identities and their place in an independent nation.

Colonial Singapore was a European city. Its ruling elite, its commercial core and its official ethos was British. But beyond the European homes, clubs and offices, the island was culturally predominantly Chinese. There was, however, a significant Indian minority, varying from 6 to 12 per cent of the population. This minority was large enough to create its own communities, where the visitor would be clearly aware of moving out of the dominant Chinese society into a "little India".

The Indian community was far from united with the major divisions between Hindus and Muslims and between southerners and northerners. These were cross-cut by further divisions of caste and region. Some of the early Indian settlers came from Penang, where there was a thriving Indian commercial community. Others migrated from India or were recruited as indentured labourers. Many thousands were forcibly transported from India as convict labourers. Until 1873, Singapore was used by British India as a penal colony. Indian convicts built the early government buildings, roads, bridges and drainage systems. In the 19th century, free Indians were primarily in public employment as clerks, teachers and policemen, or were merchants and moneylenders.

As with the Chinese majority, the political attention of Indian residents in Singapore was focused on the motherland, where Indian nationalists were locked in struggle with the British Raj. The political divisions which opened up in India in the 1920s and 1930s were reflected in the Indian community in Singapore. Muslim and Hindu, Sikh and Bengali, to name but a few, each had their own, often conflicting, view of Indian politics. While there was considerably more crossing of caste and ethnic divides in the Singapore Indian community than in India itself, nevertheless, these divisions remained important barriers. Indian communities in Singapore were linked by region, language, caste and family to the much larger Indian community in British Malaya, adding yet one more strand to the interconnection between Singapore and Malaya.

On the eve of the Pacific War, Singapore was a multiracial, multilingual and multi-religious society governed by a British elite. Social control was maintained not merely by the police and court systems but also by the pro-British Chinese business and clan heads and by the wealthy leaders of the Indian community. It was a key part of the British empire: arguably the most important commercial possession east of India and, from the 1920s, a major naval base guarding British interests in South-East Asia and providing a defence shield for Australia and New Zealand.

THE JAPANESE OCCUPATION

Singapore fell to the Japanese Imperial Army on 15 February, 1942. The loss of this strategically important island quickly led to the capitulation of the Netherlands East Indies. Thousands of Europeans, civilians as well as soldiers, were trapped in Singapore. Many were dispatched to build the infamous Burma railway. The death rate was high. More than 45,000 soldiers in the Indian and Malay regiments were urged by the Japanese to transfer their loyalties. Most refused and many paid with their lives. About 20,000 Indian soldiers joined the Indian National Army in the belief that it would be prepared by the Japanese to drive the British out of India and establish Indian independence.

While the Indian and Malay communities in Singapore suffered greatly at the hands of the Japanese, none suffered more than the Chinese. The Japanese military distrusted all Chinese and, in particular, sought to root out all who were Kuomintang supporters. Arbitrary arrests, torture and executions were commonplace. Special taxes were imposed on Chinese incomes and assets. For the residents of Singapore, the Japanese occupation was a time of struggle for survival. British rule was benign by comparison.

The Japanese occupation of South-East Asia greatly reduced European prestige. Indeed, while historians differ as to the long-term impact of the occupation in individual societies, there is general agreement that it ushered in the beginning of the end of European colonialism in the region. Japanese policies and actions clearly had an impact on individuals in Singapore. Apart from the Chinese, Indians and Malays who died in prisons, in labour camps or as a result of indiscriminate Japanese brutality, almost all who lived there suffered severe day-to-day hardships during the three-and-a-half years of Japanese occupation. The deeper, long-term impact is harder to assess. A legacy of distrust of Japan in Singapore and throughout South-East Asia may well be the most significant consequence.

TOWARDS INDEPENDENCE
Britain reoccupied Singapore in between August and September 1945. It was controlled by the British Military Administration until mid 1946 and then handed back to the Colonial Office. Post-war British policy towards Singapore differed from that towards Malaya. It envisaged Malaya moving towards independence but was determined that political reform in Singapore should be carefully controlled, with a restricted goal of limited self-government. There were three main reasons for this policy difference. First, continued direct control of Singapore was seen as vital to British commercial interests in South-East Asia. Second, Singapore was a strategic naval base in the region. Third, Singapore's ethnic Chinese majority raised fears for British interests, not just in Singapore but also in Malaya. The outbreak of the Cold War in 1947 and Mao's defeat of the Chiang Kai-Shek government in China in 1949 strengthened Britain's view of Singapore as potentially a communist fifth column in South-East Asia. It was believed that an independent Singapore would quickly come under communist control and that Singapore would then be used as a springboard to subvert Western interests in Malaya, Indonesia and elsewhere in South-East Asia.

The success of the Malayan Communist Party's (MCP) among Singapore workers in the immediate post-war years confirmed the British view of Singapore as inevitably a hotbed of Chinese communism unless strong colonial rule was maintained. The pro-British Chinese and Indian elites were equally alarmed: communism threatened their interests as much as it did the interests of the British. The MCP launched its insurrection in Singapore and Malaya in 1948, resulting in a declaration of a State of Emergency which was to last until 1960. The strength of communist-controlled labour unions in the late 1940s and early 1950s and the MCP's insurrection were viewed in the context of growing pride among overseas Chinese in the achievements of the communist government in China. The victorious communists and the vanquished nationalists, who had withdrawn to Taiwan, competed vigorously in the 1950s for moral support from the overseas Chinese. Singapore was again a vital hub in the South-East Asia campaign.

Limited self-government was introduced into Singapore in 1955. In 1959, the People's Action Party (PAP) gained a majority of seats in the Legislative Assembly, beginning a dominance of Singapore politics continuing to the present day. Led by Lee Kuan Yew, a young Cambridge-educated lawyer, the PAP was a party of a new English-educated elite emerging in Singapore in the 1950s. Strongly influenced by European social democratic ideas, the PAP produced a blueprint for Singapore's development based on a strong state and state intervention in the economy to create a new, industrialized, Singapore. Lee and his fellow PAP leaders knew that their strongest opponents were the communists, who were operating through various legal and illegal structures and, in the early 1960s, most prominently through the Barisan Socialis party. The organisational structure of the PAP mirrored that of communist parties. Its democratic centralism placed effective control in the hands of a self-selecting elite.

By the early 1960s, Britain was searching for a way to end its direct rule of Singapore while still safeguarding its strategic and commercial interests, which were seen as inextricably connected with preventing Singapore from "going communist". The pressure for Singapore's independence was strong. In addition, Britain was faced with the problem of the Borneo states of Sabah and Sarawak. In an era of decolonisation, Britain had to find a solution to its colonial problems in Singapore and Borneo.

The creation of Malaysia seemed to solve all problems. Singapore, Sabah and Sarawak would be amalgamated with Malaya to form a new state of Malaysia. The Chinese majority in Singapore would be balanced by Malay and other indigenous majorities in Malaya and the Borneo states. It was a neat political solution. It was also seen by both the British and the Singapore elite as a consummation of the strong economic interdependence that had developed between Malaya and Singapore over more than a century. Singapore would retain control over a number of crucial areas, including education and communications, in return for a lower proportion of seats in the new federal parliament of Malaysia than it was entitled by weight of population. Malay sensibilities about dominance by ethnic Chinese appeared to be assuaged and, at the same time, the PAP ensured a status for Singapore far greater than that of a mere state government.

Malaysia was formed on 16 September, 1963. Singapore separated from Malaysia in August 1965, becoming the independent Republic of Singapore. Formally, this parting of the ways was a mutual decision between the Malaysian federal government and the Singapore state government. In reality, Singapore was forced to leave. The two-year of marriage was an unhappy one. Malays increasingly feared that Singapore wanted to dominate Malaysia, and that the PAP was trying to join forces with the major ethnic-Chinese opposition party in peninsular Malaya in order to gain a majority of the seats in the federal parliament. They feared changes to the constitution, which entrenched major privileges for the Malays. It was a highly emotional period, with inter-ethnic typecasting abounding and with Malays fearing that "their" country was about to be taken over by "foreigners".

Lee Kuan Yew was shattered by this parting. The accepted wisdom in Singapore was that its economy was so closely linked to that of peninsular Malaya that economic prosperity depended on these links to continue. Singapore feared that its economy was too small and too vulnerable to anti-Chinese feelings among neighbouring Indonesians and Malays to stand alone. Now, Singapore is a major economic success story. Between independence in 1965 and the Asian economic crisis of 1997, its economy grew at an average of 9 per cent per annum. Although growth rates have since slowed, and in 2008–09 actually turned negative as a result of the global financial crisis and the country's high reliance on global trade, sound economic management is the reason for the generally high standing of the PAP government among Singaporeans, despite complaints about its style and frequent disregard for "Western style" civil liberties.

Even before independence, Lee Kuan Yew's government determined that the economy had to undergo massive structural change very quickly if Singapore was to prosper. In under five decades, Singapore has moved from an essentially entrepot economy to a predominantly industrial and services-based economy. The next decade will see Singapore consolidate its move into a post-industrial phase, with most of its wealth generated by service industries, ranging from providing regional financial and high-technology services to other South-East Asian nations to manufacturing high-technology products for a world market, utilising world's best practice. Hence, in 2001 Lee Kuan Yew, in his capacity as Senior Minister, urged Singapore to "remake itself" over the next two decades, to embrace further such industries as tourism, education and healthcare.

The remarkable and sustained economic growth in post-independence Singapore is partially explained by Singapore's strategic location at the crossroads of the ASEAN region. Until the Asian economic crisis of 1997, ASEAN countries had also experienced sustained high growth rates, to Singapore's advantage. As labour-intensive industries have moved from Singapore to other ASEAN countries, they have been replaced by a regional reliance on Singapore for more technologically sophisticated products and services. There are other important factors behind Singapore's success. First, the PAP has brought strong, stable and corruption-free government to Singapore. Above all, Singapore has been a model of planned development in every sphere. Second, through policies such as the creation of a Central Provident Fund, with Singaporean employers and employees compelled jointly to contribute a high percentage (compared with comparable schemes in western countries) of salaries to a pension fund, it has created a very high rate of national savings. Third, it has adopted social policies which have ensured that all Singaporeans have benefited from the economic growth. For example, when the PAP came to power in 1959 most Singaporeans lived in squalid housing. By the turn of the century Singapore had the highest home-ownership rate in the world, thanks to the activities of the Housing Trust and the ability of people to fund mortgages by borrowing from their contributions to the Central Provident Fund. Fourth, it has developed an excellent comprehensive education system which has produced the skilled workers needed to sustain high rates of economic growth, and which places emphasis on vocational and applied skills without the bias towards rote learning evident in some other Asian countries with advanced economies.

Government in Singapore is far more intrusive than that experienced in Western societies. The PAP has manipulated the political system to make it extremely difficult for an opposition party to challenge its power. It has used the Internal Security Act to arrest and imprison not only those who might be a threat to the state but many others who have challenged the power of the government. It had brought punitive defamation actions against dissenting opposition parliamentarians, which bankrupted them in the process and thus, according to the law, excluding them from the political process. It is a paternalistic and, at times, authoritarian government but, despite this, it does have popular legitimacy because of its delivery of clean government and its impressive social and economic achievements over nearly four decades. Its continued popular mandate is evident in the fact that the PAP easily won a landslide victory in the most recent general election in 2006.

Since independence, Singapore's government has been concerned to develop a Singaporean identity. In the first instance, this meant weaning Singaporeans away from too close an attachment to communist China. Language policy was a key part of this search for identity. In the 1960s, the emphasis was on the need for people to learn Malay and English, with government-sponsored campaigns to learn a new Malay word each day. As Singapore's prosperity grew, as the economy became more internationalised and less dependent on Malaysia, and as China became not a threat but a source of pride due to its impressive economic development and growing influence on global security issues, policy shifted towards the promotion of Mandarin instead of regional dialects (although in 2008 the government admitted the promotion of Mandarin has not been the success it had hoped for). More recently the emphasis has moved back to ensuring the survival of regional dialects alongside Mandarin and English. If Singapore's elite was uncertain about its identity in the 1960s and 1970s—were they simply Chinese overseas or a genuine part of the region?—by the 1980s they were far more confident about Singapore's future in the ASEAN region and, by the turn of the century, they were supremely confident of their ability to continue to prosper in an increasingly global economy and within the strongly developing South-East Asia region. Some commentators have talked of a "re-sinofication", not just of the Singaporeans but of ethnic Chinese communities throughout South-East Asia, as they network with each other and continue to have a dominant role in national and regional economies.

In the new millennium, Singapore is by far the most prosperous nation in South-East Asia (aside from the aberration of the tiny oil-rich state of Brunei). It is a society full of contradictions. In many ways it is a modern Confucian state—always intrusive, mostly paternalistic, sometimes authoritarian, with a strong ideology of the people's duties towards the state. It is ruled by a close-knit, meritocratic elite focused on the PAP. The state claims the right to be involved in all aspects of its people's lives: asserting the right to define family size and the nature of personal relationships, as well as to determine the structure of the economy. Thus, worried by a decline in the fertility rate of the most educated, mainly Chinese elite (brought about by the reluctance of ambitious young women to interrupt their careers), the government offers generous tax breaks and other incentives for women to have children. The state directly owns or controls large sections of the economy and, through its investment board, has shares in other Singaporean companies as well as overseas. Yet it is also the champion of free enterprise, welcoming foreign multinationals and nurturing its own multinational corporations in a competitive environment almost totally free of the corruption which bedevils other countries in the region. By 2005, bilateral free-trade agreements had been signed with the United States, Japan, Australia and New Zealand. It has an enviable record in providing low-cost housing, high-quality education and extensive health care for all Singaporeans. Yet its social security net is highly conditional, insisting that individuals must work hard and stand on their own feet. It is a state which encourages aggressive economic activity, and rewards individual ability and achievement. Yet it is a puritan state, with a state-controlled local media, censorship of foreign media and a very public concern about moral pollution of the young from Western cultural influences. In matters of national security, restrictions have been further tightened since late 2001 when a plot to launch suicide attacks by militants belonging to the regional Islamist terrorist organisation Jemaah Islamiah (JI) against a number of Singapore's critical infrastructure installations and embassies of foreign countries was uncovered. The government was highly embarrassed by the escape from custody in February 2008 of the leader of the JI network in Singapore, Mas Selamat Kastari. Kastari, an Indonesian-born Singapore national, had been deported from Indonesia in 2003 and his escape slightly tarnished Singapore's reputation as being at the forefront of regional efforts to combat the threat from terrorism.

Singapore's prosperity gives it a higher per-capita income than many Western countries and although its geographic location may be less important in the global economy with the advent of the technological revolution, in regional terms it is still as important as ever. Singapore's enthusiastic participation in a growth triangle with Malaysia and Indonesia reflects its view of itself as the economic engine of the region.

The global financial crisis of 2008–09 and the subsequent decline in world growth rates are unlikely to cause serious problems for Singapore's long-term development, due mainly to sound underlying economic fundamentals and a willingness by the government to address economic problems as they emerge rather than ignore or conceal them. Even so, in 2008 the economy slipped into recession as a result of the island's dependence upon international trade movements, in particular a sharp decline in exports to the

United States and Europe. Although painful structural and fiscal adjustments have been necessary, Singapore's economic planners and the foreign investment community are not overly concerned by slowing growth rates compared with decades past as the island has achieved a level of economic maturity comparable to the West and thus it would be unrealistic to expect that the heady growth rates could be maintained in perpetuity.

Goh Chok Tong was appointed leader in 1990 following Lee's decision to stand aside to effect a smooth leadership transition. This, Lee said, would reassure the business community and international investors, and ensure that long-term political stability would lead to continued economic prosperity. But no one doubted that during the first few years of this transition the real power still lay with Lee, who became a senior minister without portfolio. In 1992, Goh was elevated to general secretary of the PAP, and by the late 1990s he was perceived as a confident, dedicated leader with a slightly more liberal outlook than his predecessor. In 2001, Goh nominated his deputy, Lee Hsien Loong, as his successor. Lee, the son of Lee Kuan Yew, became prime minister in August 2004, with Goh taking up Lee Kuan Yew's position as senior minister. Lee Kuan Yew himself became "Minister Mentor" and is believed to retain significant behind-the-scenes influence.

The Singapore government still worries about forging a national identity, with repeated campaigns focusing on one or other aspect of the ideal Singaporean. The extent to which rising material prosperity will serve to dilute popular calls for political reform and a lessening of state paternalism will be closely watched by those who have witnessed the city-state emerge from the crisis of 1965 to become a highly-regarded regional economic powerhouse in under five decades.

10 THAILAND

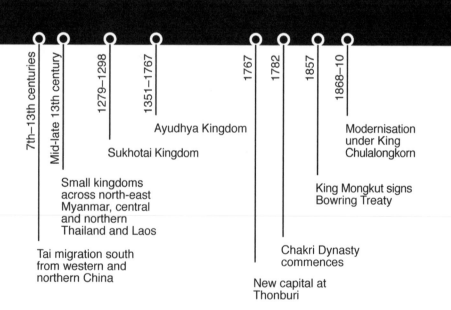

7th–13th centuries

Mid-late 13th century

1279–1298

1351–1767

1767

1782

1857

1868–10

Ayudhya Kingdom

Sukhotai Kingdom

Small kingdoms
across north-east
Myanmar, central
and northern
Thailand and Laos

Tai migration south
from western and
northern China

Modernisation
under King
Chulalongkorn

King Mongkut signs
Bowring Treaty

Chakri Dynasty
commences

New capital at
Thonburi

Ruins at Ayutthaya

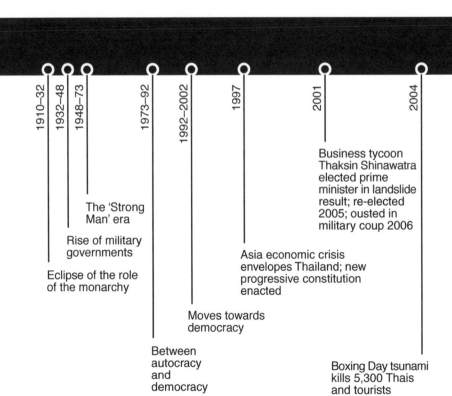

1910–32

1932–48

1948–73

1973–92

1992–2002

1997

2001

2004

The 'Strong Man' era

Rise of military governments

Eclipse of the role of the monarchy

Business tycoon Thaksin Shinawatra elected prime minister in landslide result; re-elected 2005; ousted in military coup 2006

Asia economic crisis envelopes Thailand; new progressive constitution enacted

Moves towards democracy

Between autocracy and democracy

Boxing Day tsunami kills 5,300 Thais and tourists

10 THAILAND

Thailand stands at the heart of mainland South-East Asia, yet its modern history differs strikingly from the turbulent history of the rest of the region. With the exception of the three southern-most provinces, Thailand's population of 64 million is relatively homogeneous; no major regional, ethnic, linguistic or religious rifts have threatened national coherence. Thailand does have minorities, but it is well on the way to assimilating its most significant minority, the Chinese. Uniquely in South-East Asia, Thailand avoided the disruptions of Western colonial rule and, therefore, the upheavals of decolonisation. World War II produced no serious conflict on Thai soil. After the war, and unlike in neighbouring Indochina, communism never attracted wide support in Thailand. While revolution was tearing Vietnam, Laos and Cambodia apart, and military-imposed "Burmese socialism" was stifling Burma, the country embarked upon a course of capitalist development which, in spite of the 1997 Asian economic crisis which started in Thailand, made it one of South-East Asia's strongest economies.

Historically, however, the Thais had to face serious problems. In the 18th century, Thai society had to rebuild itself after the trauma of almost total-destruction by Burmese armies of the four-centuries-old Thai kingdom of Ayudhya. In the 19th and early 20th centuries, Western pressures forced major, though necessarily delicate, adjustments to traditional Thai government, economy and social organisation. In

World War II, Thailand had to adjust to Japanese military pressures and the country suffered acute economic disruption. Afterwards, Thailand became a frontline state in the Cold War, its fortunes tied closely to US' interests.

Until 1932 Thailand was an absolute monarchy. Subsequently, it experienced a succession of unrepresentative, military-dominated, governments. A violent collision between the military and pro-democracy demonstrators on the streets of Bangkok in 1992 seemingly ushered in an era of representative democracy, but as another (peaceful) military coup in 2006 demonstrated, this is not yet assured. Resolution of conflict about the form of Thai government is urgently needed, for the country is again facing major problems. The country's economic successes have been impressive, but they have forced headlong change on Thai society. Pressing problems include inadequate infrastructure, an overburdened metropolis in Bangkok, serious pollution and ecological degradation, deplorable conditions for many workers, and widening gaps between urban and rural conditions, and between rich and poor.

Thais sum up their social coherence in the nationalist prescript "Nation, Religion (Buddhism) and King". They are proud of the history from which these nationalist symbols have emerged. This history is worth studying for clues about the ability of the Thais to handle their present difficulties.

EARLY HISTORY

In the 13th century, several small kingdoms emerged across the regions known today as northeast Burma, central and northern Thailand, and Laos. These were probably the first attempts at state-building by Tai communities. The Tais were the principal ancestors not only of today's Thais but also of the Lao peoples, the Shans of Burma, a range of upland communities in mainland South-East Asia such as the Black, Red and White Tais of Laos and northern Vietnam, and the Lü of Yunnan, China.

It used to be thought that before the 13th century, Tais had dominated a kingdom called Nanchao in Yunnan, but had been dispersed southwards by a Mongol attack in 1253. Scholars no longer hold this theory. Instead, the evidence suggests long, slow Tai migration over many centuries, beginning in western China, or even further north, and spreading southwards from the seventh century.

The Tais were wet-rice farmers clustered in *muang*—one or more villages under a chieftain. Over time some *muang* developed inter-relationships cemented by trading networks, intermarriage, security needs and talented military leaders. But the 13th century leap from linked *muang* to kingdoms was propelled by Tai adaptations of beliefs, ideas and techniques derived from the states and empires they were encountering in their southward movement. The Tais probably adopted Theravada Buddhism from Mon states in what is now central Thailand and from the Burmese kingdom of Pagan. This religion accommodated itself to Tai folk traditions and animist beliefs, but it was also an institutionalised religion with a universalist world view, and a transmitter of Mon, Burmese and Sinhalese civilisation.

The principal blueprint for Tai state-builders was, however, Angkor, the great Cambodian kingdom which at its height from the 11th to 13th centuries dominated an empire stretching from the Mekong delta to the northern Malay peninsula and as far north as the Vientiane plain. From Angkor came ideas adapted originally from Indian Brahmanical thought, particularly concepts of society as divinely ordained hierarchy and of devaraj—the ruler as immensely potent incarnation of a Hindu deity and/or Buddhist bodhisattva. Angkor also provided lessons in administering large, scattered populations and in a range of arts and technologies.

Tai attacks upon Angkor's imperial outposts, and eventually upon Angkor itself in the 14th and 15th centuries, would lead to a direct transfer of human and material resources. Meanwhile, in the 13th century the most celebrated of early Tai states was the kingdom of Sukhothai. Modern Thais regard Sukhothai as the birthplace of the Thai nation, particularly under Ramkhamhaeng, (reigned c.1279–98), whose rule is celebrated by the Sukhothai stone—an inscribed obelisk reputedly discovered in 1833 by the Thai prince, Mongkut, then a monk and scholar and later Thailand's first modernising monarch. The inscription portrays Sukhothai as an idyllic place, governed by a just, fatherly and devoutly Buddhist monarch. Possibly this is Ramkhamhaeng's self-justifying counterblast to the arrogance and avariciousness of imperial Angkor. In recent years, the stone's authenticity has been questioned, some sceptics arguing that Mongkut himself devised the inscription to give his people an appealing early history. Scholarly consensus continues to view the inscription as genuine, however.

THE KINGDOM OF AYUDHYA, 1351–1767

After Ramkhamhaeng's death Sukhothai dwindled in significance. In 1351, the establishment further south of the kingdom of Ayudhya— or Siam, as it came to be known—would provide a more lasting basis for Thai statehood. As Siam's capital, Ayudhya would survive for over four centuries, until 1767. It was founded by U Thong, who is thought to have been a Chinese merchant who acquired wealth and prestige from his trading connections with the Chinese imperial court. He was related by marriage to a prominent Thai family, and he emphasised his devotion to the Thai form of Buddhism. In him may be seen an early example of a recurring theme in Thai history—the readiness of Thai society to absorb talented Chinese and other foreigners. The people over whom U Thong claimed kingship in 1351 were perhaps predominant Tai, but "Thai-ness" was also being constructed out of Mon, Khmer, Chinese and other peoples.

Ayudhya prospered, partly because of its strategic position. It stood only 70 kilometres up the broad Chaophraya river from the sea, enabling it to become one of South-East Asia's great trading ports. Simultaneously, it commanded the vast, fertile Chaophraya plain, providing rice for a growing population and for export. The city's power was also based on its rulers' keen attention to government and social control. From the beginning, they insisted that male subjects pay many months of service each year to the state, as soldiers or labourers. King Trailok, who reigned from 1448 to 1488, elaborated to an extraordinary degree the place and duties of subjects in a rigidly hierarchical society. Codifying the structure of government and the civil law, Trailok developed the system of *sakdina*, which carefully scaled the positions of everyone in the kingdom. The pyramid social structure which resulted was intended to enforce social discipline and enable the easy mobilisation of manpower. The structure was legitimated by a parallel hierarchical organisation of the *sangha* (Buddhist monks) under royal patronage and oversight.

Elements of the *sakdina* conception of society persist in Thai thinking, and indeed, are embedded in the Thai language. However, automatic social obedience was probably never absolute in Ayudhya. The elaborate delineation of social standing bred a self-conscious concern for dignity in even the humble individual, resulting in at least passive resistance to unjust superiors. Other question marks against the cohesion of Ayudhyan society concern the regional dispersal of administrative and military power, and the difficulties surrounding monarchical succession. Ayudhyan history would be marked by rivalries between powerful families, each with bases in the provinces, and by clashes over a vacant throne.

Even so, Ayudhya's social structures proved remarkably strong and enduring. Manpower conscription enabled military-minded kings to defeat Angkor decisively, wage war on other regional rivals, and to claim an empire sometimes encompassing much of modern Laos, the Tai kingdom of Lan Na, based at Chiang Mai, and the states of the Malay peninsula. In the 15th and 16th centuries, Cambodia remained a significant antagonist, but Ayudhya's main challenges would come from the Burmese. Only the strong institutions of Ayudhyan society would enable it to survive the blows dealt it by the Burmese.

In 1568, the Burmese king Bayinnaung laid siege to Ayudhya, having extended his military power over the north as far as Laos. The city fell in 1569 and was destroyed. Yet over the next decades, Narasuan, heir to the throne, managed to reconstitute the kingdom and, as king, decisively repulsed a renewed Burmese attack in 1593. In succeeding years he clawed back much of Ayudhya's tributary empire, and by the early 17th century, Ayudhya was again a major power.

European reports provide a striking picture of 17th-century Ayudhya as a famed and wealthy trade centre. By then, Portuguese, Spanish, Dutch, French and English traders jostled there with Chinese, Japanese, Persian, Indian, Malay and other Asian traders. Ayudhya's openness to trade—and to the information and ideas that traders brought—may have been one of the sources of its strength. In 1688, however, the nobility split over the degree of foreign influence at court, particularly that of an extraordinary Greek adventurer, Constantine Phaulkon, who had become a powerful minister, and of the French, including French Jesuit missionaries. On the death of King Narai, a relatively minor official, Phetracha, organised a coup, excluded the French and had Phaulkon executed. Phetracha assumed the throne himself. Agitation over these events and the legitimacy of Phetracha's subsequent dynasty would dog Ayudhya for the next 80 years.

It was possibly ruling-class divisiveness which accounted for Ayudhya's poor response to its greatest challenge—another, and massive, Burmese siege in 1766. In April 1767, the city fell to an enemy set on destroying Thai state power forever. Ayudhya's ruling class was decimated. Tens of thousands of people and all portable wealth were carried off. The city was burned and vast tracts of territory were left as scorched earth by the Burmese forces.

THE RISE OF THE BANGKOK EMPIRE

This time of crisis saw two remarkable Thai military leaders emerge: Taksin and his leading general, Chaophraya Chakri. Taksin had a Thai mother and Chinese father. He had been raised at court and in 1767 was a provincial governor. In the leadership crisis following the destruction of the old regime Taksin rallied an army, imposed his authority on a distracted people, declared himself king and founded a new capital at Thonburi. During the 1770s, he and his armies rebuilt an empire which included Chiang Mai in the north. In 1778, armies under Chaophraya Chakri subdued Luang Prabang and captured

Vientiane. From the latter city they brought back the Emerald Buddha, subsequently Thailand's most sacred and, it is believed, most potent Buddha-image.

In his later years, Taksin undermined respect for his imposing achievements with viciously tyrannical behaviour. He may have succumbed to religious dementia, for he alienated the *sangha*. In 1782, a tax revolt evolved into a coup, and Taksin was deposed and executed. The coup leaders offered Chaophraya Chakri the throne, thus inaugurating the dynasty of Thai monarchs which continues to the present.

Rama I (reigned 1782–1809) had been born of a Thai father—a relatively minor Ayudhyan official, though of aristocratic lineage—and a Chinese mother. He would prove to have both military skills and great administrative and intellectual abilities. Militarily, his reign would see the triumphant, and final, repulsion of the Burmese in 1785 and 1786, and the consolidation of a Thai empire larger than any Ayudhya had controlled. Effectively, it covered all of mainland South-East Asia excluding Burmese and Vietnamese territory, and also included the northern Malay states. Local dignitaries ruled at the empire's perimeters—in Cambodia, Laos and the Malay states—but they did so at the Thai king's behest.

At home, Rama I supervised the construction of his new capital, Bangkok, founded in 1782, which soon became a major cosmopolitan port. From Bangkok the king rebuilt administrative structures reminiscent of Ayudhya's but arguably even stronger. Labour control now involved mass registrations and the tattooing of subjects to indicate place of residence and administrative superior. Rama I gathered about him talented officials, jurists, scholars and artists. With them he revitalised Thai culture. Their achievements included the reconstruction and reform of the *sangha* hierarchy, the production of a new, definitive text of the Buddhist scriptures, the complete revision of the kingdom's laws, and the translation of numerous literary and historical works including the Indian epic *Ramayana* (in translation, *Ramakian*). The king and his followers self-consciously renovated, rather than merely restored, old institutions. The Bangkok court thus moved into the 19th century demonstrating an intellectual and cultural acuity that would be of incalculable value in the years ahead.

BANGKOK AND THE WEST

Unlike island South-East Asia, where the Dutch had been extending their empire since the 17th century, mainland South-East Asia did not encounter intense Western pressures until the 19th century. Even

Rama I's successors, Rama II (reigned 1809–24) and Rama III (reigned 1824–51), were largely able to ignore or turn aside the problems presented by the increasing Western presence in the region. Rama III did reach vague agreement with a British emissary in 1825 (at a time when the British were conquering south-east Burma) about reducing and standardising the taxes on trade. He was unwilling, however, to grapple with the major legal and administrative changes which Western businessmen, perplexed by Thai customs and Asian ways in general, were calling for.

In key respects, therefore, Bangkok remained "traditional" in the first half of the 19th century. This was most obvious in its vigorous prosecution of its authority over its empire. By military intervention in the Malay peninsula, it risked tensions with the British, who from the 1820s, were firmly ensconced in the Straits Settlements and lower Burma. In the 1830s and 1840s, Bangkok saw Vietnam as its chief foreign threat rather than any Western power. Between 1841 and 1845, it fought an exhausting struggle with the Vietnamese over control of Cambodia, a struggle that ended in a stand-off.

Virtually at the centre of Bangkok society, however, a group of royal and noble young men were studying the West keenly, led by the example of Prince Mongkut, brother of Rama III. Then a monk, Mongkut was devoting much of his energies to the ongoing reform of Thai Buddhism. He founded the Thammayutika sect, whose goal was intellectually rigorous religious scholarship that would clear away obscurantist accretions to original Buddhist teachings. Mongkut and his circle were also studying Western languages, Western science and mathematics, and such matters as Western military organisation and technology. When Mongkut succeeded to the throne, he was therefore in a position to reorientate Bangkok positively towards the West.

King Mongkut (also known as Rama IV, 1851–68) signed the Bowring Treaty with Britain in 1855. Under this treaty, import and export duties were sharply reduced and fixed, ruling-class trading and commodity monopolies were abolished, and British subjects were granted extraterritorial legal rights. In subsequent years, Mongkut signed similar treaties with many other Western powers. The signing away of legal power over foreign subjects in the kingdom was a bitter blow and these rights would not be fully recovered until the 1930s. More crucially, the other provisions of the treaties deprived the throne and many powerful subjects of much income. The shortfall would be reversed in time by the expansion of trade and by heavy taxes on opium, alcohol and gambling, but it is testimony to Mongkut's domestic diplomatic skills, and to the cohesion of his court, that the major fiscal rearrangements passed without revolt.

Mongkut avoided other fundamental reforms. The "modernisation" of the kingdom would really only begin with his son Chulalongkorn (Rama V, 1868–1910). Even then, it would be cautiously undertaken and limited in scope. Chulalongkorn learned caution early in his reign. In 1873, at the age of 21, he announced some financial and legal reform measures which alarmed conservatives and provoked an attempted coup in 1874. The young king survived, but had to rein in his reforming enthusiasm. A strategy for the gradual abolition of slavery, also announced in 1873, continued, however. Slavery (although not always the bonds of patronage and obligation in Thai society which slavery had formalised) disappeared over the next decades,. Later, Chulalongkorn was also able to phase out corvée (forced labour for the state), replacing it with a capitation tax.

Chulalongkorn's position grew stronger as the older generation passed on and he matured into a shrewd politician, nurturing a corps of bright, Western-educated royal relatives. With them, he set about major reform of government in the mid 1880s. Specialised ministries and departments began to appear. Cabinet government was introduced between 1888 and 1892. Subsequently, the king's half-brother, Prince Damrong, undertook the delicate task of reforming provincial administration, placating the great regional families while centralising bureaucratic control in Bangkok.

The modern look to government came none too soon, for Western imperial rivalries in South-East Asia were reaching their peak. Chulalongkorn's skilled foreign minister, Prince Devawongse, could now put the case that the kingdom had no need of Western intervention – unlike its neighbours, it was stable, bent on modernisation and able to accommodate international business. Even so, Western empires stripped the former Thai empire. Already Mongkut had been obliged by the French in 1867 to abandon claims to Cambodia (except its western provinces). Now in 1893 (when French warships menaced Bangkok) and in 1902 and 1904 Chulalongkorn had to transfer to the French sovereignty over the areas which would constitute modern Laos. In 1907, he was obliged to relinquish the western Cambodian provinces. In 1909, he gave control of four northern Malay states formerly under his suzerainty to the British (leaving, nevertheless, a Malay-Muslim minority within his kingdom). Meanwhile, an 1896 treaty between France and Britain had marked a crucial turning-point in the disposition of Thai territory. This treaty, designed primarily to head off Anglo-French confrontation in South-East Asia, guaranteed the independence of most of the territory which today forms Thailand. Chulalongkorn's core kingdom had been secured.

He proceeded with modernisation until his death in 1910, laying the foundations of a modern military, improving communications—particularly with an extensive railway system—and continuing law reform. Western-style education became common for royal and upper-class children, and an elementary Western-style syllabus was introduced to the temple schools. Chulalongkorn resisted full-tilt modernisation, however. He rejected any thought of introducing democracy. Economically, he presided over the development of a quasi-colonial state. Ordinary Thais became commodity producers for the world market, rice accounting for over 70 per cent of exports in the early 20th century. Other items included tin, teak and rubber. There was no significant industrialisation. Western and Chinese interests dominated the country's financial and commercial life. Chinese numbers swelled to about ten per cent of the population. Indeed the size and power of the Chinese community began to disturb many Thais.

THE ECLIPSE OF THE MONARCHY, 1910–1932

During the reigns of Chulalongkorn's successors, Vajiravudh (Rama VI, 1910–25) and Pradjahipok (Rama VII, 1925–35), disgruntlement with Thailand's equivocal modernisation and economic subjection would grow amongst the expanding, though still small, Western-educated elite. Vajiravudh's dilettante approach to kingship also provoked criticism. His inner circle at court consisted of male favourites. His extravagance contributed to government deficits and a balance-of-payments crisis in the 1920s. On the other hand, his contributions to the emergence of Thai nationalism probably strengthened his reign. It was he who introduced the trinity of "Nation, Religion (Buddhism) and King" as the focus of popular loyalty, and promoted organisations and public spectacles designed to inculcate nationalist pride. In the 1920s, he also sponsored successful diplomatic efforts to end the extraterritoriality provisions of Mongkut's treaties and recover national control of tariffs.

Prajadhipok (Chulalongkorn's 76th child—Vajiravudh died heirless) took an earnest approach to his duties, but was hamstrung by the financial problems bequeathed to him and even more by the Great Depression. In the early 1930s, national income slumped and cuts to government expenditures heightened discontent. For him the promotion of nationalist thinking proved to be a double-edged sword. The concept of "Nation" alongside that of "King" soon encouraged modern-minded Thais to distinguish between the two.

On 24 June 1932, plotters in the military and bureaucracy staged a coup and, in the name of the nation, obliged Prajadhipok to surrender the monarchy's absolute powers and accept constitutional status. In 1935, Prajadhipok abdicated in favour of his nephew Ananda (Rama VIII, 1935–46) who was then at school overseas and would remain abroad until 1945.

THE RISE OF MILITARY GOVERNMENT, 1932–1948

The promoters of the 1932 revolution consisted of both civilians and military men. Their professed goal was the staged introduction of parliamentary democracy, and they set up a National Assembly of appointed and elected members. By the late 1930s, however, the parliament appeared doomed to virtual irrelevancy. For 60 years after 1932, in fact, the military would dominate Thai government.

For several reasons, military dominance would not prove stifling nor produce wholly negative effects. Firstly, Thai military leaders faced no serious problems of national integration; history had bequeathed to them a country of relatively minor cultural, religious, ideological or ethnic tensions, and they could usually enforce their will with a relatively light hand. Secondly, they would generally be willing to accommodate other elites in the power process, and those elites—business, bureaucracy and civilian politicians—would generally acquiesce in military pre-eminence. Thirdly, ossification of the power structure would be avoided, crudely but not ineffectively, by rivalries within the military and changes of government by intra-military coup. Finally, successive military-dominated governments would pursue modernisation, economic growth and the expansion of education and other services. For several decades this would seem to justify military rule—though it would eventually undermine it. Economic development and a better-educated society would finally produce broad-based pressures for more representative government.

In the 1930s, Thailand was still overwhelmingly a country of peasant farmers. The military was its best-organised, most cohesive modern institution. The military's crucial role in the 1932 revolution was underscored in October 1933, when pro-royalist protesters marched on Bangkok. They were repulsed by troops commanded by a Lt-Colonel Phibun Songkhram. The following year, Phibun became defence minister, and would hold various posts until he became prime minister in 1938, when he headed a cabinet of predominantly military men Phibun and his supporters, unimpressed by the floundering Western democracies of the period, were attracted to other political models—fascist Italy, Germany and, above all, Japan, the one Asian country which seemed to offer Thailand a pattern for modernisation. Phibun rapidly adopted some features of dictatorship, arresting opponents, promoting himself as Thailand's great leader and exciting nationalist emotions. A series of "cultural mandates" attempted instant economic and social change. Domestically, his most dramatic move was legislation targeting the Chinese in Thailand. State corporations took over commodities such as rice, tobacco and petroleum, and Chinese businesses found themselves subject to a range of new taxes and controls. Chinese economic know-how was, in fact, too valuable for anti-Chinese measures to be pushed far, but Phibun's policies would have lasting effects. They stimulated Chinese assimilation into Thai society, through Sino-Thai business partnerships, intermarriage, and Chinese acceptance of Thai language, education and culture. They also set in train heavy state involvement in the economy, which would blur the lines between business and those who held political and bureaucratic power.

Pursuing his nationalist goals, Phibun changed his country's name from Siam to Thailand in 1939 (the name Siam would be briefly resumed between 1945 and 1949). Phibun pointed out that "Siam" was originally a term for the area used by Chinese and other foreigners, but the change also had irredentist implications—should "the land of the Thais" include "Tai" people who lived beyond its borders, many as a result of Western pruning of the old Bangkok empire? Phibun answered this question in November 1940, when Thai forces invaded Laos and western Cambodia. The Japanese, who now held base and transit rights in French Indochina, stepped in to mediate, awarding Cambodia's western provinces and portions of Laos to Thailand.

This victory was popular in Thailand. Phibun's subsequent relations with the Japanese would become more controversial, however. In December 1941, the Japanese moved troops into Thailand, demanding transit rights for their attacks on British Burma and Malaya. Thai troops resisted but, within hours, the Phibun government called for a ceasefire. Subsequently, it entered a military alliance with Japan and, in January 1942, declared war on the United States and Britain. Division about these events within Thai ruling circles was indicated most obviously by the refusal of the Thai minister in Washington, the aristocratic Seni Pramoj, to advise the US government of the declaration of war. A Free Thai movement began to grow amongst overseas Thais and, eventually, underground within Thailand itself.

At first, however, Phibun's actions were widely supported, and Thailand was rewarded by Japan with the Shan states of Burma in 1942 and the four northern Malay states in 1943. Disillusionment began to set in as the tide of war turned against Japan, and Thailand experienced acute economic disruption because of the war. In July 1944, Phibun quietly resigned the prime ministership, leaving the National Assembly with the problem of preparing Thailand for an Allied victory.

The politicians were restrained by the Japanese presence until August 1945, but then all agreements with Japan were repudiated (including those which had transferred territory to Thailand). Though the goal of democratic government was reasserted, a range of factors would combine to frustrate its achievement. The British and French were at first bitterly hostile to Thailand. The economic difficulties of the war years persisted and political infighting prevented effective, or even stable, government.

In the midst of the turmoil, King Ananda, who had returned to Thailand in December 1945, died of a gunshot one morning in June 1946. His death has remained shrouded in mystery. The young king enjoyed collecting guns and most likely the shot was accidentally self-inflicted but the political scene was inflamed by murder theories. The prime minister, Pridi Phanomyong, famed as the chief civilian promoter of the 1932 revolution but viewed by conservatives as a radical leftist, resigned amidst mounting hysteria against "communists". The government continued to flounder until the military stepped in with a coup in November 1947. Initially, they retained a civilian prime minister but forced him to resign in April 1948. He was replaced by Phibun.

THE "STRONG MAN" ERA, 1948–1973
The resumption of military dominance over government instigated a succession of authoritarian leaders who were unchallenged by forces outside the military until 1973. Their power was enhanced by US patronage and aid. Washington wanted strong, anti-Communist, leaders who would both repress domestic communism (never more than a fringe phenomenon in Thailand, in fact) and join in American-led strategies for the containment of Asian communism. From the 1950s, US aid to Thailand was substantial. It enabled a great deal of social and economic development, notably in communications, infrastructure and social-welfare projects, but it also bolstered military and police power.

Even so the goal of stable government was not necessarily secured. American aid created new opportunities for corruption in Thai government and administration, and stimulated competition for the prizes of power between rival political networks anchored in the military but reaching into business and the bureaucracy. American appeals for some evidence of democracy in Thailand produced in the short term only cynical political manipulation, rigged elections and rubber-stamp parliaments from time to time.

After 1948, Phibun resumed many of his former repressive policies. He mounted another anti-Chinese campaign, and also attempted to impose cultural uniformity forcefully on the Malay-Muslims of the far south. The latter resisted the arrival of Thai officials, the introduction of Thai-language education and the substitution of Thai law for customary law. A separatist movement grew which, despite conciliation by later Thai governments, persists to this day.

Despite the tough image which Phibun once more projected, his power was not in fact secure. He faced several attempted coups from within the military between 1948 and 1951. All were defeated, but at the price of the emergence of two further "strongmen"—army commander, subsequently Field Marshal, Sarit Thanarat (whose later spectacular wealth would be grounded in his control of the government lottery), and police chief, Phao Siyanon (who would make his fortune from opium trafficking). In 1955 Phibun eased the controls on political activity and promised elections. He may have been under American pressure to do so, or he may have hoped to out-manoeuvre his rivals by winning popular endorsement. However, his party was accused of massive fraud during the 1957 election and Sarit won popularity by resigning, supposedly in disgust, from Phibun's government. In September 1957, Sarit staged a coup, driving Phibun and Phao into exile.

In October 1958, Sarit declared martial law, silencing the experiments in open politics. He justified his authoritarianism in two ways: he argued for a return to Thai traditions of social order, and he accelerated economic development and social modernisation. Under the former banner, the monarchy was given renewed prominence. King Bhumibol Adulyadej (Rama IX, 1946–present) attended public ceremonies, toured the provinces and patronised development projects, becoming a revered figure in the process. Under the banner of development, Sarit introduced to government a new generation of economically liberal technocrats, encouraged private and foreign investment, launched major rural development programmes and rapidly expanded educational facilities.

When Sarit died in December 1963 power transferred peacefully to his close associates, Generals Thanom Kittikachorn (who became prime minister) and Praphas Charusathian (deputy prime minister). Thanom and Praphas basically maintained Sarit's style of government and economic policies, which produced GNP growth rates of over eight per cent per year during the 1960s. At the same time, the military's place in the Thai political landscape seemed to loom larger than ever. US aid increased sharply because of the Indochina conflicts. From 1964, Thailand provided bases for the US airforce and committed its own troops to action in Vietnam and Laos. US aid was also forthcoming to combat a communist insurgency which had taken root amongst alienated tribal groups in the country's north and northeast.

The era of unquestioned "strong man" rule was drawing to a close, however. Economic development, wider education and better communications were rapidly increasing the numbers of the politically aware. In 1968, Thanom proclaimed a new Constitution, and an election the following year established a new parliament. The political public was shocked when he reversed direction in 1971, dissolving the parliament and banning political parties once more. By the early 1970s, several other issues were raising concern. The leaders' presumed successor, Narong Kittikachorn (Thanom's son and Praphas' son-in-law), was not regarded highly inside or outside the military. Thailand's close involvement with the US obviously required rethinking as the US moved to disengage from Vietnam and the region. The OPEC "oil shock" and rising prices sent tremors through the economy.

It was the educated young who precipitated the downfall of the Thanom-Praphas regime. In October 1973, student protests against political repression (inspired to some extent by the western student radicalism of the era) escalated into massive confrontation with the police on the streets of Bangkok. Popular sympathy for the students increased when several of their number were killed or wounded by the police. In the first subtle indication of royal political opinion in many years, the King permitted student first-aid stations on royal ground. The demonstrators triumphed when the army withheld its support from Thanom, Praphas and Narong, who fled into exile.

BETWEEN AUTOCRACY AND DEMOCRACY, 1973–1992

The "Students' Revolution" unleashed an extraordinary burst of political activism. Political parties mushroomed, hitherto banned ideas circulated freely, trade unionism flourished, and numerous organisations of all shades of opinion set out to politicise the people. Even the Buddhist *sangha*, long a compliant supporter of government, revealed radical dissent within its ranks.

An interim civilian government arranged for a fully elected parliament to be created by elections in January 1975. The result was an unstable coalition government which collapsed within 12 months. Another ineffective coalition emerged from elections in April 1976. Meanwhile, the problems of a destabilised economy were not being addressed and neither were the apparent threats to Thailand from the communist victories in Cambodia, Vietnam and Laos in 1975. Conservative opinion, outraged by the political disorder from the beginning, increasingly became popular opinion. In October 1976, the military resumed power, unopposed, permitting right-wing organisations to torture and kill student radicals gathered at Thammasat University in Bangkok. Many leftist and moderate leaders fled the city, some to join the communist insurgents in the north-east. For the moment it appeared that Thailand faced more authoritarian government than ever before. The policies of the first post-coup prime minister, a civilian but a rigid right-winger, deepened rather than healed the divisions in the country. Even civil war seemed possible, if the newly expanded insurgent forces could attract popular sympathy.

Within the military, however, opinions varied about the future of Thai politics and the military's relationship to government. At one end of the spectrum stood those keen to retain the autocratic discipline of the "strongman" years. At the other stood, those who saw the development of democracy as desirable, even inevitable; clearly Thai society was now unwilling to be politically passive. In the middle of the spectrum, key military figures concluded that "managed democracy" was possible—an option which has remained attractive to military politicians ever since. Management could include a range of strategies: the maintenance of a Constitution which allowed for an appointed prime minister; appointments to other senior posts and a part-appointed parliament; the nurture of political parties sympathetic to military interests; the promotion of the military to the public as an efficient national institution more likely to deliver government in the common good than self-interested (civilian) politicians. The strategy of managed democracy also seemed to require, however, that the military should retain the right to the ultimate weapon of political management, the coup.

In October 1977, General Kriangsak Chomanand assumed the prime ministership, promising a new constitution and elections in 1979. He also offered amnesty to repentant insurgents, which hastened the collapse of an insurgency movement increasingly disillusioned by the falling out between Cambodia, Vietnam and China, and by the revelations of the horrors of Khmer Rouge rule in Cambodia. (Ironically it would be the Thai military, rather than the insurgents, who would develop a liaison with the Khmer Rouge, after Vietnam's occupation of Cambodia in 1979.)

Not long after the 1979 elections Kriangsak was succeeded by General Prem Tinsulanonda, whose particular form of managed democracy would attract the label "Premocracy". Prem was an appointed prime minister (under the 1978 Constitution) but he took care to base his authority on parliamentary support, persuading MPs from a range of parties to back him. Generally, Prem maintained a reputation for being "clean" and making appointments to senior posts on the basis of merit. Military elements twice tried to overthrow him, in 1981 and 1985, but on both occasions he survived with the explicit support of the King and of loyal military forces.

Prem retired in 1988 and elections brought to power a civilian prime minister, Chatichai Choonhavan, heading a coalition identified with civilian political and business interests. The Chatichai government was buoyed by economic boom conditions and, initially, by popular enthusiasm; the military took a wait-and-see attitude. Military leaders grew alarmed, however, when Chatichai manoeuvred to diminish their influence behind the scenes. Pro-military media publicised with relish examples of his government's inefficiency and undoubtedly grave corruption. In February 1991, a quiescent public observed a well-planned coup which overthrew Chatichai, parliament and the Constitution.

The principal figure behind the coup was army commander General Suchinda Kraprayoon. Other leading figures included the navy and air force chiefs and the deputy commander of the army. Their alliance dated back to their education at Chulachomklao Military Academy, where they had graduated as members of "Class 5", a generation of cadets which had come to dominate many key positions of power. Suchinda was known to despise democracy. Nevertheless, the coup group—calling themselves the National Peacekeeping Council (NPC)—set out to explore new methods of managed democracy, promising another Constitution and elections, and establishing an interim government headed by Anand Panyarachun, a respected businessman and former diplomat. The NPC's stance may have been prodded by more than domestic considerations. Many countries expressed dismay at the 1991 coup and international business registered some alarm at the capriciousness of the Thai political scene.

As interim prime minister, Anand performed effectively but controversy grew over the new Constitution, announced in December 1991, which favoured the military by allowing for an appointed prime minister and an appointed upper house (the Senate) with power over legislation. The NPC leadership proved able, however, to command the lower house too. Elections in March 1992 gave a narrow majority to a coalition of parties supporting, or willing to align themselves with, military-dominated government. Only the question of a prime minister seemed to remain unresolved.

The military's initial choice for prime minister, a civilian lower-house MP, had to withdraw when the US government publicised his links to the drug trade. General Suchinda stepped into the vacuum—to the outrage of Thailand's frustrated democrats. Mass demonstrations began in Bangkok, led by the Buddhist ascetic Chamlong Srimuang, an ex-military officer and former Bangkok governor. Chamlong had a reputation for incorruptibility. With his political party, Palang Dharma and its supporters, he now campaigned for clean, democratic government. In Bangkok and major provincial centres they enjoyed wide support.

Disastrously, Suchinda ordered troops to use force against the demonstrators. Between 17 and 20 May, at least 50 protesters were killed (several hundred according to rumour at the time) in scenes of mayhem and military brutality that shocked television viewers around the world. On 20 May, the King intervened. A truce was negotiated which led to Suchinda's resignation as prime minister after he had declared an amnesty for "all parties" involved in killing and injuring demonstrators. Anand returned as interim prime minister, minor modifications were made to the Constitution, and fresh elections in September 1992 resulted in a narrow majority for anti-military parties. From these, a civilian coalition government headed by the Democrat Party's Chuan Leekpai was formed, and this for nearly three years before collapsing in 1995 after a scandal over land-reform rights on Phuket Island. However, Chuan was returned to power in 1997 during elections under a new, progressive Constitution and led the country until he was replaced in 2001, in a landslide result by one of the country's most successful business tycoons, Thaksin Shinawatra. Indeed, Thaksin liked to quip that he was the nation's chief executive officer, and the business savvy he brought to the role initially proved to be a refreshing change for many Thais, especially those in the rural areas who have traditionally benefited far less from economic development than their city-dwelling counterparts. However, Thaksin had many (increasingly outspoken) domestic critics wary of his populist appeals and "one-man-band" leadership style which, they maintained, was fine for running a company, but not appropriate for running a whole country.

A trigger for the unrest that eventually toppled Thaksin occurred in January 2006 when he sold his family's controlling interest in telecommunications giant Shin Corporation to Temasek, an investment company owned by the Singaporean government. The multi-billion-dollar sale alienated many Thais not only as it was to a foreign company, but also because it was structured so that Thaksin received the proceeds tax-free.

Anti-Thaksin protesters crystallised around a loosely-based coalition, the People's Alliance for Democracy (PAD), comprising businessmen and the urban middle class, and demanded the prime minister's resignation. Following a series of PAD-led anti-government demonstrations, on 19 September 2006 a military coup (apparently with royal approval) overthrew the government while Thaksin was overseas. Martial law was imposed and a new constitution was drafted which was endorsed by referendum in August 2007. To the alarm of liberal critics, the new constitution weakened the influence of elected politicians and increased the power of the judiciary (which had been purged of pro-Thaksin elements). Thaksin himself stayed in exile overseas, but was sentenced in absentia to two years in prison in October 2008 for abuse of power, to be served should he return to Thailand. He was also accused of attempting to undermine the revered monarchy.

New elections were held in December 2007 and to the dismay of the military and the PAD, were convincingly won by a pro-Thaksin coalition led by the People's Power Party (PPP). In November 2008, continuing protests culminated in a week-long blockade by PAD supporters of Bangkok's two key airports that left 350,000 passengers stranded. The blockade was lifted in December after the Constitutional Court ordered the dismantling of the PPP, holding that its leadership was guilty of electoral fraud. The court also handed a five-year political ban to the then prime minister Somchai Wongsawat (Thaksin's brother-in-law), who immediately resigned. Thaksin's allies then regrouped behind a new political party and seemed poised to return to power. However their plans were thwarted when a number of political leaders previously loyal to Thaksin defected to PAD-aligned parties, and they were able to form a new government in late 2008. Nevertheless the current political tussles between pro- and anti- Thaksin supporters would seem too far from over.

THAILAND IN PROSPECT
The wave of domestic and international revulsion against the violence of May 1992 was thought by many commentators to have diminished the likelihood of further direct military intervention in Thai

government, but the military coup of 2006, albeit peaceful, proved them wrong. Clearly the wish of democratic reformers to detach the military from politics and other non-military spheres of public life is by no means assured. Long years of military dominance have taught the present officer corps to expect influence, careers and rewards beyond the strictly military realm. The military's political influence remains particularly strong in rural Thailand (which ironically is where Thaksin drew, and continues to draw, his most vociferous support), where the armed forces present an image of practical concern for development and for the needs of the poor. Meanwhile, civilian politicians still need to convince many Thais that they put clean, stable and effective government ahead of their personal interests. Corruption is a spectre which hangs over both civilian and military politics.

It must also be a matter of concern that the monarchy has had to involve itself in politics in the past two decades. The present King (who celebrated the 60th anniversary of his ascension to the throne in 2006 but whose health is rumoured to be poor) has acted judiciously and maintained broad national respect, but royal intervention in politics presents risks, for the monarchy and for social stability if a future intervention were to be misjudged. Thailand's political system cannot be seen as stable or mature while resort to royal arbitration remains an occasional necessity.

Today some Thais also fear for another traditional source of social stability – Buddhism. In pre-modern Thai society, Buddhism, as well as providing religious inspiration and solace, was probably the chief form of "social cement". Buddhist temples were centres of education and social activity as well as of worship. Royal and aristocratic patronage of Buddhism ensured that the traditional social order enjoyed religious legitimation. In 1902, King Chulalongkorn formalised the administration of the *sangha*, in effect making it an arm of the state. Post-1932 governments perpetuated this strategy; both Phibun and Sarit reorganised *sangha* administration, at least in part, for political purposes.

In the short term, this strategy enhanced social order. In the longer term, it has produced scepticism amongst many Thais towards established Buddhism and its conservative teachings. This has led in some cases to indifference; in others, to the growth of movements and sects challenging mainstream Buddhism. Modern education and rising affluence have, of course, contributed to the diversification of attitudes towards religion.

Instabilities in Thai society can be exaggerated, however. Despite the intermittent political crises at the top, Thai society has remained serenely stable when compared with some of its neighbouring countries. This stability has enabled economic and social development on a breathtaking scale. The political discord of recent decades may have reflected strains and tensions arising from rapid social change but, to date, it has not endangered Thailand's development more than fleetingly.

For over three decades, Thailand achieved average growth rates of around seven to eight per cent, reaching over ten per cent in the late 1980s. Since 2000 (following negative growth in 1998–99), this figure has been a still-respectable five per cent. The country has been a favoured destination of foreign investment, led at present by Japan and China, with Taiwan, the United States and Singapore also posting significant shares. Meanwhile, Thai investment also now flows to other countries of the region. What was once rice-growing mono-economy before World War II, Thailand's economy is now broad-based, producing a range of agricultural products, many of them processed in Thailand. Mining, oil and liquefied natural gas constitute a growing sector.

The growth of manufacturing, however, has been the most spectacular aspect of the development. Negligible till the 1950s, manufacturing accounted for 29 per cent of export earnings in 1980. By 2002, this had risen to 85 per cent. Over the same period, agricultural export earnings fell from 68 per cent to just seven per cent. With such growth, Thailand has become a key regional financial centre and Thai business expects to play a significant role in the development of southern China, Vietnam, Laos, Cambodia and Myanmar.

Within Thailand, other major changes have been taking place. The population stood at 38 million in 1970 and 64 million in 2008 (the growth rate is now down to 0.6 per cent, however). Improved medical and other services have significantly reduced the death rate and the incidence of malnutrition, tuberculosis and tropical diseases. In education, enrolment rates have grown at all levels, far outstripping population growth at secondary level (up fivefold between 1970 and 2000) and tertiary level (up eightfold). A trend to urbanisation, reflecting economic shifts, has meant that over 40 per cent of Thais now live in Bangkok or provincial towns. In the capital and other urban centres, the emergence of a substantial consumer-oriented middle class is strikingly evident. The old Thailand, where small royal, aristocratic or military elites could dominate a quiescent population of subsistence farmers, has gone.

Thai government must now grapple with an increasingly mobile, affluent and educated society. Other problems loom as large. The agenda of issues confronting any Thai government today seems, indeed, disconcertingly long and urgent. On a macroeconomic level, Thailand must move on from industrial development based on cheap labour and foreign-owned technology. Economic growth has produced extreme disparities of wealth, both vertically and horizontally. The affluent share the cities with workers on minimal wages and often work in atrocious conditions. In per-capita terms, however, urban Thais are vastly better off than those in rural areas. Poverty is particularly pronounced in the north, north-east and far south.

Poverty again became an issue at the forefront of national concerns following the sudden plunge in living standards brought on by the Asian economic crisis, which had itself been precipitated by the government's decision to sharply devalue the baht in mid 1997. Soon afterwards, the currency went into free-fall and, by early the following year, its value had been halved and the stock market had fallen by 75 per cent. These upheavals resulted in the loss of a million jobs and the number increased as the tough "shock therapy" prescribed by the International Monetary Fund to address the problems that caused the "correction" in the first place took effect. These structural weaknesses included an unsustainably large current-account deficit, chronic public infrastructure problems (including some of the world's worst traffic jams in Bangkok), and high private-sector borrowing for speculation in the property market. Thailand's system of corrupt "money politics", whereby politicians rely on vote-buying and favours from powerful regional strongmen, was also put under the spotlight. According to the World Bank, between the 1997 crisis and 2001, poverty rose from 11 per cent to 16 per cent of the population, though this is fairly low by regional standards. It has since fallen.

By the turn of the century, the country had turned a corner and entered a recovery stage, winning praise from the IMF. In 2003 Prime Minister Thaksin Shinawatra announced that the government had made the final repayment of an IMF emergency loan package negotiated in 1998. By then, Thailand's prospects again seemed buoyant, with annual growth averaging five per cent, despite short-term setbacks caused by declines in tourist numbers as a result of the regional outbreak of Severe Acute Respiratory Syndrome (SARS) in 2003, avian influenza (bird flu) in 2004 and, most tragically, the consequences of the 2004 Boxing Day tsunami, in which 5,300 Thais and tourists died in the south. But the effects of the political convulsions of 2006–08, combined with the global economic downturn of 2008–09, will impact negatively on growth levels as foreign investors and tourists reevaluate Thailand as a preferred destination. In 2007 alone, foreign investment reached nearly US$10 billion and the tourism industry was valued at US$16 billion. Both figures are predicted to fall sharply.

Serious social problems remain to be addressed. They include the perpetuation of a dual economy in which most industrial development is focused on the capital, which accounts for over 50 per cent of the nation's GDP although it has only an estimated 15 per cent of the population. Bangkok's infrastructure is straining to cope with the expansion but, despite major development schemes, rural infrastructure remains inadequate to attract much business and industry away from the capital. Pollution and environmental degradation have become urgent issues in both urban and rural areas. AIDS has become the country's most pressing health issue, with several million Thais estimated to be HIV-positive; though, due to campaigns by government and non-governmental organisations, AIDS-awareness among young Thais is now among the highest in the developing world and the problem does seem to be under control. The drug problem also created international headlines when, in February 2003, the government launched a "war on drugs". Unprecedented in its severity, an estimated 3,000 people were killed within the first three months, mostly by over-zealous police. While the campaign met with overwhelming public support, in December 2003 the King publicly chastised Thaksin over the number of extra-judicial killings and called for an investigation.

In 2003, separatist violence broke out in the three Malay-Muslim-dominated southern states of Pattani, Yala and Narathiwat, resulting in martial law being imposed. The violence worsened in April 2004 when the police killed 107 alleged militants after being tipped off about planned attacks. In December 2004, 78 Thai Muslims who were detained following a protest rally suffocated to death in military custody; an event which sparked strong international condemnation of the government. The security situation remains uncertain in the south with both sides accused by human rights groups of committing abuses.

Despite these problems, Thailand's history over the centuries tends to induce optimism for its future; albeit noting the confluence of the global financial crisis with continuing political tussles between pro- and anti-Thaksin forces (and all the serious underlying issues behind these) may put extraordinary pressure on its citizens in the near future. So far however, Thai history can be read as the story of a people with an unusual capacity for social cohesion, for resolving or evading conflict, and for confronting unavoidable challenges creatively.

11 VIETNAM

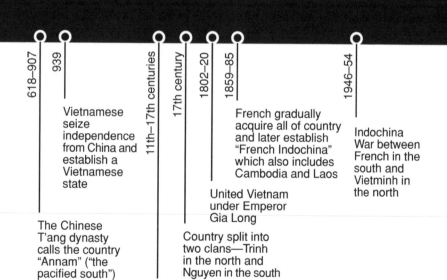

618–907

The Chinese T'ang dynasty calls the country "Annam" ("the pacified south")

939

Vietnamese seize independence from China and establish a Vietnamese state

11th–17th centuries

Acquire central part of the country from the Kingdom of Champa and Mekong delta from the Khmers

17th century

Country split into two clans—Trinh in the north and Nguyen in the south

1802–20

United Vietnam under Emperor Gia Long

1859–85

French gradually acquire all of country and later establish "French Indochina" which also includes Cambodia and Laos

1946–54

Indochina War between French in the south and Vietminh in the north

Ruined Gateway at Hue

1954

1960s

"Vietcong" control over much of the south leads to United States increasing aid and US troops sent to support RVN

Country partitioned—Democratic Republic of Vietnam (DRV) in the north and Republic of Vietnam (RVN) in the south

1973

Paris Peace Agreements signed

1975

RVN falls; Vietnam unified and refugees flee country

1978

Vietnam's invasion of Cambodia leads to attacks on northern borders by China

1986

Policy of *doi moi* (renovation) adopted and overhaul of political and economic systems begins

1990

Collapse of USSR and loss of foreign aid propel further economic change towards a free-enterprise system

1995

Joins ASEAN; resumes diplomatic relations with US

2000

First stock market launched; visit by US President Clinton

Admitted to World Trade Organization

2007

11 VIETNAM

The Vietnamese were ruled by the Chinese for over a thousand years, from the second century BC until the 10th century AD. After winning their independence, the Vietnamese continued looking to China as their cultural model, their prime source of concepts of government, social organisation and the arts. Culturally, Vietnam thus belonged to the Confucian world of East Asia, which distinguished it sharply from neighbouring states with Theravada Buddhist or Islamic cultures. The difference in cultural outlook between Vietnam and her South-East Asian neighbours has long contributed to conflict in the region.

But the Vietnamese regard for China also made for conflict within Vietnam itself. It proved difficult to reconcile with another Vietnamese impulse—to protect their distinctive character as a people and to uphold uniquely Vietnamese cultural traditions. Whether to adopt or to resist Chinese ideas became a perennial source of social and cultural stress within Vietnam's ruling class, and also between ruling class and people.

The Vietnamese state was an expanding one, which only intensified such cultural stresses though it took 700 years. The expansion—known as the "march to the south" eased the country's population pressures and made Vietnam a major power in South-East Asia. But it also bred deep regional differences and rivalries within

Vietnamese society. Vietnam in 19th century was in poor shape to face the challenges posed by the West's political, economic and cultural expansion.

The Western impact, in the shape of French colonial rule and subsequent American intervention, aggravated the historic tensions and also cut bitter new divisions in Vietnamese society. Communism in Vietnam, as in China, won wide popular support, with its promise of national independence and a reintegrated and just society. It delivered on the first promise; it failed on the second. As in China, communism in Vietnam as an overarching state ideology now drifts uncertainly, though most observers are optimistic about the future of Vietnam's 86 million people living in a state under Communist Party control but with a free-enterprise economy.

EARLY HISTORY

The earliest Vietnamese state occupied only the Red River Delta, today the heart of northern Vietnam. In the second century BC this state was absorbed into the empire of Han-dynasty China, the Chinese calling it Nan-yüeh or Nan-viet. Thus began over 1,000 years of Chinese rule, during which the Vietnamese became familiar with Chinese political and social institutions, the Chinese writing system and Chinese learning and arts.

They were also influenced by the Mahayana forms of Buddhism then flourishing in East Asia, another factor which would set them apart from their neighbours in South-East Asia amongst whom Hinduism and, subsequently Theravada Buddhism flourished. Mahayana Buddhism tended to blend with Confucian and Taoist thought and, in Vietnam, with local popular religious folklore and beliefs. It never developed the strong institutional networks of temples and monasteries which gave considerable political strength to Theravada Buddhism.

The high-water mark of Chinese influence upon the Vietnamese was probably reached during the T'ang dynasty (618-907 AD), whose rulers termed the country of the Vietnamese "An-nan", or "Annam"—"the pacified South". The Vietnamese, however, never lost their sense of separate identity. In 939 AD, they took advantage of political disorder in China to seize their independence and re-establish a Vietnamese state. In later centuries, the Chinese attempted on several occasions to reassert their authority—leading to a Vietnamese perception of themselves as a permanently threatened nation—but they were successfully resisted. The early Ming did manage to take and hold Vietnam for 20 years (1407–1428) but were ousted by forces led by one of Vietnam's greatest heroes, Le Loi, the founder of the Le dynasty, which was to last from 1428 until 1789.

The history of Vietnam after independence in the 10th century would be marked by two principal, and conflict-provoking, tendencies. The first of these was the development of a Confucian state and high culture modelled on China. By the 15th century, Vietnam had a system of government similar in all but size to that of its mighty northern neighbour. The Vietnamese emperor, at the capital, Hanoi, presided over a mandarin bureaucracy educated in the Confucian classics. Law, administrative structures, literature and the arts all followed Chinese forms. The educated class also tended to prefer to use Chinese rather than the Vietnamese language. In theory, the adoption of the Confucian model of social organisation should have conferred enlightened government on Vietnam. In practice, it produced a ruling class culturally alienated from their subjects. This problem was compounded by the grip on the country's commercial life maintained by Chinese merchants allied with the Vietnamese ruling class.

Nevertheless, popular Vietnamese culture absorbed many attitudes and values of Chinese derivation, through acceptance of codes of law and morality promulgated by government and spread by scholars. Thus, ordinary Vietnamese displayed such characteristically Confucian traits as respect for hierarchy, emphasis on an individual's social obligations, intense family loyalty and reverence for education and scholarship. Even so, Vietnamese popular culture always remained self-consciously distinct, hostile to China and wary of the country's Sinophile upper class.

The second main tendency in the history of Vietnam after it gained independence from China was southward expansion, and this would compound the cultural tensions. Military in organisation, the expansion was driven basically by the need to find farming land for a growing population. Between the 11th and 17th centuries it gradually extinguished the kingdom of Champa, in what today is central Vietnam. It then took the Mekong Delta from the Khmers and, during the 19th century would probably have overwhelmed the whole of Cambodia had not the Thais challenged the Vietnamese advance and the French brought it to a halt by establishing a "protectorate" over Cambodia in 1863.

The "march to the south" allowed rival power blocs to develop within Vietnamese society and the 16th century saw intermittent civil war in Vietnam. In the 17th century the country was split between two powerful clans: the Trinh in the north and the Nguyen in the south.

The frontier established between them was only a few kilometres from the site of the demilitarised zone which would separate North and South Vietnam from 1954 until 1975. In the 17th and 18th centuries, the Nguyen rulers in the south became responsible for the country's continued expansion.

The cultural differences between northerners and southerners popularly recognised in modern Vietnam may have their origins in the "march to the south". The circumstances of the "frontier" southerners contrasted with those of "stay-at-home" northerners. In the south, settler families were thrown on their own resources, in a tropical environment unlike that of the temperate north. Deference towards officialdom declined. Village organisation of economic and administrative matters—elaborate in the north—also declined in the south. On the southern frontier, facilities for the reinforcement of Confucian culture were virtually non-existent. At the same time, the southern settlers were encountering alternative ideas, particularly religious concepts, in the cultures of the Chams, the Khmers and upland tribal (montagnard) groups. Here perhaps were the beginnings of the cultural dichotomies popularly perceived today. Northerners are noted for their conservatism, deference to the group, reserved manners and respect for the intellectual life; southerners for their outgoing approach to life, free-wheeling attitudes towards authority, outspoken manners and eclectic religious life.

Whatever the developing differences, the Vietnamese perception of themselves as being fundamentally one people remained unquestioned. This was dramatically demonstrated in the Tay Son Rebellion which broke out in Vietnam in 1771. A vast "revolution from below", the rebellion swept away the Nguyen and Trinh regimes which had divided Vietnam, and removed what was by that stage a nominal Le imperial dynasty. The rebels also repelled a Chinese invasion, and turned on Chinese merchants in Vietnam. They faltered only when faced with the tasks of practical government. A member of the southern Nguyen clan, Nguyen Anh, raised forces and, by 1802, managed to subdue the rebel forces. He became the emperor Gia Long, first of Vietnam's Nguyen emperors and the first ruler to preside over a united Vietnam for more than two centuries.

THE 19TH CENTURY CONFUCIAN REVIVAL

Emperor from 1802 to 1820, Gia Long recognised what an administrative and defence nightmare Vietnam's geography had become—two fertile deltas, 1,000 kilometres apart, connected by a narrow coastal corridor. Ignoring Hanoi (and thus incurring northerner resentment), he established his capital in the centre of the country, at Hué. There he built a palace complex that was a scaled-down replica of Peking's Forbidden City. The symbolism was appropriate—Gia Long and his son, Minh Mang (emperor from 1820 to 1841), would attempt to establish in Vietnam the most thorough copy yet seen of Chinese administrative concepts and methods. Though honourably intentioned, the attempt would prove a disaster.

From the 1830s onwards, rebellion flared frequently in protest at the level of bureaucratic intervention in daily life, the rigidities and absurdities of mandarinal decrees and, above all, at the level of taxation demanded by the system. The renewed concern with Confucian models also diminished the ability of Nguyen imperial government to deal realistically with the growing challenges from the West. Some members of the Vietnamese scholar class recognised the need to study the West, but they were in the minority. Disastrously, Emperor Minh Mang and his successors (Thieu Tri, emperor 1841–47, and Tu Duc, emperor 1847–83) chose to confront and repress the religion of the West, Christianity.

French Catholic missionaries had been active in Vietnam since the mid 17th century. They had helped Gia Long defeat the Tay Son rebels and establish his imperial dynasty, assisting him with men and resources. By the mid 19th century there were an estimated 450,000 Catholic converts in Vietnam. Vietnamese government had always been wary of organised religion in any form, seeing it as a potential threat to Confucian authority, and now Christianity seemed to present a serious challenge. In successive campaigns of repression, thousands of Christians and their priests were killed and Christian villages were levelled. The persecutions shocked Catholics in France, and unwittingly provided a pretext for French intervention in Vietnam.

COLONIAL HISTORY

In 1859, a French naval expedition seized Saigon, following an unsuccessful attempt on the then more significant port of Da Nang, which was close to Hué. Emperor Tu Duc faced rebellion in the north and, in 1862, conceded to the French, who gained by treaty Saigon and its three surrounding provinces. In 1869 the French seized three further adjoining provinces, thus completing the territory of the colony they would call Cochin China.

The French conquered the remainder of Vietnam between 1883 and 1885, in the course of a complicated conflict in the country's north. The north had collapsed in chaos fomented by both

Vietnamese and expatriate Chinese rebels. The Vietnamese imperial government had lost all capacity to control events. Both China and France regarded Vietnam as being within their respective spheres of influence and sent forces, with the French eventually repelling the Chinese.

The French then declared "protectorates" over northern Vietnam (Tonkin) and central Vietnam (Annam), where they would retain a line of "puppet" Nguyen emperors until 1926. In 1885, some Vietnamese mandarins, outraged at the French intrusion, organised a resistance movement called Can Vuong ("Aid the King"), which would persist for several years. After it was pacified, the French would rule relatively securely until 1940.

French colonial rule would bring many elements of modernity to the country, amongst them handsome cities with sewers and electric lighting, the Saigon-Hanoi railway, modern port facilities, a network of metalled roads, and modern education and medicine for those—a small minority—who could afford them. Under the French, the city's rice output was greatly expanded and Vietnam linked into the world economy on the basis of exports of rice and, to a lesser extent, rubber and other products. Colonialism's most significant impact, however, was to increase divisiveness in Vietnam, administratively, economically and socially.

Administratively, "Vietnam" disappeared off the map. The country was divided into Cochin China Annam and Tonkin, whose administrative centres were Saigon, Hué and Hanoi, respectively. This had the effect of outraging Vietnamese nationalists and enhancing regionalist tendencies. The three segments became parts of French Indochina, along with Cambodia and Laos. Differing approaches to administration north and south also seemed to encourage regionalism. Cochin China, constitutionally a French colony, experienced French administrators and French legal forms. Saigon became the leading and most Westernised city of Indochina, an alluring showpiece of modern fashions and culture. In the "protectorates" Tonkin and Annam, by contrast, the French endeavoured to retain indigenous administrative and legal systems, if only for the sake of reducing costs. As a result, Hanoi and Hué remained much quieter places than Saigon.

Colonial economic policies also pulled the country apart, though the fundamental reasons for this lay in the circumstances inherited by the French. In Vietnam's north, the French found a ready-made economic crisis—a densely crowded population dependent on subsistence rice agriculture. By 1929, the average population density in the countryside of the Tonkin Delta would be 975 per square kilometres. The whole system depended on an elaborate but ancient and dilapidated complex of irrigation dykes. Most families held inadequately small plots and were in debt. The French were unwilling to industrialise in Vietnam—industry was for metropolitan France, not for her colonies—and thus had no fundamental answers to these problems. By the 1930s only about 120,000 people were classified as industrial workers in Vietnam, many of these being miners in the north's coal, zinc and tin mines. Some northerners moved to the south's rubber plantations as indentured labour, often in scandalously exploitative conditions, but this labour traffic had little impact on the north's basic economic problems.

In contrast, Cochin China was the success story of French colonialism. When French rule began the Mekong Delta was still relatively lightly populated, though much of the land was still swamp. From the 1870s, water control and irrigation programmes made available vast new areas of farming land. Later the French would boast that they had boosted Vietnam's rice lands by 420 per cent. By the 1920s, the development of the Mekong Delta had enabled Vietnam to become one of the world's leading rice exporters, although the absolute primacy of rice—accounting for over 70 per cent of colonial Vietnam's exports—made the economy precariously unbalanced. It was also debatable, ironically, whether the southern farmers were much better off than their northern cousins. Most southerners became sharecroppers on the vast estates created out of the reclaimed lands; as such, they enjoyed little security or prosperity.

Vietnamese histories recall with horror French taxation policies, claiming that the Vietnamese were the most highly taxed people in the colonial world. That is debatable, but French defence, administrative and public works costs were high and so, therefore, were their taxes. The promotion of a government opium monopoly, as late as the 1930s, is remembered with particular distaste. Other imposts included a poll tax and taxes on alcohol and salt.

CULTURE AND POLITICS IN COLONIAL VIETNAM

Socially and culturally, colonial Vietnam was a place of ferment. The collapse of Confucian government and the triumph of the "barbarian" West had thrown all traditional Vietnamese beliefs and values into question. The Vietnamese upper and middle classes pursued modern (as against Confucian) education avidly, and more than made up for their small numbers with the intensity of their debates on the way forward for Vietnam.

Here, too, divisiveness grew. Some opted for various Western models of thought and behaviour. Others looked to China for ways of reconstructing a shattered Confucian world, but found only conflict there, too. Still others looked to Japan. By the 1920s, however, the Vietnamese intelligentsia reached consensus on the adoption of *quoc ngu*, a relatively simple romanised written form of Vietnamese invented by French missionaries, in preference to the traditional but cumbersome Chinese-style characters (*Chu Nom*). *Quoc ngu* helped the growth of an impressive modern Vietnamese literary culture, and the production of popularly accessible newspapers and political literature.

Even so Vietnamese political enthusiasts made little popular headway before World War II. The moderates of the Constitutionalist Party, who favoured gradual development of democratic structures, were considered too pro-French by most Vietnamese and, in any case the French were dismissive of their plans. In 1927, some radical-thinking Vietnamese established the VNQDD (Viet Nam Quoc Dan Dang), a party moulded on China's Kuomintang. However, their numbers were decimated following an abortive uprising in 1930. In the same year, some young Vietnamese attracted to the teachings of Marx and Lenin founded the Indochina Communist Party (ICP), but also became targets of French surveillance and usually severe repression, although they were able to operate semi-openly in Cochin China during the Popular Front era in French government, 1936 to 1939. They were embarrassed, however, by the policy twists and turns in their orders from Stalin's Comintern, and many Vietnamese left-wingers turned to Trotskyism. The extent of either Marxist group's popular appeal in Vietnam in the 1930s is debatable. The ICP's achievements before World War II are probably exaggerated by modern official histories, though certainly not the courage and determination of its pioneer members.

The most imposing popular movements before World War II, in numerical terms, were in fact religious movements. Cao Dai, a sect founded in the south in 1925 and claiming to harmonise the East and the West and unique Vietnamese traditions, had over a million adherents by the late 1930s. A Buddhist sect, Hoa Hao, was also attracting large numbers in the south by that time. Christianity had also grown in Vietnam, by the 1930s claiming around ten per cent of the population (then about 30 million). These and other flourishing religious movements would pose problems for Vietnamese nationalism after World War II.

WORLD WAR II AND THE FIRST INDOCHINA WAR, 1940–1954

Japanese forces entered French Indochina in 1940 and quickly reached an agreement with the colonial government similar to that reached between Nazi Germany and the Vichy regime in France. Thus, French colonial authority survived—but only until March 1945, when the Japanese interned all French in Indochina. The Japanese then set up a nominal Vietnamese government under the emperor Bao Dai and other dignitaries.

By early 1945, Vietnam was sliding towards chaos. The wartime disruptions to the economy, Japanese seizures of rice and other goods, plus disastrous weather which wrecked two successive harvests combined to produce famine in Tonkin and Annam. The death toll from famine possibly exceeded a million by the time the war ended precipitously on 15 August and produced what was, in effect, a power vacuum in Vietnam. The stage was set for the "August Revolution" of the Vietminh.

The Vietminh (Viet Nam Doc Lap Dong Minh: League for the Independence of Vietnam) had been set up in 1941 as a front organisation of the ICP, whose leadership was then gathered at Pac Bo, an isolated spot high in the mountains on the Sino-Vietnamese border. Here they had been joined by Ho Chi Minh, now in his 50s. Although as Comintern agent for South-East Asia in the late 1920s and 1930s he had maintained intermittent contact with Vietnam's communists, this was the first time he had been back in Vietnam since 1911.

Henceforth, Ho would be free from Moscow's control and though he would always try to maintain good relations with both Soviet and Chinese communists, if only for the aid they might offer him, he would cut his own revolutionary path in Vietnam. Ho would prove to be a brilliant, if devious, revolutionary tactician, a skilled leader of the many talented young Vietnamese attracted to communism, and a hugely popular political leader, speaking and writing in terms that moved and exhilarated large numbers of his countrymen and women.

During the war, the Vietminh developed a strategy for its cadres and guerrilla forces to seize power at the war's end, when Vietnam could expect to be in disarray. Within days of the Japanese surrender, Vietminh forces (under the banner of national independence rather than socialism) took control of most of northern and central Vietnam. They were less successful in the south where Vietminh organisers were recognised as ICP members and found themselves opposed by political, business and religious forces. Nevertheless, on 2 September in Hanoi, Ho Chi Minh declared Vietnam's reunification and independence.

Vietnam was fated to remain divided, however. In the north, the Allies had appointed Chinese nationalist forces to replace the Japanese. The Chinese occupied the north until May 1946, and, crucially, left the French there interned while tolerating Ho Chi Minh's government, thus enabling it to consolidate its power. By contrast, in southern Vietnam the Japanese were relieved by British Indian troops. Their commander, dismayed at the political mayhem in Saigon, released and rearmed the French. By late 1945, French forces again controlled southern Vietnam. During 1946, Ho's government anxiously negotiated with the French, buying time as both sides prepared for war, which finally broke out in December 1946.

By early 1947, the French, fighting a conventional war, appeared to have all strategic positions in Vietnam under their control. The Vietminh, however, had settled down to an underground "people's war", organising and educating the population to support what could turn out to be a long guerrilla campaign. The turning point came in 1950, when first the new communist government of China and then the USSR began to assist the Vietminh with arms and other material. International communist support for the Vietminh precipitated direct US aid for the French war effort but, by the early 1950s, the French were beginning to weary of the inconclusive conflict. The fall of the French garrison at Dien Bien Phu in May 1954—a brilliant victory for the Vietminh's military strategist, Vo Nguyen Giap—effectively signalled the end of France's attempt to hold Vietnam.

VIETNAM PARTITIONED AND THE VIETNAM WAR, 1954–1975

As Dien Bien Phu fell, the great powers were meeting at Geneva to seek a settlement of the war. The result was a ceasefire and partition of Vietnam at the 17th parallel. The North, to be known as the Democratic Republic of Vietnam (DRV), would be governed by Ho Chi Minh and his group, who since 1950 had emerged as unequivocal communists, dedicated not only to national independence but to socialist revolution. The South would be headed by Bao Dai, who had abdicated as emperor in 1945 but become nominal "chief of state" under the French in 1949. Ho's victorious forces settled for partition presumably because the Geneva conference had also heralded elections in 1956 to establish government for a reunited Vietnam. As national heroes they were confident of winning such elections.

The elections never took place. France withdrew from Vietnam and the United States backed Ngo Dinh Diem, a Catholic and staunch anti-communist, as prime minister under Bao Dai. With American aid, Diem suppressed or bought off rival southern anti-communist leaders and their disparate followings. In 1955, Diem won a referendum to determine whether he or Bao Dai should head the South. Bao Dai left Vietnam and Diem declared himself President of the Republic of Vietnam (RVN). With American support, Diem refused to discuss the proposed nationwide elections.

In the North, the DRV government, appealing to long-cherished community values, pressed ahead with its socialist agenda, including the collectivisation of agriculture. Those deemed "capitalists" and "rich peasants" suffered, sometimes brutally, but the majority—the poor—seem to have accepted socialism's promises. Popular support for Ho Chi Minh's government remained enormously high.

By contrast, Diem was never to be genuinely popular in the politically and religiously fragmented South, except perhaps amongst his fellow Catholics (almost a million northern Catholics were shipped south by the US navy in 1954). Diem, as indifferent to economics as he was to democracy, offered little hope to the southern poor, and spent most of his US aid on his security forces, which were under the command of his brother Ngo Dinh Nhu. Other members of his avaricious family also provoked resentment.

In 1959, the DRV government, observing the build-up of popular opposition towards Diem the "American puppet", sponsored a new Vietminh-style front organisation for the South. This was the NLF (National Liberation Front—called "Vietcong" by its opponents). Coy about its degree of control by communists, the NLF appealed to Vietnamese patriotism and morality, promising to oust American influence and to set up fair and honest government.

By the early 1960s, NLF guerrilla forces were in command of wide areas of the southern countryside, and had won sympathisers at all levels of society. Alarmed, US President Kennedy stepped up aid to Diem and sent American military "advisers"—17,500 of them by 1963. By mid 1963, however, Diem and his brother had antagonised almost every sector of Southern society. The world was startled when Buddhist monks began burning themselves to death in protest against the regime. Plotters within South Vietnam's military concluded that Diem and Nhu had to go and, in October 1963, they were murdered.

Four years of unstable government followed in South Vietnam until General Nguyen Van Thieu emerged as president in 1967. A skilful manipulator of the vast patronage which American aid made possible, Thieu would remain president until 1975. Meanwhile, in the United States, Kennedy's successor, Johnson, had decided to confront the NLF directly with US power. In early 1965, the US air force began bombing targets in both South and North Vietnam and US ground troops landed in the South. What came to be called "the Vietnam War" was now unequivocally under way.

A process of "escalation" followed: China, the USSR and the Eastern Bloc raised their aid to the DRV, which raised its commitment of materiel and men to the NLF. In turn, the US raised the stakes further, increasing the number of its troops to a peak of 525,000 by 1967. The US received some support from Australia, New Zealand and some anti-communist Asian governments, but its major allies stayed aloof from the conflict.

In 1968, at Tet, the lunar new year, NLF/DRV forces launched a massive offensive throughout the South. This was repelled, but its strength shocked both the Johnson administration and the American public, which had been led to believe that the war was being won. Richard Nixon, elected president in 1968, and his special adviser, Henry Kissinger, had to find alternative strategies. They pursued what could be called "Vietnamisation" of the war, reducing US troop levels and encouraging the South with ever-increasing aid to increase its own levels. By 1973, the South's armed forces numbered 1.1 million—half the country's male population between the ages of 18 and 35.

The Nixon/Kissinger strategies also included increased aerial warfare. American bombing of both North and South, and of Cambodia wreaked social, economic and ecological devastation. By the end of the war, 60 per cent of southern villages would be destroyed or rendered unsafe; only 35 per cent of an essentially peasant population would still live in rural areas. However, the bombing never proved decisive to the course of the war. It even failed to interdict the legendary Ho Chi Minh Trail, the network of mountainous trails down which the DRV supplied its war effort in the South.

Some American opinion consistently urged the expansion of the ground war into the North, but neither Johnson nor Nixon was ever willing to take that course, fearing that it might precipitate full-scale American confrontation with the USSR and China. Thus, the DRV, despite the bombing, always remained a secure base for the DRV/ NLF-war effort in the South.

Meanwhile, Nixon and Kissinger also pursued diplomacy. Talks between United States and DRV/NLF representatives had begun in Paris in 1968. For years they dragged on inconclusively but, in January 1973, the Paris Peace Agreements were signed by the US, the Saigon government (reluctantly, under intense US pressure), the DRV and the PRG (the Provisional Revolutionary Government of the NLF).

Crucially for the DRV/NLF, the first article of the agreements recognised the "independence, sovereignty, unity and territorial integrity" of Vietnam. Other articles called for a ceasefire, at which point the contending Vietnamese forces could claim whatever territory they held in the South, pending elections to determine the South's future government. The agreements also called for the total withdrawal of US troops and military personnel within 60 days. This article proved, in fact, to be the only one of the Paris Agreements which was fully carried out. The American troops went home, but in South Vietnam war continued unabated.

The morale of the Southern forces began to slide, particularly after Nixon's resignation in August 1974 over the Watergate scandal. His successor as president, Gerald Ford, had little influence over a Congress now disillusioned with the war and reluctant to sustain US aid to the Saigon regime. In contrast, the DRV/NLF forces, legitimately ensconced in the South under the Paris Agreements, were increasingly confident that victory was in sight. Guerrilla war had long since given way to conventional military tactics. By now the amount and sophisticated nature of their weaponry, supplied by their allies, matched that of the Southern forces.

Even so, the speed with which the war ended stunned both sides. DRV/NLF forces launched a limited offensive in the South's central highlands in mid March 1975. RVN forces panicked when ordered to retreat, creating a country-wide rout which was slowed by Southern detachments in only a handful of places. The Southern government collapsed, and DRV/NLF forces entered Saigon on 30 April. The last Americans remaining in South Vietnam had been evacuated just hours before, along with some Southerners closely identified with the American presence.

VIETNAM SINCE 1975

The major question in April 1975 concerned the speed with which Vietnam would be reintegrated. Since the 1950s, the historic differences between north and south had been hugely magnified. The northerners had existed under an austere, disciplined socialism which re-emphasised their traditional regard for social hierarchy and community obligation. The southerners had been introduced to a quasi-capitalist consumer economy, sustained by American aid, and to the trappings of American popular culture.

In 1975, the victorious DRV government revealed a profound distrust of even pro-communist southerners, and moved swiftly to subordinate the south. The NLF and its provisional government were disbanded, and administrative control was imposed directly from Hanoi. In 1976, the country was renamed the Socialist Republic of Vietnam (SRV), though in practice it was a "greater DRV", dominated by northerners. In the same year plans for the collectivisation of southern agriculture were announced, and the reorganisation of the south's entire economy along socialist lines, integrating it with the northern economy, proceeded swiftly in the next two years.

Heady from their military triumphs perhaps, Vietnam's leaders envisaged equally dramatic results from their decisive action in the economic sphere. Instead, the organisation engendered acute economic crisis, made worse by flood and other natural disasters in 1977 and 1978. Ambitious industrial targets were not met. Most seriously, rice and other agricultural outputs plummeted and food rations had to be slashed.

In late 1978, Vietnam invaded Cambodia and ousted the socialist but virulently anti-Vietnamese Pol Pot regime. In retaliation, China attacked Vietnam's northern frontier zone. Traditional regional antagonisms and rivalries had quickly reasserted themselves over the apparent international socialist comradeship of the years before 1975. In Vietnam, these hostilities exacerbated the domestic crisis. In the early 1980s, many Chinese and Sino-Vietnamese fled Vietnam, either to China or as "boat people" to overseas countries, sharply boosting the statistics on people fleeing Vietnam since 1975.

The scale of the economic crisis forced some softening of policy as early as 1979, but hardline neo-Stalinist opinion essentially prevailed within Vietnam's ruling group until 1985, when Gorbachev's reforms in the USSR heartened reformers in Vietnam. In 1986, the Sixth National Congress of the Vietnam Communist Party formally approved the policy of *doi moi*, or "renovation".

During the mid-to-late 1990s, Vietnam's economy benefited from a rapprochement with its regional neighbours and even its old enemy, the United States. Washington lifted its 30-year trade embargo in 1994, and agreed to a full normalisation of diplomatic relations in July the following year, though it was not until 1997 that Congress ratified the appointment of an ambassador. For this role, they chose Pete Peterson—a Vietnam War pilot who had spent time as a prisoner of war in the infamous Hanoi Hilton. The major sticking point in relations between the two countries had been Washington's insistence that Hanoi fully account for 1,600 US servicemen posted as missing in action during the war. Hanoi pledged full cooperation and has assisted military investigation teams with information and logistical support. In 2001 the two countries signed a bilateral trade agreement and the United States is now the country's largest export market, followed by Japan, China, Australia and Singapore.

Vietnam entered ASEAN in 1995 and was elected its chairman in 2001, a source of considerable national pride considering that the grouping was originally set up as an umbrella organisation to oppose communist expansion in the region. Relations with China have also blossomed. The growing importance of this bilateral relationship was illustrated in 2007 when newly-elected President Nguyen Minh Triet visited China one month before his first official visit to the United States. Nonetheless tensions remain, many of them historical. Both sides lay claim to the Spratly Islands in the South China Sea, which may be a source of future conflict if commercial quantities of oil are discovered.

The Asian economic crisis which rocked South-East Asia in 1997 and the subsequent hi-tech crash and global economic slowdown have had only an indirect impact on Vietnam, though this had more to do with the limited extent to which the economy had been opened up and integrated regionally under *doi moi*, than on any strong economic fundamentals working to buttress investor confidence. Whilst many factors relevant to economic recovery are outside of its control, there are pressures on the government to implement further wide-ranging economic reforms to counter systemic problems arising from an un-wieldy bureaucracy, the persistence of widespread corruption in both Party and government, and a Soviet-era legal system which requires reform in order to shore up foreign investor confidence by guaranteeing private property. The government has also been urged by Western donors to increase measures to encourage the private sector, in order to ease the reliance on foreign aid. Indeed the impressive growth of the private sector was demonstrated by the fact that by 2007 it accounted for over 50 per cent of GDP and was responsible for generating 90 per cent of jobs created over the period 2002-06. In January 2007 Vietnam was admitted into the World Trade Organization, a source of con-siderable pride and satisfaction among the leadership as membership conferred foreign recognition of the country's transition to a market-based economy which was increasingly integrated into the global economy.

Politically, *doi moi* has led to the emergence of a new, younger leadership, the streamlining (relatively) of the country's administrative apparatus, reforms in the Party's structure, and moves towards the rule of law, accountable government and greater freedom of expression. It was precisely with this in mind that in 2004, the Central Committee of the Communist Party held its major mid-term conference and identified the major tasks for the next decade as being to privatise state-owned enterprises, to reduce poverty, maintaining political and economic stability, and achieving annual economic growth of 8 per cent. GDP doubled between 1995 and 2005. The country is progressing from an agricultural-based economy towards an industrial one.

At the Tenth Party Congress in 2006, members were treated to unprecedented frankness on the corrosive effects that corruption by party and state officials was having on popular support for the government. Such rare candour followed a series of corruption scandals involving senior officials, which the usually tightly controlled press had been encouraged to report on. The 2006 Party Congress also confirmed the appointments of Nguyen Tan Dung as the new prime minister and Nguyen Minh Triet as the new President. Both men had been the sole nominees to their respective positions and both hail from the more free-wheeling south, reflecting an emphasis on continued economic (if not political) reform.

Economic change has gone much further than political reform, propelled by the collapse of the Soviet Union and the Eastern Bloc's abandonment of socialism. In practical terms, this has meant the loss to Vietnam of aid which accounted for up to 30 per cent of the state budget. China's example has also been a major, if unacknowledged, factor in determining Vietnamese policy. Like China, Vietnam is now a hybrid: a state under one-party control—in theory, socialist—but with a free-enterprise economy operating alongside state enterprises.

As with China, some analysts question the long-term stability of such a system. Free-enterprise economic activity is perhaps intrinsically pluralist. In Vietnam, the historically more pluralist south has shot ahead of the north economically since *doi moi*. Some are worried the country's pull-apart tendencies could re-emerge. On the other hand, Vietnam's current rulers are firmly in command as the rightful heirs of the socialist patriots who overcame France and the United States and reunited the fatherland. The challenge they face is not at present to their power, but to their capacity to persist with reforms begun under *doi moi* and now yielding impressive results, to see through the myriad social and cultural, as well as economic and political, changes demanded by *doi moi* and, in the process, to maintain stability in a country where until recently stability has rarely been experienced.

FURTHER READING

GENERAL

Kelly, David and Reid, Anthony — *Asian Freedoms: The Idea of Freedom in East and Southeast Asia.* Cambridge: Cambridge University Press, 1998.

McVey, Ruth T (ed) — *Southeast Asian Capitalists.* Ithaca: Cornell Southeast Asia Program, 1992.

Osborne, Milton — *Southeast Asia: An Introductory Illustrated History.* Sydney: Allen & Unwin, 1995.

Reid, Anthony — *Southeast Asia in the Age of Commerce, 1450–1680.* New Haven: Yale University Press, 1988.

Reid, Anthony — *Southeast Asia in the Early Modern Era: Trade, Power and Belief.* Ithaca NY: Cornell University Press, 1963.

Steinberg, David J (ed) — *In Search of Southeast Asia.* Sydney: Allen & Unwin, 1987.

Wang, Gungwu — *Community and Nation: China, Southeast Asia and Australia.* Sydney: Allen & Unwin, 1992.

BRUNEI

Ranjit Singh, D S — *Brunei 1834–1983: The Problem of Political Survival.* Singapore: Oxford University Press, 1984.

Turnbull, C Mary — *A History of Malaysia, Singapore and Brunei.* Sydney: Allen & Unwin, 1989.

CAMBODIA

Chandler, David — *A History of Cambodia,* 2nd edition. Sydney: Allen & Unwin, 1982.

Kiernan, Ben	*How Pol Pot Came to Power.* London: Verso, 1985.
Osborne, Milton	*Sihanouk: Prince of Light, Prince of Darkness.* Sydney: Allen & Unwin, 1994.

INDONESIA

Booth, Anne (ed)	*The Oil Boom and After: Indonesian Economic Policy and Performance in the Soeharto Era.* Singapore: Oxford University Press, 1992.
Legge, J D	*Sukarno: A Political Biography.* Sydney: Allen & Unwin, 1985.
Liddle, R William	*Leadership and Culture in Indonesian Politics.* Sydney: Allen & Unwin, 1996.
MacIntyre, Andrew	*Indonesia.* Sydney: The Asia-Australia Institute, UNSW, 1993.
MacIntyre, Andrew	*Business and Politics in Indonesia.* Sydney: Allen & Unwin, 1990.
Ricklets, M C	*A History of Modern Indonesia Since c. 1300.* London: Macmillan, 1993.
Vatikiotis, Michael	*Indonesian Politics under Suharto.* London: Routledge, 1993.

LAO PDR

Brown, MacAlister and Zasloff, Joseph J	*Apprentice Revolutionaries: The Communist Movement in Laos, 1930–1985.* Stanford: Hoover Research Institution Press, 1986.
Dommen, Arthur J	*Laos: Keystone of Indochina.* Boulder: Westview Press, 1985.
Stuart-Fox, Martin and Kooyman, Mary	*Historical Dictionary of Laos.* Metuchen, NJ: Scarecrow Press, 1992.

MALAYSIA

Andaya, Barbara & Leonard	*A History of Malaysia.* London: Macmillan, 1982.
Crouch, Harold	*Government and Society in Malaysia.* Sydney: Allen & Unwin, 1996.

Kahn, Joel S and Loh, Francis Kok Wah (eds)
Fragmented Vision: Culture and Politics in Contemporary Malaysia. Sydney: Allen & Unwin, 1992.

Mahathir, M
The Malay Dilemma. Singapore: Times Books International, 1970.

Means, Gordon P
Malaysian Politics: The Second Generation, Singapore and New York: Oxford University Press, 1991.

MYANMAR

Aung-Thwin, Michael
Pagan: The Origins of Modern Burma. Honolulu: University of Hawaii Press, 1985.

Badgley, John
Myanmar in 1993: A Watershed Year. Asian Survey, 34: 2: February 1994: 153–59.

Lintner, Bertil
Outrage: Burma's Struggle for Democracy. Hong Kong: *Far Eastern Economic Review,* 1990.

Osborne, Milton
Burma. Sydney: UNSW, Asia-Australia Institute, Asia-Australia Briefing Paper, 1994.

Osborne, Milton
Southeast Asia: An Illustrated Introductory History. Sydney: Allen & Unwin, 1990.

Silverstein, Josef (ed)
Independent Burma at Forty Years: Six Assessments. Ithaca: Cornell Southeast Asia Program, 1989.

Smith, Martin
Burma: Insurgency and the Politics of Ethnicity. London: 1991.

Taylor, Robert
The State in Burma. Honolulu: University of Hawaii Press, 1988.

PHILIPPINES

Friend, Theodore
The Blue-Eyed Enemy: Japan Against the West in Java and Luzon, 1942–1945. Princeton: Princeton University Press, 1988.

Hawes, Gary — "Marcos, His Cronies, and the Philippines Failure to Develop", in Ruth T McVey, *Southeast Asian Capitalists*. Ithaca, NY: Cornell University, 1992.

Ileton, Reynaldo — *Pasyon and Revolution: Popular Movements in the Philippines, 1840–1910*. Manila: Ateneo de Manila Press, 1979.

McCoy, Alfred W and d Jesus, C (eds) — *Philippine Social History*. Sydney: Allen & Unwin, 1982.

McCoy, Alfred W (ed) — *Southeast Asia Under Japanese Occupation*. New Haven: Yale University Southeast Asian Studies, 1980.

Paredes, Ruby R (ed) — *Philippine Colonial Democracy*. New Haven: Yale University Southeast Asian Studies, 1988.

Pinches, Michael — "The Philippines: The Regional Exception". *The Pacific Review*, 5: 4: 1992: 390–401.

Reidinger, Jeffrey — *The Philippines in 1993*. Asian Survey, 34: 2: February 1994: 139–52.

SINGAPORE

Carnegie, Georgina and Sharpe, Diana — *Singapore*. Sydney: The Asia-Australia Institute, UNSW, 1993.

Chua, Beng-Huat — *Communitarian Ideology and Democracy in Singapore*. London: Routledge, 1995.

Minchen, James — *No Man Is an Island: A Portrait of Singapore's Lee Kuan Yew*. Sydney: Allen & Unwin, 1990.

Rodan, Gary — *The Political Economy of Singapore's Industrialisation*. Kuala Lumpur: Forum, 1989.

Siddique, S and Sholam, N — *Singapore's Little India*. Singapore: Institute of Southeast Asian Studies, 1982.

Turnbull, C M — *A History of Singapore, 1819–1988*, Singapore: Oxford University Press, 1992.

THAILAND

Suehiro, Akira

Capital Accumulation in Thailand, 1885–1985. Tokyo: The Centre for East Asian Cultural Studies, 1989.

Hewison, Kevin

Politics and Power in Thailand: Essays in Political Economy. Manila: Journal of Contemporary Asia Publishers, 1989.

Wright, Joseph J

The Balancing Act: A History of Modern Thailand. Bangkok: Asia Books, 1991.

Wyatt, David K

Thailand: A Short History. New Haven: Yale University Press, 1984.

VIETNAM

Duiker, William J

Historical Dictionary of Vietnam. Metuchen, NJ: Scarecrow Press, 1989.

Jamieson, Neil

Understanding Vietnam. Berkeley: University of California, 1993.

Karnow, Stanley

Vietnam: A History. London: Penguin, 1984.

Kolko, Gabriel

Vietnam: Anatomy of War 1940–1975. London: Allen & Unwin, 1986.

Lockhart, Greg

Nation in Arms. Sydney: Allen & Unwin, 1989.

Porter, Gareth

Vietnam: The Politics of Bureaucratic Socialism. Ithaca: Cornell University Press, 1993.

Turley, William S

The Second Indochina War: A Short Political and Military History. Boulder: Westview Press, 1986.

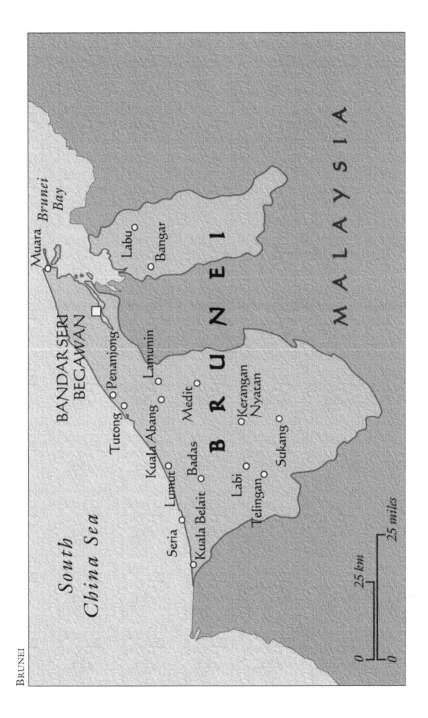

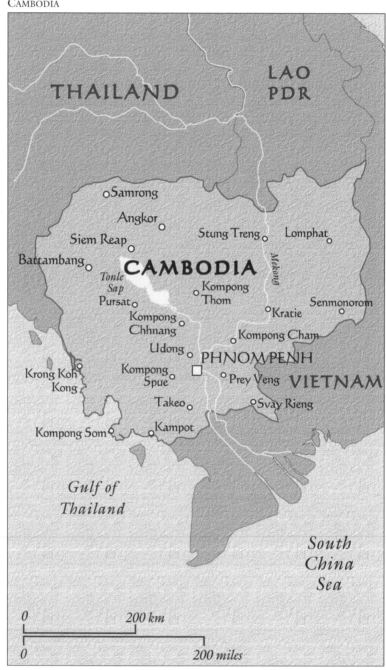

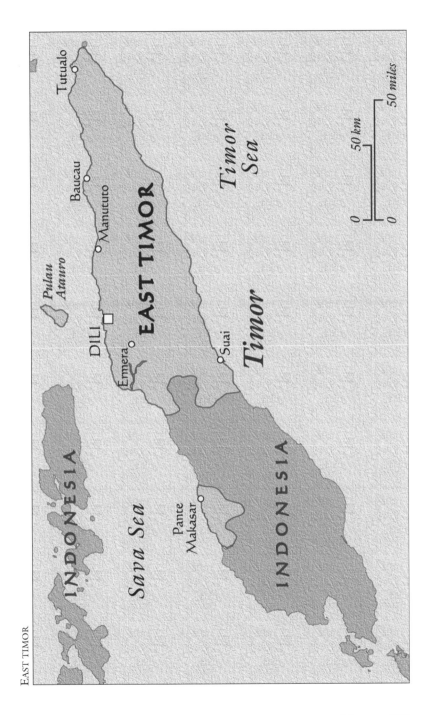

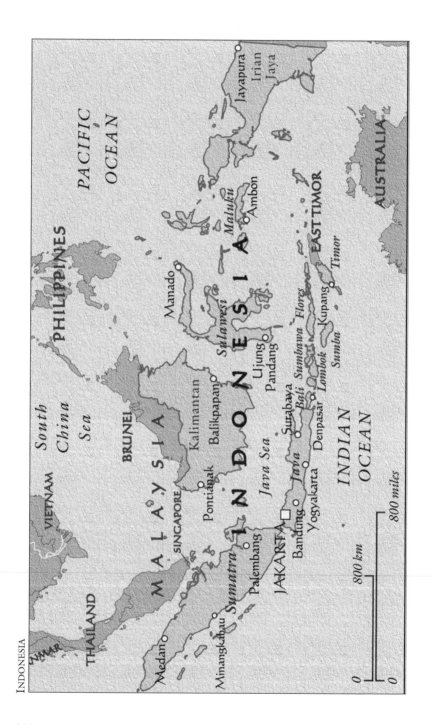

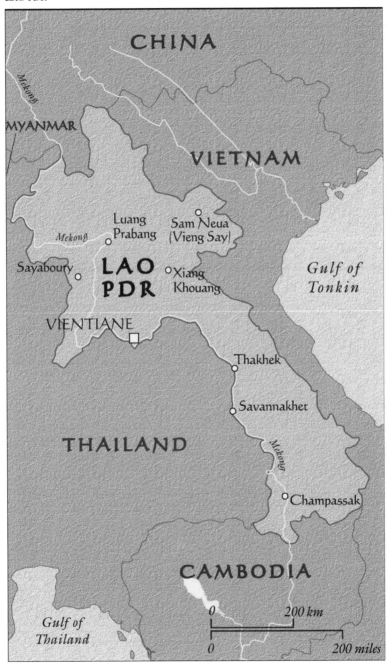

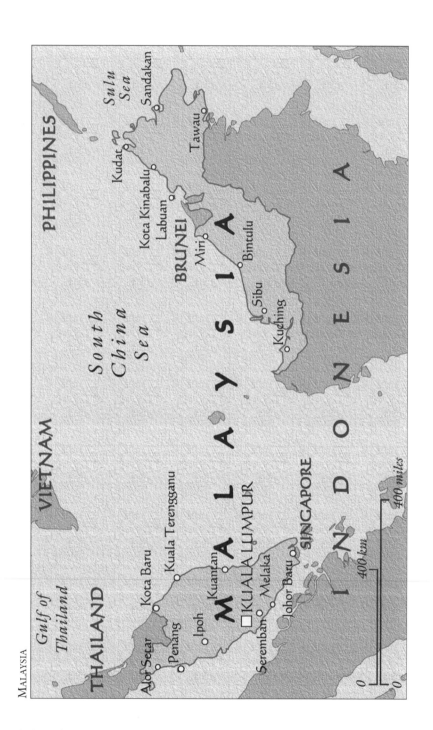

MALAYSIA

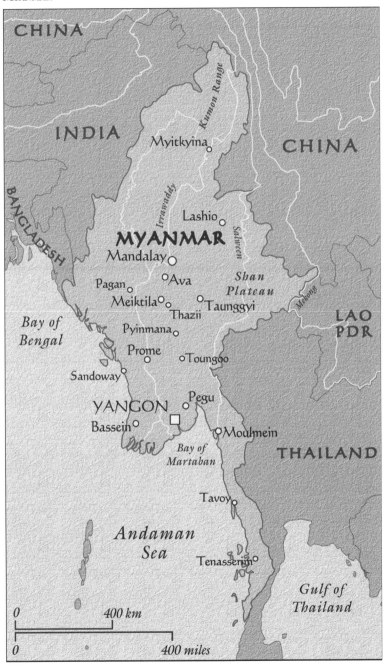

0 | 200 km
0 | 200 miles

Batenes Islands

Babuyan Islands

Laoag
Aparri
Vigan
Tuguegarao

San Fernando

Baguio

Philippine Sea

Lingayen

Luzon

Tarlac

Subic

Quezon City

MANILA

Lipa

Batangas

Naga

Legaspi

South China Sea

Mindoro

Marinduque

Sarsogon

Burias

Tablas

Sibuyan

Basuanga

Masbate

Cathalogan

Samar

Panay

Roxas

Tasloban

PHILIPPINES

Iloilo

Leyte

Palawan

Bacolod

Cebu

Puerto Princesa

Negros

Bohol

Damaguete City

Butuan

Sulu Sea

Ozamiz

Cagayan de Oro

Mindanao

Zamboanga

Davao

Cotabato

MALAYSIA

Sulu Archipelago

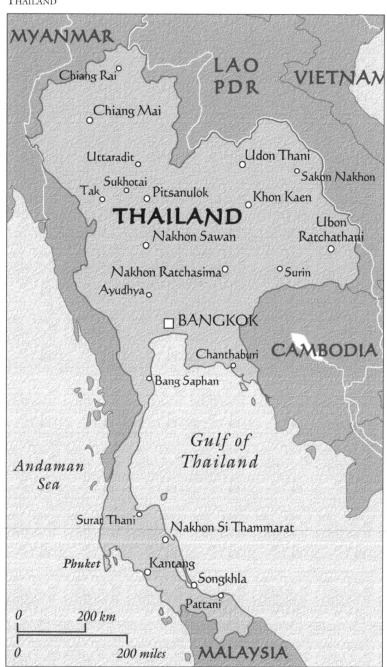

MYANMAR

Chiang Rai

Chiang Mai

LAO
PDR

VIETNAM

Uttaradit

Udon Thani

Sakon Nakhon

Tak

Sukhotai

Pitsanulok

Khon Kaen

THAILAND

Nakhon Sawan

Ubon
Ratchathani

Nakhon Ratchasima

Surin

Ayudhya

BANGKOK

Chanthaburi

CAMBODIA

Bang Saphan

*Gulf of
Thailand*

*Andaman
Sea*

Surat Thani

Nakhon Si Thammarat

Phuket

Kantang

Songkhla

Pattani

0   200 km

0   200 miles

MALAYSIA

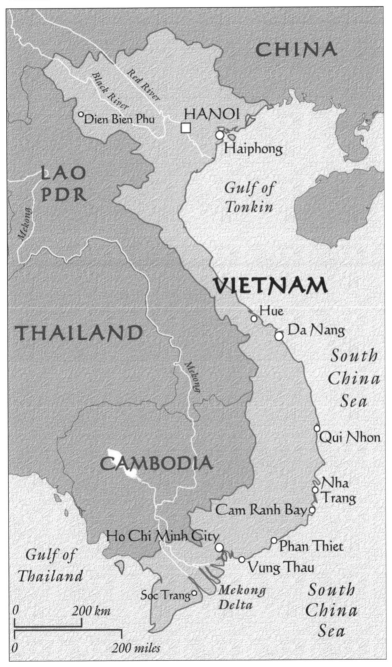

About AFG Venture Group

AFG Venture Group is an Australian and Asian corporate advisory firm with activities throughout Australia, South East Asia and India (www.afgventuregroup.com). AFG Venture Group has a number of core sector competencies, including Education, Health and Life Sciences, Mining and Resources, IT&T, Retail, Services (including Environmental and Clean Technology) and Manufacturing and Engineering.

AFG Venture Group was created by the merger of Asean Focus Group, with its 20 year history of creating alliances, relationships and transactions in Asia and in particular in South East Asia and India, and Venture Group, with its 14 year history of corporate and equities advisory in Australia.

AFG Venture Group's principal offices are in Sydney but it has representative and joint venture offices throughout Asia including Bangkok, Chennai, Hanoi, Ho Chi Minh City, Hong Kong, Hyderabad, Jakarta, Manila, Mumbai, New Delhi, Singapore, Vientiane (Lao PDR), and Yangon (Myanmar).

Blake Dawson

Blake Dawson (www.blakedawson.com) is one of Australia's largest law firms with over 1,500 people, including more than 180 partners and 625 lawyers offering expertise to private and public sector clients in over 30 areas of law. It maintains a network of offices across Australia in Sydney, Melbourne, Brisbane, Canberra, Perth and Adelaide and has extensive experience in acting for clients across the Asia Pacific region. The 2009 opening of a Singapore office further expands on its existing regional capability and on the ground client services from its own or affiliated offices in Jakarta, Indonesia, Shanghai, China and Port Moresby, Papua New Guinea. The firm also has significant experience in other Asian and the Middle East markets.

It is the provider of legal services to Australia's top Stock Exchange listed companies, global corporations and government and in 2007 was named "Best Financial Law Firm 2007" (FinanceAsia Achievement Awards) and in 2008 "Law Firm Of The Year: Australia & Oceania – PLC Which lawyer? Law Firm Awards". It has 89 Best Lawyer listings in Best Lawyers Australia, 2008 across 41 different areas of commercial practice, the equal most listings in Australia. Blake Dawson was also nominated as Employer of Choice 2008 (for the 8th consecutive year) by the Equal Opportunity for Women in the Workplace Agency.

INDEX